Managing Service Firms

Routledge Interpretive Marketing Research

EDITED BY STEPHEN BROWN AND BARBARA B. STERN,
University of Ulster, Northern Ireland and
Rutgers, the State University of New Jersey, USA

Recent years have witnessed an 'interpretative turn' in marketing and consumer research. Methodologists from the humanities are taking their place alongside those drawn from the traditional social sciences.

Qualitative and literary modes of marketing discourse are growing in popularity. Art and aesthetics are increasingly firing the marketing imagination.

This series brings together the most innovative work in the burgeoning interpretative marketing research tradition. It ranges across the methodological spectrum from grounded theory to personal introspection, covers all aspects of the postmodern marketing 'mix', from advertising to product development, and embraces marketing's principal sub-disciplines.

Romancing the Market
Edited by Stephen Brown, Anne Marie
Doherty and Bill Clarke

Consumer Value: A framework for analysis and research
Edited by Morris B. Holbrook

Marketing and Feminism: Current issues and research
Edited by Miriam Catterall, Pauline
Maclaran and Lorna Stevens

Managing Service Firms

The Power of Managerial Marketing

Per Skålén

Routledge
Taylor & Francis Group

LONDON AND NEW YORK

Published 2010 by Routledge
2 Park Square, Milton Park, Abingdon, Oxon OX14 4RN
52 Vanderbilt Avenue, New York, NY 10017

Routledge is an imprint of the Taylor & Francis Group, an informa business

Typeset in Sabon by IBT Global.

Library of Congress Cataloging-in-Publication Data
Skålén, Per.
      Managing service firms : the power of managerial marketing / by Per Skalen.

      p. cm. — (Routledge interpretive marketing research ; v. 11)
      Includes bibliographical references and index.
      1. Service industries.   2. Marketing — Management.   I. Title.
      HD9980.5.S55 2010
      658.8 — dc22
      2009040648

ISBN13: 978-0-415-47326-2 (hbk)
ISBN13: 978-0-203-85449-5 (ebk)

To
Jaspar, Bruno, and Nelson

Contents

Preface

This book is a sociological, empirically based power analysis of marketing, service marketing and management, in particular. In contrast to mainstream marketing research, it does not seek to prescribe more managerial practices to practice. Rather, it focuses on studying how service marketing and management practices affect service firms and their members. Rather than producing more managerial marketing practices, the focus is on studying marketing as practice. This provides the marketing discipline with an alternative, sociologically informed foundation and marketing managers with knowledge about the role of marketing in organizations. The book should be of interest to scholars, students, and managers of marketing.

The bulk of the book was written during my 2008 tenure as a guest researcher at the 'Scandinavian Consortium of Organizational Research (SCANCOR)', at Stanford University. I wish to extend my gratitude to SCANCOR director Woody Powell and to all the SCANCOR scholars who came and went during that year for creating such a stimulating research environment. I gratefully acknowledge the fact that my year at Stanford was made possible by means of scholarships awarded by the 'Sweden-American Foundation' and by the 'Jan Wallander and Tom Hedelius Foundation'. Part of the book was also written at my permanent affiliation, 'The Service Research Center', at Karlstad University. I am very pleased to be a part of the CTF team and to be able to work in such a stimulating and accommodating academic environment. Language editing was covered by a grant from the Swedish Council for Working Life and Social Research.

I would like to extend my special thanks to those who have read and commented on the manuscript. Per Echeverri and Richard Ek read the whole manuscript. Your insightful and supportive comments helped me to improve several vital parts of the text. I also thank Esther Barinaga, Markus Fellesson, Martin Fransson, Hans Hasselbladh, Johan Quist, Henrietta Huzell, and Bo Enquist, who have also made insightful comments. I would also like to acknowledge the 'Financial Institute', the anonymous organization where the empirical study that the present book is based on was conducted. Without the involvement of the employees of the 'Financial Institute', the book would not have been possible. I am particularly grateful to my contact person, referred to in the book by the fictitious name David, and to my other main informants, referred to by the fictitious names Mary, Alice, John, Barbara, and Ann.

I would like to point out that the book was written while I was writing an article published in the *Journal of Marketing Management* as 'Service Marketing and Subjectivity: The Shaping of Customer-Oriented Employees' (Vol. 25 No. 7–8, 2009, pp. 795–809). The book and the article have informed each other. The book can be seen as a continuation of the studies of the history of marketing thought that I have been conducting in collaboration with Martin Fougère and Markus Fellesson and which have been published in book form as *Marketing Discourse—A Critical Perspective* by Routledge (2008), and in article form by the *Scandinavian Journal of Management* (see Vol. 22 No. 4, 2006, pp. 275–91) and the *Journal of Organizational Change Management* (see Vol. 20 No. 1, 2007, pp. 109–25). Despite the fact that Martin and Markus have not been involved in writing the present book, our previous joint effort has informed the writing. The errors of judgment that remain are, of course, my own.

Last but not least, I would like to thank my wonderful wife Sofia. The book is dedicated to our children Jaspar, Bruno, and Nelson. Now that I have this book in my hand, it will be a whole lot easier to answer the question: 'What do you do all day long Daddy?'

1 Introduction

Marketing is largely a positivistic and managerially prescriptive academic discipline. Knowledge production has been framed, at least since the 1960s, by a positivistic understanding of science and a managerialistic worldview. The emphasis has been on prescribing marketing practices to organizations and not on studying marketing as practice (see, for instance, Arndt 1985; Hollander 1986; Hunt 1976; Skålén et al. 2008). In an attempt to counterbalance the positivistic and managerial hegemony, *critical* perspectives were introduced into marketing toward the end of the 1980s (see, for instance, Arndt 1985; Fuat Fuat Firat et al. 1987; Murray and Ozanne 1991). In the middle of the 1990s, Alvesson and Willmott conducted an overview of critical research within the management disciplines, summarizing the status of critical research into *marketing* thus: 'marketing is perhaps the sub discipline of management to which CT [Critical Theory] (and related intellectual traditions) can contribute most, and yet it is also in this specialism that the influence of critical analysis is weakest' (Alvesson and Willmott 1996: 128). Most contemporary commentators seem to argue that critical marketing research has still not really kicked off.[1] Although frameworks for pursuing critical research into marketing have been introduced (see, for instance, Arndt 1985; Brownlie et al. 1999; Burton 2001; Hackley 2009; Saren et al. 2007a; Skålén et al. 2006; 2008; Tadajewski and Brownlie 2008), and although a critical analysis of marketing texts and the discipline's history has been conducted (see, for instance, Brownlie and Saren 1997; Hackley 2003; Marion 2006; Morgan 2003; Skålén et al. 2006; 2008; Skålén and Fougère 2007; Tadajewski 2006), few, if any, systematic *empirical* studies of marketing practice have been conducted from a critical perspective. In the words of Brownlie and Hewer (2007: 59): 'It is now time to put critical aspirations into action', which is something that I intend to do in this book.

Before jumping right into this project, at least two qualifications are needed. Firstly, the image of the object of study needs to be sharper: What do I mean by marketing? What kind of marketing practice do I intend to study empirically? Secondly, the angle that marketing is going to be illuminated and analyzed from is in need of some elaboration: What critical perspective do I intend to draw on? What do I mean by critique?

SERVICE MANAGEMENT AND MARKETING

Academic marketing can be divided into two broad, yet overlapping, research streams, one of which is devoted to studying *consumer behavior* and the other to studying *strategic marketing* (Sheth et al. 1988). Consumer research is oriented toward studying consumer choices on the market, and how organizations might gain knowledge of and affect these choices, whereas strategic marketing is more preoccupied with organizational and management issues, in particular with how organizations should become customer oriented. It is within strategic marketing that the lack of critical research is most acute. Consumer research is to some extent counterbalanced by critical and sociological approaches. The sociology of consumption is a research field in its own right which systematically studies the role of consumption in society, implicitly and explicitly addressing marketing issues (see, for instance, Bauman 1998; Bourdieu 1984; Featherstone 1991). Furthermore, even though managerial approaches dominate within the narrower boundaries of consumer research, this field also includes research that critically approaches consumption practices associated with the managerial side of consumer research (see, for instance, Arnould and Thompson 2005; Mick et al. 2004). However, strategic marketing research lacks this type of empirical critical sociological inquiry almost completely. The fact that strategic marketing research is sometimes referred to using the notion of 'managerial marketing' is telling.

The present book focuses on studying strategic marketing—it is not a study in consumer research.[2] The more exact focus is on analyzing, both conceptually and empirically, practices associated with research into *service marketing* or *service management*—here jointly referred to as service marketing and management (SMM)[3]—which together with, for example, 'the marketing management', 'the commodity', 'the functional', 'the institutional', 'the scientific', and 'the organizational dynamics' schools of thought (see Bartels 1988; Sheth et al. 1988; Skålén et al. 2008) make up the research stream of strategic marketing. SMM emerged as a field of research in the late 1970s (Berry and Parasuraman 1993). Today, SMM needs to be perceived as an institutionalized school of thought in marketing, with a distinct research program.[4] Some even claim that SMM is the school of thought that will come to dominate academic marketing research and lead the discipline into the future (see following and, for instance, Grönroos 2007a; Vargo and Lusch 2004).

The Emergence of SMM

SMM can be perceived as a reaction to, and a problematization of, marketing management, the school of thought which, most would agree, has been dominating strategic marketing research since the middle of the 1960s. Sharing with marketing management the fundamental idea that 'the marketing concept'—'the notion that the firm is best off by designing and directing its activities according to the needs and desires of customers in chosen target markets' (Grönroos 1997: 324)—should order academic marketing research and that marketing should be a managerial and applied discipline, SMM research has put forward other views on how to put the marketing concept into practice (Skålén et al. 2006; 2008). This is a central theme as early on as in Shostack's (1977) article, which contributed significantly toward making space for SMM research. Shostack (1977: 73) complained, pointing her finger toward marketing management, that 'service industries have been slow to integrate marketing into the mainstream of decision-making and control because marketing offers no guidance, terminology, or practical rules that are clearly relevant for services'. More to the point, Shostack claimed that the central managerial practices of marketing management research, e.g. the 4Ps marketing mix, fostered the customer orientation of products but not people, making it inapt for service organizations. Similar claims were put forward by Grönroos (1978; 1982; 1984) in a series of early discipline-shaping SMM papers pointing out the 'need for [the] development of service marketing theory' (1982: 30).

The point of departure for the problematization of marketing management was the claim that service firms are different from consumer goods companies; that these differences have implications for the development of marketing knowledge and practice, but that marketing management research had failed to take them into account. Although the production and consumption of goods constitute distinct processes, services are produced and consumed simultaneously. According to Grönroos (1982: 32), consumers of services even enter 'the production process of the service firm . . . [and] have an impact on the production process itself'. Accordingly, Shostack (1977: 79) argues that 'services are often inextricably entwined with their human representatives. In many fields a person is perceived to be the service'. Grönroos (1978: 598) holds a similar position: 'The performance of the personnel is considered to a great extent to·shape the service that is offered'. More particularly, Grönroos (1982: 32) argues that 'the consumer's opinion of the service firm and its services . . . [is] determined by what happens in the buyer-seller interactions of the simultaneous production and consumption'. Accordingly, it is neither sufficient to localize the customer orientation logic of the marketing concept to the marketing department nor to be satisfied with ensuring that the products are customer oriented, as marketing management discourse prescribes. Rather, the logic of customer orientation needs to be dispersed throughout the organization and to inform, particularly, what is referred to as the 'interactive marketing function' (Grönroos 1982; see also Gummesson 1977): that is, the employees' customer interaction.

Based on this premise of the centrality of human resources and customer interaction in service marketing and management practice, and the fact that, at the point in time (the late 1970s / early 1980s) when Shostack and Grönroos were writing their discipline-shaping papers many industrialized countries were on the threshold of entering a service-based economy, Shostack and Grönroos drew the conclusion that, if academic marketing research wanted to stay managerially relevant, it would need to shift its managerial attention away from the products that companies make and toward the individuals they employ. As the title of Shostack's (1977) paper suggests, the time for 'breaking free from product marketing' had finally arrived. Shostack (1977: 79) wrote: 'the potential power of more deliberately controlling or structuring [the human resource] element is clear . . . The point is that service marketers should be charged with tactics and strategy in this area, and must consider it a management responsibility'. Grönroos (1978: 593) corroborated: 'the administration of the human resources must be considered an important means of competition in service marketing' (cf. Heskett et al. 1997). Thus, Shostack and Grönroos envisioned marketing as a discipline devoted to producing the knowledge, methods, and practices needed for managing the human resources and their customer interaction from the perspective of customer orientation as prescribed by the marketing concept. In this regard, their intervention was very successful. Many of the subdisciplines of SMM—e.g. service quality (see Schneider and White 2004) and service orientation research (see Lytle et al. 1998)—that emerged after their intervention focused on developing practices for customer orienting the employees and their interaction skills. Similar ambitions have also guided research streams closely associated with SMM, e.g. relationship marketing (see Gummesson 2008) and market orientation research (see Kholi and Jaworski 1990; Narver and Slater 1990).

Toward a Service-Dominant Logic

The idea that the employees should be the main target of the managerialism of SMM is elaborated on in the influential works on the service-centered view which synthesize and elaborate on the central findings of SMM and closely related fields of research (Lusch and Vargo 2006; Lusch et al. 2007; Vargo and Lusch 2004; 2008a; 2008b; 2008c; Vargo and Morgan 2005; see also *Marketing Theory* 2006; *Journal of the Academy of Marketing Science* 2008). The service-centered view is articulated in the distinction between '*operand resources*', that is, 'resources on which an operation or act is preformed', e.g. 'land, animal life, plant life, minerals and other natural resources' and '*operant resources*', which are most prominently 'skills and knowledge' that are 'employed to act on operand resources (and other operant resources)' (Vargo and Lusch 2004: 2). Based on this distinction, two dominant logics (or worldviews) are articulated: the goods-dominant logic (G-D logic), where operand resources are considered primary, and the service-dominant logic (S-D logic), where operant resources have primacy. The basic argument of the service-centered view is that 'operant resources are the fundamental source of competitive advantage' (Vargo and Lusch

2008a: 6). Therefore, marketing research, practice, and education need to evolve into an S-D logic.

According to proponents of the S-D logic, the fundamental problem with previous marketing research is that it has been informed by the G-D logic. Previous marketing research has departed from the idea that oper- and resources, rather than operant resources, are the most important ones. This is particularly true for the marketing management school of thought which, as noted previously, has been mostly concerned with the customer orientation of products. However, SMM research has to some extent also been informed, according to Vargo and Lusch (2008b), by the G-D logic. In SMM, service and services have traditionally been defined as a residual of goods—service and services have been seen as something that goods are not—and have thus indirectly been premised upon the G-D logic. More particularly, the intangibility, heterogeneity, inseparability, and perishabil- ity of service production has been emphasized (Edvardsson et al. 2005; Lovelock and Gummesson 2004). 'In S-D logic service is defined as the application of specialized competences (operant resources—knowledge and skills), through deeds, processes and performances for the benefit of another entity or the entity itself' (Vargo and Lusch 2008b: 26). This implies that the employees, as in previous SMM research, are considered the prime managerial object. But it also implies that the S-D logic, in relation to some previous SMM research, reconsiders employees from perceiving them to be 'replaceable operand resources' to viewing them as 'operant resources'. In the S-D logic discourse, the employees 'become the primal source of inno- vation, organizational knowledge, and value' (Lusch et al. 2007: 15). The employees are turned into pure operant resources; that is 'pure knowledge and skills'. It is primarily this knowledge and skill that needs to be man- aged. Or putting it another way; by regulating the knowledge that employ- ees draw on when 'co-creating value' with their customers, the actions of the employees can be effectively managed and controlled.

However, because of the managerial orientation of SMM research, and the general lack of critical self-reflexive studies within this strand of research, little attention has been devoted to studying how organizations use and utilize the managerial practices that have been developed to cus- tomer orientate employees and their customer interaction. Like mainstream marketing research in general, SMM has largely focused on developing and prescribing managerial practices to organizations, but has not focused on systematically studying the effects of its prescriptions in practice. This is in spite of the fact that SMM practices have impacted extensively on the man- agement and organization of the work of service firms (see, for instance, Morgan and Sturdy 2000; Peccei and Rosenthal 2000; 2001). The mea- surement of service quality, the service orientation of corporate culture, and relationship marketing databases are only three examples of initiatives, associated with the SMM discourse, that have been widely drawn on by contemporary organizations.

The intention behind this book is to make the balance between managerially prescriptive and empirically critical marketing research more even by drawing on an empirical study of a Swedish financial institution—referred to herein as the FI—which is mainly active on the home loans market. FI management introduced SMM practices in order to customer orient the organization, i.e. the customer interaction of the frontline employees (FLEs), in particular, during the early years of the 21st century.[5] The practices associated with SMM research that were utilized included strategic service and market orientation, customer-perceived service quality measurement, coaching, and relationship marketing. In combining a critical conceptual analysis of the SMM practices which were drawn on at the FI, as represented in the academic literature by a critical analysis of the empirical findings, I ask the following question: *How do SMM practices facilitate the customer orientation of employees—particularly FLEs—and their customer interaction?* The next section introduces the perspective from which this question will be illuminated.

CRITIQUE AND POWER

The managerial and positivistic orientation of marketing and SMM research makes it similar to the broader field of management theory, largely occupied with developing organizational forms, management models, and practices 'proven' to contribute to economic performance in a better way than alternative frameworks. However, management theory is counterbalanced by the field of organization studies which is partly devoted to analyzing the forms of knowledge, methods, and practices that have been developed within the boundaries of management theory from a sociological and critical perspective (Hinings and Greenwood 2002). Whereas efficiency and effectiveness are the prime concerns of management theory, *power*, according to Hinings and Greenwood (2002), is the central concern of organization studies (see also Clegg et al. 2006). According to Merlo (et al. 2004; see also Gummesson 2008), power has been a neglected, almost absent, theme in empirical marketing research. When power has been dealt with, the analysis has mainly been framed by a managerialistic research agenda. The purpose has not been to challenge the potentially perverse effects of marketing practices on organizations and their members. Rather than questioning the power embedded in marketing discourse, the research into power within the boundaries of the marketing discipline has reproduced the power inherent in it. Indeed, some marketing scholars have claimed that marketing research has not focused very much on studying the role of marketing within organizations, from any perspective at all. Webster (2002: 69), for example, argues that 'There has been surprisingly little solid research on the organization of the marketing function, probably reflecting the complexity of the issue . . . [and] the general lack of training in the organizational theory area by academic marketing specialists'. In a similar manner, Harris and Ogbonna (2003: 483) claim that 'the topic of marketing organization is surprisingly understudied'. Despite this, Harris and Ogbonna (2003: 483) continue 'practitioners appear bombarded with conflicting and contradictory prescriptions for the organization of marketing' (see also Svensson 2007).

One of the broad aims of this book is to contribute toward establishing, together with other works on marketing that share a similar research orientation, a research stream whose relationship with (strategic) marketing theory and knowledge is similar to the relationship that organization studies have with management theory. In this book, I intend to turn power into a central analytical concept for marketing, as opposed to the managerial focus on customer orientation which has dominated marketing research for the last 50 years. Thus, in addition to studying, from a critical perspective, how SMM practices facilitate the customer orientation of employees and their customer interaction, *the present book also addresses the role of marketing in organizations, more broadly defined, and discusses why so little is known about this issue.* In line with Webster (2002), part of the problem will be attributed to academia. *Consequently, the book aims to contribute toward articulating an alternative identity for the academic marketing discipline: an identity which, by alluding to organizational studies, can be thought of in terms of marketing studies.*

Critical Management and Marketing Studies

But is power, as suggested by Hinings and Greenwood (2002) and Clegg et al. (2006), really the central notion of organization studies?[6] Institutional analysts (see, for instance, DiMaggio and Powell 1983; Meyer and Rowan 1977) might argue that it is not power but 'legitimacy' that is the central sociological notion of organization studies. Students of organizational culture (see, for instance, Alvesson 2002; Smircich 1983) might maintain that 'values' or perhaps 'symbols' should be given this privileged position, whereas scholars focusing on organizational sensemaking (Weick 1979; 1995) might argue that 'cognition' ought to have this position. Thus, if organizations and the organized are approached from a political, institutional, cultural, or cognitive perspective, different analytical concepts emerge as most central to organizational analysis (cf. Morgan 1986). I will argue that, rather than being the central notion of organization studies, power is the central notion of *critical* management studies (CMS)—the institutionalized label of this type of research. The type of analysis that I am pursuing here is not, thus, described most adequately as marketing studies, but as *critical marketing studies.* Another way to put it would be to say that I am pursuing critical management studies of the regime of knowledge and form of practice referred to as marketing and, more particularly, SMM.

CMS was formed as a field of inquiry in opposition to mainstream management theory in the late 1980s / early 1990s. Since then, it has grown in importance, particularly in the UK. Today, CMS has its own conferences, journals, interest groups, and websites, etc. It has been institutionalized as a field of academic inquiry in its own right. The distinguishing feature of CMS is that analysis of organizations is informed by thought traditions that question the prevailing order, e.g. critical theory and post-structuralist approaches. 'Critical' can, accordingly, mean slightly different things, depending on what framework that is being drawn on. However, the common concern for CMS is 'to interrogate and challenge received wisdom about management theory and practice. This wisdom is deeply coloured by managerialist assumptions—assumptions that take for granted the legitimacy and efficacy of established patterns of thinking and action . . . In contrast, critical perspectives on management share the aim of developing a less managerially partisan position' (Alvesson and Willmott 2003: 1). That power plays a key role in the critical project is clear from the following quote taken from an edited volume entitled *Critical Marketing— Defining the Field* (Saren et al. 2007a). In the introduction, it is stated that the purpose of critical research, including critical marketing research, is to 'make explicit certain ideologies and assumptions . . . [in order] to reveal the *power* relations and contested interests that are embedded in knowledge production' (Saren et al. 2007b: xviii, emphasis added). A key aim of CMS and critical marketing studies is, thus, to question managerialistic management and marketing theory and practice based on different forms of power analysis.

Although systematic, critical empirical research into SMM practices is nonexistent in critical marketing studies, a critical discourse on service firms has emerged within CMS. However, this discourse originated decades before the CMS label was invented. C. Wright Mills addressed the management and nature of service work early on in his classic book *White Collar* (Mills 1951). Arguing that the 'personality' of the 'white-collar worker' affected how the customers perceived the service, Mills took a point of departure similar to the pioneers of SMM. But contrary to the SMM scholars, Mills did not perceive the management of 'personality' as an unproblematic and unexploited managerial possibility. Rather, he was critical of the state of affairs. Mills (1951: xvii) wrote: 'When white-collar people get jobs, they sell not only their time and energy but their personalities as well. They sell by the week or month their smiles and their kindly gestures, and they must practice the prompt repression of resentment and aggression. For these intimate traits are of commercial relevance and required for the more efficient and profitable distribution of goods and services'. It is indeed possible to read Mills as though he argues that the need to advance critical research grows even stronger when human beings and their subjectivity become the main and direct object of a managerial regime or discourse, as is the case with SMM, than when a regime or discourse of management directly targets the material reality such as products, as in marketing management.

Mills has served as a main source of inspiration for sociologists studying service management and work critically. Several of his themes, e.g. emotional labor (Hochschild 1983), the routinization of service work, and the bureaucratization of service organizations (Leidner 1993; Ritzer 2004), have been elaborated on. Indeed, many of the empirical studies within CMS have focused on service firms. Some studies have even investigated, at least partly, themes associated with SMM discourse (see, for instance, du Gay 1996; du Gay and Salaman 1992; Fitchett and McDonugh 2001; Hodgson 2000; 2002; Manley 2001; Morgan and Sturdy 2000; Sturdy 1998). In addition, studies lacking an explicitly critical framework, but which still have implications for critical research, have focused on the extent and ways in which managerial regimes, including SMM, affect service work (see, for instance, Batt 2000; Harris and Ogbonna 1999; 2000; 2003 Lachman 2000; Peccei and Rosenthal 2000; 2001; Rosenthal et al. 1997). Although these studies have contributed toward articulating a critical discourse on service management and work, they still suffer, to varying degrees, from three shortcomings vis-à-vis the present study. Firstly, the studies are based on too shallow a conceptual and empirical analysis of SMM discourse and practices. SMM are often grouped together with other managerial discourses, e.g. TQM, HRM, and marketing management, resulting in the common managerial implications of the practices of all these discourses, rather than the particular implications of SMM practices, being focused upon. The aim has not primarily been to advance a critical analysis of SMM and marketing discourse. Secondly, the studies do not focus to any great extent on *how* SMM practices facilitate the customer orientation of the employees. The focus has instead been on the effects of SMM practices, and other customer orientation practices, on the employees and particularly the FLEs. However, because SMM are grouped together with other managerial regimes, the specific effects of SMM remain somewhat obscure. Thirdly, the analysis has not been able to capture how SMM practices operate as a form of power. This is largely due to the studies having been informed by frameworks not designed to analyze this aspect of SMM, and when the relevant frameworks have been drawn on, neither the conceptual nor the empirical analysis has been taken far enough.

A Foucauldian Power Analysis

I have chosen to draw on the notion of power articulated by Michel Foucault in order to critically analyze how SMM practices customer orient the employees and their interaction. Foucauldian-inspired frameworks have been drawn on extensively in empirical and conceptual analyses of management practices within CMS (see, for instance, Covaleski et al. 1998; Knights and McCabe 1999; Willmott 1993) and have been introduced into marketing in order to conduct conceptual analyses of marketing texts and history (see Shankar et al. 2006; Skålén et al. 2006; 2008; Skålén and Fougère 2007). In relation to the aims of the present study, several good reasons can be given for choosing to depart from Foucault's notion of power; two of which I want to mention right here. Firstly, Foucault studied how knowledge ordered the social and academic disciplines. The work of Foucault focuses on how discourses such as medicine, social medicine, psychology, crime, and sexuality (Foucault 1967; 1970; 1973; 1977; 1981a; 1985a; 1985b) order reality and how the prerogatives built into these discourses order knowledge production within, and the formation of, the academic disciplines themselves. Foucault's work provides a framework for studying how SMM practices order organizations and their members and how marketing orders itself as an academic discipline. Secondly, a particular focus of Foucault's was how power and knowledge order the subjectivity of people. Because subjectivity, for Foucault, is formed with reference to discourse, e.g. marketing, discourse is never neutral. Rather, discourse always has power effects. Therefore, Foucault prefers to speak about regimes of *power/ knowledge,* not power and knowledge as separated concepts. As opposed to traditional power theories (see, for instance, Lukes 1974), power is not, thus, coupled with an agency and not seen as something that agents or institutions can use to force people to do things against their will. Rather, power resides in knowledge and power/knowledge frames subjectivity and self conception. By working knowledge into people's self-understanding, knowledge has power effects by informing people how to view the world and by making them align themselves with the normativity built into systems of knowledge. Given that SMM scholars have argued that the marketing discipline should focus on outlining practices for managing employees (see previous references to Shostack and Grönroos), and that employees have recently been redefined in SMM discourse as operant resources, or pure *knowledge* and skills (see previous references to Vargo and Lusch), the power/knowledge framework is well suited to empirically studying how SMM practices order, on the one hand, employees and their subjectivity and, on the other, the marketing discipline and its 'identity'.

A Foucauldian analysis is critical because it makes explicit the political nature of discourses or systems of truths. It exposes discourses such as marketing as regimes of power/knowledge and problematizes the subject positions they prescribe. The aim is 'to question truth on its effect of power and question power on its discourses of truth . . . critique would essentially insure the desubjugation of the subject in the context of what we could call, in a word, the politics of truth' (Foucault 1997: 32). By uncovering what kind of power/knowledge effects a discourse and its associated practices has, it becomes possible for people to move away from the hold that a discourse has on them.

Within the boundaries of CMS, the main alternative to a Foucauldian approach is critical theoretical analysis, which also aims to uncover hidden power structures. In contrast to critical theoretical approaches, a Foucauldian analysis ends when these power structures have been uncovered. It does not propose emancipation by promoting a certain worldview, as does critical theory (see Alvesson and Willmott 1992; Alvesson and Willmott 1996). Foucault took the stance that it was not desirable to replace one normativity with another because of the risk of not seeing the potential power implications of the new normativity.

OUTLINE OF THE BOOK

The book is structured as follows. In the second chapter, there is a fuller presentation of the Foucauldian framework. This presentation is intertwined with a critical discussion of marketing management discourse and SMM. Pastoral and disciplinary power emerge as central analytical notions for conducting the conceptual and empirical analysis of the SMM practices drawn on by the FI. Before presenting this analysis, Chapter 3 describes the nature of the FI as an organization prior to the introduction of the SMM practices in 2002. Chapter 4 is devoted to an empirical and conceptual pastoral-power-informed analysis of the strategic service and market orientation program of the FI and of the service and market orientation literature. The focus is on explicating the ethic that such programs elicit and how this ethic governs the FLEs of the FI in a pastoral fashion. Chapter 5 conceptualizes the service quality discourse as a form of disciplinary power and suggests that the disciplinary effect of the measurement of service quality at the FI convinced management that the FLEs were reactive but needed to be more proactive. In order to accomplish such a shift in FLE subjectivity, management introduced coaching and relationship marketing. Coaching is related to service quality discourse and positioned as a form of pastoral power in Chapter 5, also suggesting the ways in which the coaching practices used at the FI ingrain the subject position of proactivity into the FLEs. Chapter 6 is devoted to relationship marketing. The conceptual analysis argues that relationship marketing discourse fosters change in people through disciplinary and pastoral power. The empirical analysis of the relationship marketing project conducted at the FI suggests the extent and way in which these forms of power affect the FLEs. In the seventh and concluding chapter, the implications of the preceding analysis vis-à-vis SMM research, the role of marketing in organizations, and academic marketing research are discussed. Questions pertaining to methodology and method may be found in the Appendix.

2 Power and Marketing

In his inaugural speech at the *Collège de France* in 1971, Foucault (1981b) argued that his previous works had dealt with power despite the fact that the word power had not been explicitly used frequently. At the beginning of the 1980s, he stated: 'It is not power, but the subject, that is the general theme of my research' (Foucault 2000a: 327). It is true that, at different points in time, Foucault put more emphasis on one or the other of the notions of power and subjectivity. But I would like to suggest that it is hard to understand the work of Foucault without relating his notion of power to his notion of subjectivity, and vice versa, because of the interdependency of these two concepts in his writings. Power and subjectivity are thus central to the analytical framework presented in the present chapter. However, other key notions such as pastoral and disciplinary power, managerial rationalities and practices, and technologies will also be discussed.[1]

The emerging framework is related to the central tenets of marketing research. The analytical focus of the present book—SMM discourse and practices—is the center of attention. However, because SMM, as suggested in the introduction, is partly a problematization and critique of marketing management and because it partly builds on and elaborates marketing management discourse, SMM discourse will be juxtaposed with marketing management. The two bodies of knowledge will be presented as forms of power/knowledge and, more particularly, as forms of pastoral and disciplinary power. The focus will also be on what managerial rationality is fostered by academic managerial marketing discourse, what type of subject position it elicits, and what practices and technologies it has developed in order to foster subjectification.

POWER/KNOWLEDGE AND MARKETING

According to Foucault (1977; 1981a; 1997; 2007), power has three central anchoring points: Law, Science, and Christianity. These three anchoring points are associated with three different forms of power: *Sovereign power* (Law); *Disciplinary power* (Science), and *Pastoral power* (Christianity), of which the latter two will be discussed in detail toward the end of this chapter. The conceptualization of power that still dominates in social theory is sovereign power (Clegg 1989), associated with the works of Machiavelli, Hobbes, Marx, Weber, and Dahl, among others. A sovereign understanding of power presupposes that power belongs to certain actors and that these actors can use their power to force other persons and groups of persons to carry out actions against their will. Sovereign power is interwoven with certain formal and informal positions in the societal structure, which legitimizes the exercising of power (see Lukes 1974 for an overview). It is possible to interpret the literature on the service-centered view as associating the G-D logic, and thus marketing management, with sovereign power. This is the case, for example, when leadership is discussed: 'The leadership of many G-D logic organizations is based largely on the manipulation of rewards and punishments and is, accordingly, a coercive form of leadership. It is also based on asymmetric information with the leader and organization holding much information private and out of the reach of employees' (Lusch et al. 2007: 15). In a G-D logic organization leaders have power which they use to force people to do things they would not otherwise do.

Foucault criticized the notion of sovereign power, arguing that, during modernity, with its focus on rationality and objective truths, on the one hand, and its belief in common ethics such as the Christian worldview, on the other, it would be unrealistic to assume that power could be exercised arbitrarily by a sovereign against the will of the masses. This claim caused Foucault to depart from the dominant power theory in two key ways. Firstly, rather than being just a negative force, power, to Foucault (and many other recent power theorists; see Clegg et al. 2006 for an overview), is both positive and negative, productive and destructive. This reconceptualization enables us to find power in social domains and discourses which, according to a sovereign understanding of power, would be considered power-free zones. It enables us, for example, to find power in the discourse of S-D logic despite the fact that the researchers behind the framework seek to constitute it as free from power by implicitly associating the opposing G-D logic with and disassociating the S-D logic from a sovereign conceptualization of power (see Lusch et al. 2007; Vargo and Lusch 2008b). However, at the same time as the S-D logic is disassociated from sovereign power, the framework is associated with a positive understanding of power. This is evident, for example, when Lusch et al. (2007: 15, emphasis added) write about leadership from an S-D logic point of view, arguing that 'when employees are viewed and treated [as operant resources] they become empowered in their role as value co-creators . . . The role of the leader [according to S-D logic] is to be a *servant-leader* who is there to serve the employees, rather than employees serving the leader'. This is in line with Lytle et al. (1998) who talk about the importance of 'servant leadership' for service orienting organizations. Building up and empowering people's subjectivity by being kind and gentle, as 'servant leadership' implies, is as much a demonstration of power as being cruel and forceful because it directs people's attention and action in certain ways (Cruikshank 1994; Foucault 2007).

Secondly, and in addition to viewing power as both negative and positive, Foucault 'de-commodified' power by arguing that, rather than being the property of a sovereign, power is situated between people; in the discourses it is embedded in—it is relational. During modernity, sovereign power as well as disciplinary and pastoral power, he argued, always have to be legitimated with reference to an objective truth or common good, hence the notion *power/knowledge* (Foucault 1977; 2007). Power, according to Foucault, is always embedded in, and operates through, forms of discourse or knowledge and knowledge/discourse always has potential power effects. Given that my focus in this book is to study marketing and, in particular, SMM discourse/knowledge from a power perspective in combination with the operant resources—knowledge and skills—being the main managerial object of SMM, at least according to the S-D logic perspective, the close coupling between power and knowledge in the Foucauldian framework makes it appropriate for the present study.

DISCOURSE AND MARKETING

Central to a Foucauldian analysis of power is, thus, the notion of *discourse / knowledge* systems. Very generally, discourse can be defined as 'a particular way of talking about and understanding the world (or an aspect of the world)' (Phillips and Jørgensen 2002: 1). In order to define discourse more precisely, I draw on Laclau and Mouffe (1985) who make a distinction between two forms of 'differential positions' or signs—'elements' and 'moments'—in order to theorize what a discourse is. Elements are signs whose meanings have not been fixated in discourse, whereas moments are signs with a fixed meaning. 'Articulation' entails 'any practices establishing a relation among elements such that their identity is modified as a result of the articulatory practice' (Laclau and Mouffe 1985: 105). If the elements acquire a fixed meaning through articulations, they are turned into moments. 'The structured totality [of moments] resulting from the articulatory practice, we will call discourse' (Laclau and Mouffe 1985: 105). According to Laclau and Mouffe, discourse consists of signs that have acquired a precise meaning through articulatory practices: Discourse can be 'understood as the fixation of meaning within a particular domain' (Phillips and Jørgensen 2002: 26). Marketing became a discourse, and more precisely a managerial discourse, with the marketing management school of thought and the articulation of the marketing concept. The latter still is the most important nodal point—the privileged signs of discourse that give discourses a coherent meaning (Laclau and Mouffe 1985)—of marketing discourse (see Skålén et al. 2008). To some degree, actors can choose which discourse to position themselves in and see the world through, which discourses to embrace, and which discourses to reject or resist, but actors can never meaningfully conceive of the social world outside of discourse. Laclau and Mouffe (1985) do not suggest—as some of their critics have claimed—that the social world is discourse. They suggest that the social world is always mediated by, and only meaningfully conceivable through discourse.

As Foucault (1967; 1970; 1972; 1973; 2006) and 'post-Foucauldians' such as Rose (1996; 1999) and Dean (1999) have suggested, the social and behavioral sciences are important for fixating the meaning of the language referring to particular social domains and thus for constructing discourses and regimes of power/knowledge. Indeed, the figure of the researcher can be thought of as one of the more important 'discourse and power/knowledge producers' in contemporary society. This is also why academic discourse becomes an important object of study in both Foucauldian and other discourse analytical approaches. Academic discourse is not only conceived of as describing the world, but also as prescribing the world—it is perceived as performative creating the object it describes (Phillips and Jørgensen 2002). The privileged position given to academic discourse as standing outside of the social reality representing it is deconstructed in Foucauldian discourse analysis, implying that academic discourse is never approached by asking the positivistic and empiricistic question about how well the propositions of a theory account for the empirical reality. Rather, the focus is on the truth effects that a certain theory has and the kind of reality it envisions. Rather than focusing on whether or not academic theories are true, the focus is on the potential and actual ordering effects of the truth they prescribe (Foucault 1970). As pointed out in the introduction, the aim is critical, it is to question and problematize the effects of truth and support the subject in breaking free from truth (see Foucault 1997). This anti-positivistic and critical standpoint vis-à-vis the nature of academic discourse and truth has methodological and analytical implications for studying how practices associated with academic discourse order organizations and their members. The focus of this book will be studying the SMM practices that are drawn on by the FI by means of situating them as forms of power/knowledge and by focusing on what ordering effect they have on FI employees, not on whether or not these practices describe reality in an accurate way. Accordingly, I will not focus my attention on whether or not these practices are true, but on their truth effects. The ontology and epistemology of the present study thus break radically with mainstream academic marketing research.[2]

Marketing's Managerial Rationality

The discussion in the previous section suggests that academic managerial marketing discourse can be perceived as a form of power/knowledge which simultaneously describes and prescribes social reality. Like other behavioral and social sciences (Rose 1996; 1999), marketing can be envisioned as filters suggesting what actions that are possible and plausible. More to the point, academic marketing can be perceived as a regime of government—as a type of *governmentality*—prescribing customer focus to organizations and employees. The notion of governmentality surfaced in Foucault's lectures at *Collège de France* in the latter half of the 1970s (Foucault 2007). Governmentality is a neologism derived from the terms 'government', 'mentality', and 'rationality' (Dean 1999; Townley 1994). Governmentalities are discourses that promote certain rationalities (ways of knowing) that further certain mentalities (ways of thinking) that inform specific types of government or management: that is, a more or less calculated direction of human conduct (Dean 1999; Foucault 1981a; 1985a; 2007; Rose 1999). In using the term *managerial rationality,* I refer to the various ways of knowing the object of management which management, leadership, and marketing discourses address.

The G-D and S-D logics of marketing can be perceived as two distinctive governmentalities, albeit with a common point of departure (cf. Zwick et al. 2008). This common point of departure is the marketing concept plus the managerial rationality of market and customer orientation associated with it, being central to both 'logics' (Vargo and Lusch 2008b). In this book, this management rationality will be referred to using the notion of *customerism.* It will be argued, furthermore, that the managerial rationality of customerism prescribes *customeristic* subjectivities and ways of approaching reality.

> Customerism is a form of governmental rationality that, through prescribing certain practices and technologies, aims to establish customer needs and demands as the point of reference for management, organizational behavior, the design and development of organizational forms and the products and services that organizations offer. Within marketing discourse, customerism is signified by concepts such as customer orientation, marketing orientation, market orientation, service dominant logic, and the marketing concept.
>
> (Skålén et al. 2008: 152–53)

The G-D and S-D logics can be perceived as governmentalities because they promote 'dominant' logics which seek to direct human conduct in specific ways by promoting distinctive ways of knowing (rationalities) and thinking (mentalities). The notion of dominant logic is indistinctly defined in the work of Vargo and Lusch, but they argue that 'a worldview or dominant logic . . . more or less seeps into the individual and collective mind-set' (2004: 2). A dominant logic of marketing implies, furthermore, a 'shift in perspective for marketing scholars, marketing practitioners, and marketing educators' (Vargo and Lusch 2004: 1). The G-D and S-D logics are thus marketing frameworks that provide collectives of marketing practitioners with worldviews—that is, ways of knowing and thinking about the world or expressed more simply: governmentalities. Whereas the former perceives value to be embedded in operand resources and focuses attention on units of output, the latter holds that value is realized in use and co-created by the employees and customers; that is, co-created by different 'operant resources'.

Vargo and Lusch (2008c) argue that the marketing management school of thought is informed by the G-D logic (governmentality) of marketing. This is in spite of the fact that the pioneers of marketing management, in Keith's words, argued that the implementation of marketing management implied a 'mental revolution' (Keith 1960; see also, for instance, Alderson 1957; Borsch 1957; Drucker 1954; Levitt 1960; McKitterick 1957 for similar positions). One is led to think that it is the employees who are the main target—or the object that is to be known—in this form of managerialism. However, a thorough reading (see Skålén et al. 2008) of the marketing management literature suggests that this is not the case. The practices—or ways of knowing—that are promoted in marketing management discourse to foster the customerism that the marketing concept prescribes, e.g. segmentation, targeting, and the marketing mix, all focus on products rather than people. In addition, 'as directed by G-D logic [such as marketing management], they [employees] are considered operand resources, and thus potentially viewed as replaceable and treated transactionally . . . In G-D logic, not only are . . . employees often undervalued, they are often undercultivated, if not mistreated' (Vargo and Lusch 2008b: 33). In marketing management, the focus is on the operand resources and the employees are treated as one such resource among others.[3]

As suggested in the introductory chapter, this is not the case in SMM research. The ground-breaking papers of Shostack (1977) and Grönroos (1978; 1982; 1984) turned the employees and their customer interaction into the main object of knowing/management (cf. the notion of interactive marketing) whereas the equally ground-breaking papers of Vargo and Lusch and colleagues (see Lusch et al. 2007; Vargo and Lusch 2004; 2008a; 2008b; 2008c; Vargo and Morgan 2005) turned the employees into operant resources—'pure knowledge and skills'. The major reason for focusing on the employees in SMM discourse is the belief that value is produced when interacting with the customers and that the employees, particularly the frontline employees (FLEs), are the most important organizational agents in this interactive value-creation process. This supposition has resulted in the production of practices and ways of knowing (rationalities) the employees, such as the strategic service and market orientation, customer-perceived service quality measurement, coaching, and relationship marketing studied in the present book, intended to instill a customeristically informed way of thinking (mentalities) into the employees with the ultimate aim of making them co-create services or interact with the customers in ways aligned with the managerial rationality of customerism. In summary, the opposition between the G-D and S-D logics of marketing can be seen as a struggle between two competing governmentalities striving for hegemony in managerial marketing discourse.

SUBJECT POSITIONS IN MARKETING DISCOURSE

It should be noted, however, that how and to what extent the managerial rationality associated with a particular discourse orders reality usually needs to be directly empirically studied—through interviews or observations. Or formulated differently: without systematic empirical studies, it cannot be taken for granted that a discourse really orders a particular social domain. Indeed, a justified criticism leveled at some Foucauldian discourse analysis is that it only relies on archival data failing to check whether texts and rhetoric materialize, thus downplaying individual agency (see, for instance, Thompson and Ackroyd 1995). However, empirical studies need not be the departure point of discourse analysis. Rather, discourse analysis of a particular field can start with an elucidation of the rationality of a discourse by focusing on textual representations of it acknowledging that this rationality is what the discourse promotes and elicits, not what the social world ends up being (Dean 1999). Such conceptual analysis might pave the way for and direct firsthand empirical studies. If the object of textual analysis is the social, human, or behavioral sciences, such as in the present case where SMM is the object of analysis, one central focus will be the *subject positions* that the regime of power/knowledge elicits and promotes. This is so because the object of knowledge of these sciences is humans. They offer people possibilities and plausibilities to constitute their *subjectivity,* which is the main way that power/knowledge orders the social.

To Foucault (1977; 1981a; 1985a), subjectivity is not associated with the stable constellation of attributes, beliefs, values, motives, and experiences which resides in the individual and constitutes the person. Foucault thus breaks away from the notion of identity that is inherent in modern psychology (Foucault 2006; Rose 1996). Rather, subjectivity, according to Foucault, is externalized; inherent in discourses or regimes of power/ knowledge are subject positions—ways of being and acting in the social world—which actors draw on in order to constitute themselves. For Foucault, the subject is 'a position that can be filled in certain conditions by various individuals' (Foucault 1977 quoted in Bergström and Knights 2006: 354). Accordingly, Foucault's notion of subjectivity has been utilized in critical management studies to analyze what possibilities the different management discourses—including (but not restricted to) total quality management (Knights and McCabe 1999; Quist et al. 2007), human resource management (Townley 1993), and management by objectives (Covaleski et al. 1998)—provide managers and employees with when constituting their selves, as well as how they make these possibilities a part of themselves. To contradict the interpretation of Foucault's work by some of his critics, Foucault did not argue that subjectivity is determined by discourse but that subjectivity arises as an interaction between human agency and discourse. Therefore, as pointed out previously, it cannot be taken for granted, without empirical investigation, that the subject positions promoted by marketing, for instance, become central to the employees' subjectivity (Bergström and Knights 2006; McCabe 2007).

Foucault's notion of subjectivity is tricky. The notion of subject positions, in particular, might lead the wrong way. One can get the impression that people can only choose between distinct, complete 'subjectivity packs' regulating every aspect of human beings. That discourses provides humans with such comprehensive 'subjectivity packs' can be the case, but seldom is. In order to bring precision to the notion of subjectivity, I, along with Latour (2005), argue that discourse provides humans with 'plug-ins', a metaphor borrowed from the language of the Internet. When you surf the Internet, you might not always gain access to a specific site because your computer lacks the right 'plug-in'. A friendly warning will appear on your screen suggesting that you need to download a piece of software which 'once installed on your system, will allow you to activate what you were unable to see before' (Latour 2005: 207). In the same way that the Internet provides your computer with the necessary plug-ins, discourse provides you with 'plug-ins' whenever you 'need' them. Subject positions are thus differential positions—not complete 'personalities'—which discourse provides actors with in order for them to constitute themselves (cf. Laclau and Mouffe 1985). In order 'to obtain "complete" human actors, you [the researcher] have to compose them out of many successive layers, each of which is empirically distinct from the next' (Latour 2005: 207). This also implies that the person can recompose him- or herself by drawing on various available 'plug-ins' or positions at different points in time operating with a particular subjectivity at any one given moment but with a different one during the next. It also implies that the 'plug-ins', or positions provided by a particular discourse, will give rise to different effects when blending together with the layers that the person already consists of. Subjectivity cannot be dictated by discourse.

Along with marketing management, marketing turned into a general managerial discipline but, as we have seen, a managerial discipline that had products or operand resources as its primary object rather than people or operant resources. Therefore, it cannot be claimed that marketing management offers customeristic subject positions or 'plug-ins' of customer and market orientation to all kinds of employees. This was not the case. The managerial rationality of marketing management did not, for instance, target blue-collar staff, nor did it target most white-collar staff either: these staff categories did not need to behave and think in a customeristic way. The types of staff being targeted by marketing management were workers in marketing and sales. It can be argued that marketing management provided subject positions and 'plug-ins' in order for people to constitute themselves as modern marketers focused on activities associated with marketing research, advertising, and segmentation and modern marketing managers focused on deriving policies detailing how to produce products suited to the targeted markets (Skålén et al. 2008). In SMM discourse, in contrast, every employee is turned into a marketer. Or, expressed differently; according to SMM discourse, all employees need to think and act in a customeristic way. Because, in SMM discourse, the employees of service organizations are largely preoccupied with co-creating services and products with their customers and because these customers, in the terminology of Grönroos (1978), not only evaluate *what* they get but also *how* service production is carried out, the managerial rationality of marketing needs to be embodied in each and every employee. Evert Gummesson's concept of 'the part-time marketer' is illuminating in this respect, prescribing that all employees needs to see themselves as marketers in service organizations, at least on a part-time basis (Gummesson 1991). In SMM discourse, every organizational member thus becomes an object of the managerial rationality of marketing, but the FLEs are targeted in particular because they are the ones who do most of the interacting with customers. Exactly what subject positions and 'plug-ins' that are promoted by SMM discourse will be a central focus of the conceptual analysis in Chapters 4, 5, and 6.

MARKETING'S MANAGERIAL PRACTICES AND TECHNOLOGIES

However, social, humanistic, and behavioral discourse / science not only embeds subject positions and 'plug-ins', it also promotes *technologies* and *practices* facilitating the construction of subjectivity. It is thus important when analyzing such a discourse, e.g. SMM, to explicate which technologies and practices are being promoted. Based on Rose (1996), I understand technologies as detailed, often standardized, examinations and methods that promote a certain type of control of human behavior. Practices are less detailed prescriptions of how things should be done or descriptions of how things should be acted upon, as well as thought and felt about, but work in the same way as technologies. The distinction between practices and technologies is fluid and blurred. Practices may be produced by, and may in turn produce, technologies; but practices may also lack a 'technological foundation'. In such cases, they may be regarded as specifications of broader ideals (Hasselbladh and Kallinikos 2000). The 'technologies of the self' which, according to Foucault (1977; 1997; see also Townley 1998), are inherent in most other technologies and practices are the *confession* and the *examination,* and these will be discussed in relation to the notions of pastoral and disciplinary power in the next section.

In many discourses, e.g. marketing, technologies and practices are not normally treated as control devices, therefore a power/knowledge analysis needs to reposition them as such. More precisely, the analysis needs to suggest what assumptions about human beings technologies and practices pre-require as well as how they 'operationalize' the managerial rationality of the discourse they are embedded in, e.g. customerism, when it comes to marketing discourse. Because these assumptions are based on knowledge that is considered true, the technologies and practices are infused with power: they are the tools of power/knowledge. However, on the basis of these assumptions, technologies and practices also produce 'true' knowledge, establishing norms of appropriate behavior, thinking, and emotion and offering approaches that regulate people toward norms.

The most important practices associated with marketing management discourse are market segmentation, targeting, and the marketing mix. As previously noted, these do not directly target the employees and thus probably have only a limited capacity to reshape the whole organization in line with the managerial rationality of customerism. As an effect of turning the employees into the main target of the managerial rationality of marketing in SMM, a vast number of sophisticated technologies and practices for regulating the conduct of employees have been developed, e.g. strategic service and market orientation, customer-perceived service quality measurement, coaching, and relationship marketing studied conceptually and empirically in this book.

THE DISCIPLINARY AND PASTORAL POWER OF MARKETING

I opened this chapter by arguing that Foucault theorized power as a negative and positive force residing in discourse and as a regulator of relationships between people. Therefore, Foucauldian power analysis should be distanced from notions of sovereign power and informed by the concept of power/knowledge. I also argued that the former view of power informs the G-D logic and associated the S-D logic with power/knowledge—the latter view of power thus being central to the present analysis. Foucault discussed two main forms of power/knowledge—*disciplinary* and *pastoral power*—and these will be the main analytical concepts for conducting the conceptual and empirical analysis of the SMM practices drawn on by the FI in Chapters 4, 5, and 6. Disciplinary power and pastoral power order the social reality and direct the social construction of subjectivity in different ways. More specifically, Foucault argued that these two forms of power/knowledge direct the construction of subjectivity by drawing on two 'technologies of the self', i.e. technologies or practices of a heuristic nature which are inherent in most other technologies and practices and which can therefore be used to shed light on how power works more generally.

In several studies, Foucault (1977; 1981a; 2007) showed that disciplinary power operates through *examinations* and that pastoral power operates through *confessions*. The present section suggests that the managerial practices associated with SMM are more purely pastoral and disciplinary power practices than are those associated with marketing management.

Marketing and Disciplinary Power

Disciplinary power (Foucault 1977; 2000a) defines subjectivity from 'the outside in' (Covaleski et al. 1998). Functioning like examinations, practices of disciplinary power turn people into objects of knowledge. Examinations embody the norms promoted by the regimes of power/knowledge that they are embedded in and reveal, by generating knowledge about the person that they have as their object, gaps between the person's present state and that norm: i.e. gaps between actuality and possibility. This enables management of people in order to foster a movement toward the norm: by closing gaps between the actual self and the ideal subject position, the person, by means of disciplinary power, becomes both a subject of knowledge and subjected to knowledge. Disciplinary power, hence, subjectifies by fostering normalization. Medical examinations are an excellent example of the operation of disciplinary power. The physician examines the patient in relation to medical discourse and seeks to 'normalize' the patient by prescribing a cure that is consistent with the recommendations given by medical discourse.

Examinations manifest disciplinary power through their ability to compare. 'Generally there are two systems of comparison: the creation of an order through a taxonomy, a sequence of descriptive language (taxinomia); or the establishment of an order through measurement (mathesis)' (Townley 1994: 30, drawing on Foucault 1972; 1977). Informed by 'truths' produced within the social and behavioral sciences, as well as by experts such as consultants, taxinomia and mathesis order people into categories and groups which provide them with a potential subjectivity. Taxonomies and measurement practices are not only technologies associated with a certain type of power, they also facilitate the production of knowledge—they provide, in accordance with the power/knowledge they are embedded in, information about who the person 'really' is. As Townley (1994: 32) argues: 'Both taxinomia and mathesis facilitate management or governance. They provide for the arrangement of identities and differences into ordered tables and create a grid, a configuration of knowledge, which may be placed over a domain'.

Despite the fact that marketing management discourse does not address human beings directly, it can be conceived of as a form of disciplinary power, albeit an incomplete one. The most central practices promoted in order to realize the marketing concept—segmentation, targeting, and the marketing mix—are classification systems which suggest that they function as examinations and, more particularly, as taxonomies. The four Ps—the best known version of the marketing mix—is, for instance, a practice for determining what *products* to produce, what *prices* they should be sold at, what *promotional* activities should be carried out in order to sell them, and at which *places* the products should be offered (Borden 1964). Analyzing a particular product by drawing on the four Ps framework enables the marketing personnel at a specific firm to get to know that the product has the wrong color and too low a price, and that it is being promoted through the wrong marketing channels and sold in the wrong places. In this way, the four Ps framework reveals a gap between the present and ideal states and enforces the power that marketing management has on the product. In order to reduce this gap, the marketers need to change their ways of perceiving the products, as well as their ways of marketing them, because dissimilar categories of products need to be marketed differently. Reducing the gap that disciplinary power practices have made visible thus entails, to some extent, changes in the people using them. More particularly, the marketing mix presupposes that marketing staff are 'mixers of marketing ingredients'. Thus, when marketers use the marketing mix, they are positioned as particular types of marketers. The marketing mix positions marketers as 'bartenders' of marketing (cf. Borden 1964).

Some of the central technologies and practices of SMM can be perceived as purer forms of disciplinary power. Customer-perceived service quality measurement models, for example, directly target human beings, focusing on factors such as the empathy, appearance, and reliability of the staff (see Skålén et al. 2006; 2008; Skålén and Fougère 2007). Building on a factor analysis of which organizational constituents are able to explain variances in service quality—many of these factors directly addressing human behavior—standardized measurement scales and surveys (i.e. examinations) have been developed in the service quality literature. Service quality models typically invite the customers of the focal organization to rank the level of perceived service quality on ordinal scales. Normally, the customers' replies concern how they want the employees to behave—their expectations about behavior—and how the staff actually behave—the actual customer-perceived behavior—by means of answering the same types of questions. Accordingly, the results can be used to check whether or not the customers feel that the employees behave in a way the customers want them to. If this is not the case, gaps between the ideal and the actuality is made visible. Suggestions for reducing the gaps, by changing the employees, are suggested by the models (see Schneider and White 2004 for an overview). In this way, customer-perceived measurement models, like other types of SMM technologies and practices, can be seen as forms of disciplinary power subjectifying from 'the outside in'.

Marketing and Pastoral Power

Rather than defining subjectivity, from 'the outside in', as disciplinary power, pastoral power defines subjectivity from 'the inside out' (Covaleski et al. 1998). The word pastoral is usually associated with Christianity, but pastoral power and two of its central functions—confession and avowal—shed light on how power is manifested and executed in many societal domains, hence being able to serve as a metaphor for conceptualizing how power is exercised more generally (Foucault 1977; 2007; Townley 1994). Thus, the notion of pastoral power should not be seen as a literal description of how power is realized in most contemporary congregations or of how pastors work, but as a notion focusing attention on certain power relations which, in their form, contain certain general commonalities with an ideal typical understanding of the Christian pastoral. The specific type of manager whom we refer to when using the word pastor wields power over a collective of people. The role of the pastor is to guide and lead a flock of sheep who, within organizations, are the employees. The pastor thus signifies a type of manager who primarily focuses on managing people. Pastoral management focuses on material reality only if it influences how people conduct themselves. The pastor manages by means of her/his inner qualities, which are considered superior to the inner qualities of the people constituting the 'flock'. The objective of pastoral management is to secure the managed subjects aligning themselves with an implicit or explicit ethic such as customerism (Foucault 2000b; 2007). One mark of a pastoral discourse is that it prescribes such an ethic to a particular domain.

In order to orient people toward a certain ethic, the operation of pastoral power is dependent upon knowing the innermost thoughts of the sheep. Based on this knowledge, the pastor will be able to direct and lead the collective of people he or she is appointed to lead (Foucault 1985a; 2000a; 2000b). Pastoral power thus depends upon technologies and/or practices in order to make individuals talk about themselves; it requires *confessional* technologies and practices. By means of the avowals that confessional technologies generate, it is possible for the pastor to guide and lead the confessor 'from the inside out' in ways that the manager believes to be appropriate. But confessing and avowing subjects will also subjectify themselves without the support of an outside force. When speaking about themselves, they will reveal, to themselves, what types of people they are (Covaleski et al. 1998). If they are not satisfied with who they are—a satisfaction contingent on the ethic informing the operation of the particular type of pastoral power—they may try to change themselves in order to accord with the governmental ethic better. Accordingly, pastoral power promotes and makes possible self-reflexive subjectification (Clegg et al. 2002).

Marketing management discourse turned customerism into the central ethic of marketing. As such, it can be treated as a pastoral discourse delineating a distinct rationality. In addition, marketing management discourse has distinguished between 'pastors' and 'sheep' by giving different roles to the marketing managers and to the marketers. The marketing manager is given the role of guiding and leading the marketing department and the marketers. As such, marketing managers can be envisioned as pastors with the role of interpreting actions and information in the light of the pre-scribed customeristic ethic, adapting this ethic to the local organization. The marketer, on the other hand, can be seen as constituting the flock of sheep that ought to be guided and directed in accordance with the mar-keting manager's perception of customerism. Other factors speak against marketing management discourse being perceived as a pastoral discourse, at least a fully fledged one. In particular, the practices and technologies associated with this form of knowing—e.g., segmentation, targeting, and the marketing mix—can hardly be used by managers to make employees confess their innermost thoughts, which is a prerequisite for pastoral power to operate effectively (see preceding). The technologies and practices associ-ated with marketing management cannot perform the function of making the employees talk about themselves. As pointed out previously, they do not even target the marketer but the customer and / or consumer.

As we have seen, SMM discourse has remained true to the customeristic ethic of marketing management, but has elaborated on it and redirected it toward the employees of the focal organization. Because SMM discourse presupposes that value is produced during the interaction between employ-ees and customers, making the employees customeristic became just as important, if not even more so, than making products in accordance with customer requirements. The management of human resources was no lon-ger just a human resource management issue, it had also become a mar-keting issue. The understanding that customers coproduce services with employees, that customers see employees as a part of the service, and that customers take employee behaviors into account when evaluating service production formed the foundation which the field of SMM was built upon (Grönroos 1978; 1982; 1984; Shostack 1977). Accordingly, the technolo-gies and practices of SMM were designed in order to gain knowledge of whether or not the employees were customeristic. Service quality measure-ment models, discussed previously, are one example, relationship market-ing practices another. Such models and regimes of power/knowledge help managers to detect deviations from the rationality of customerism in their employees, and they help employees to detect such deviations in themselves. As such, they inspire and guide managers to talk to their employees in ways that facilitate employee confessions that are contingent on the customeristic managerial rationality of marketing. Or, in the words of Lusch et al. (2007: 15), leadership in the S-D logic implies that 'employee-manager interaction compromises conversation and dialog and the development of norms of relational behaviour such as trust, open communication and solidarity'. Organizations permeated by the S-D logic are thus characterized by a con-fessional and avowing climate. The avowals generated in such an organiza-tion are a prerequisite for leading and guiding the 'servant' subject and for these subjects to lead themselves reflexively toward the customeristic ethic embedded in marketing discourse.

SUMMARY OF THE ANALYTICAL FRAMEWORK

This chapter has introduced the Foucualdian power/knowledge framework, which will be drawn on in order to shed light on the aims of the present study: that is, to illuminate how SMM practices facilitate the customer orientation of employees, to discuss the role of marketing in organizations, and to articulate an alternative identity for the marketing discipline. Indeed, this chapter has already contributed to this critical project by positioning SMM and marketing management discourse as regimes of power/knowledge. This chapter has also introduced the notions of disciplinary and pastoral power, which will be drawn on in order to conduct the empirical and conceptual analysis of the studied SMM practices in Chapters 4, 5, and 6. Before embarking on this analysis, the case of the FI will be presented in Chapter 3. There will be a particular focus on the nature of the organization prior to the introduction of SMM practices in 2002.

3 The Bureaucratic Organization and the Reactive Employee

This chapter introduces the case organization—the Financial Institute (FI)—and provides a short description of its history. It analyzes the nature of the organization and the subjectivity of its FLEs prior to the introduction of SMM practices in 2002. As such, the chapter provides an image that the empirical analysis of the SMM practices in Chapters 4, 5, and 6 is mirrored against. The chapter does not intend to provide a comprehensive overview of the FI nor of the financial markets it operates on, but rather to review the aspects of the organization relevant to understanding the dynamics associated with the introduction of SMM practices at the FI. As should be clear from the previous chapters, the present study is devoted to (strategic) marketing: it is not a study of the nature of financial service firms (see, for instance, Morgan and Sturdy 2000 for the latter). Because the chapter provides a broad empirical backdrop to the introduction of SMM practices, the Foucauldian analysis is not as elaborated on as in subsequent chapters. In addition, other theoretical frameworks are drawn on, e.g. labor process theory.

The chapter opens with a brief description of the history of the FI and introduces its formal organizational structure. This is followed by a section showing that the FI, when expanding extensively during the 1990s, mostly hired efficient but reactive FLEs with an administrative orientation. Then comes a section about the technical and bureaucratic control which reproduced the reactive orientation of the FLEs. This is followed by an analysis of what can be referred to as the corporate culture, or collective subjectivity, of the FI. The conclusion of the chapter is that the FI, prior to the introduction of SMM practices in 2002, should be described as a traditional bureaucracy populated by reactive bureaucrats. As will be suggested in the subsequent chapters, one major goal with the introduction of SMM practices was to customer orient the organization and to make the employees more proactive.

FORMAL ORGANIZATION AND BRIEF HISTORY

As a company wholly owned by the Swedish government, the FI was founded in 1985 to finance a special kind of government home loan on offer to some home owners. In 1989, the FI started to administrate these loans, and in 1991, it was granted the right to offer them in its own name. In the mid-1990s, the government ordered the FI to offer regular home loans at margins lower than those of the commercial banks. The resulting low-price strategy led to a very favorable market position and rapid growth. Today, the FI has approximately 10 percent of the Swedish home loans market, with a net annual profit of SEK462m (approx. €50m). In 2006 and 2007, when I was conducting my study, the FI had between 375 and 410 employees, of whom approximately 60 percent were women (Annual Report 2006; 2007).

The formal organizational structure of the FI is hierarchical and divisionalized (see Figure 3.1). At the 'top', we find the executive board and the CEO, the latter managing the organization with the help of six support functions: Business Development, Credit, Finance, Human Resources, Law, and Business Support. The operational part is divided into three divisions: borrowing, business-to-business loans, and consumer loans. Together with the CEO, the heads of the three divisions and the heads of the six support functions constitute the executive body of the FI. Of the three divisions, this book focuses solely on the consumer loans division. Unless otherwise stated, the company label Financial Institute and the abbreviation FI will in what follows be used to refer to the consumer loans division, the FI's largest, which had approximately 200 employees during the time of the study (Annual Report 2006; 2007). This includes the divisional manager, the customer service center manager, support functions, and the customer service center staff who are organized into six groups of approximately 15 FLEs each and headed up by a team leader. In addition to these formal organizational boundaries, the consumer loans division is distinct from the head office by means of its geographical location. The former is located in a small town in Sweden, which I have chosen to label Middletown, located approximately 300 kilometers from the Swedish capital, Stockholm, where the head office is located. The top management of the consumer loans division is located at the head office.

If the focus of the present study is the consumer loans division, there is a particular focus within that division on the customer service representatives, or the FLEs, of the division. It is among the FLEs where, according to research into service work (see, for instance, Korczynski 2002; Morgan and Sturdy 2000; Peccei and Rosenthal 2000; 2001), we find the distinguishing feature of service organizations, namely extensive interaction with their customers. Consistent with the SMM literature (see, for instance, Grönroos 1978; 1982; Parasuraman et al. 1985; Shostack 1977; Vargo and Lusch 2004), the FLEs were also the main target of the SMM practices. The FLEs interact mainly with their customers by phone, but also by email and fax. No face-to-face interaction occurs with the customers.[1] Of the 41 interviews I conducted with staff from the FI, 22 were conducted with FLEs and 7 with their team leaders. These interviews largely revolved, as did

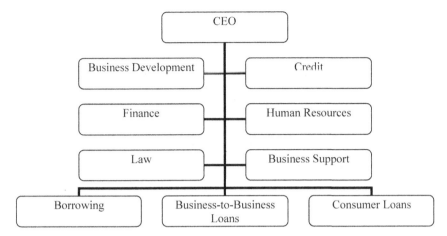

Figure 3.1   The formal organization of the FI.

the remaining 12 interviews with back office staff and managers, around the work and management of the FLEs (see more about methods in the Appendix).

FORMATION OF THE ORGANIZATION AND THE EMERGENCE OF THE REACTIVE FLE

In order to facilitate and enable the building of detached houses, something called interest subsidies existed in Sweden during the 1980s and up to the mid-1990s. This meant that the Swedish government waived part or all of the interest on mortgages for Swedish citizens who built new homes. Accordingly, as one of my informants—team leader John[2]—said: 'these loans were very popular in the 1980s because . . . it was money straight into people's pockets'. However, in order to obtain these interest subsidies, people who were planning to build new homes needed to apply to special Regional Housing Boards, of which there were 24; one in nearly every county in Sweden. Apart from that, new or future home owners needed to have a special kind of home loan issued by the government in order to obtain the interest subsidy. Originally, these home loans were financed directly by the Swedish treasury, but it was eventually decided to create a special administrative body that would be responsible for financing them through regular channels, e.g. housing bonds issued on the market. The FI was created to do that in 1985 as a corporation wholly owned by the Swedish government.

For four years, the FI's only task was to finance these loans, while they were administered by a government agency called the National Board of

Housing, Building, and Planning and the 24 Regional Housing Boards. The former was responsible for disbursement and notifications whereas the latter were responsible for reviewing and granting applications, as well as administrating outstanding loans and interest subsidies. After a while, it became evident that this was not the ideal way of organizing this form of housing support. One of the FLEs, who held a position on one of the Regional Housing Boards, before joining the FI in 1992, said in an interview: 'I worked for the Regional Housing Board for 2 years after finishing school [between 1990 and 1992]. At this point, it was realized that the organization wasn't good. It's very expensive, this entire financing system, and it was a good thing that the choice was made to separate subsidies and loans. The FI got the loans and the Regional Housing Boards got the subsidies'. The FI was given the task of administrating all issues connected with loans and the Regional Housing Boards were given the task of reviewing and approving applications and administrating interest subsidies. However, in 1992, the then government decided to stop offering these special kinds of subsidies and loans. Loans issued already would still exist and be valid and would need to be administrated. From January 1993, the FI assumed full responsibility for these loans. In order to do that, and as an effect of regional political considerations, a central customer support office staffed by 30–40 employees was set up in Middletown in 1992. The consumer loans division I studied evolved from this support office. In 2008, about 200 hundred people were working there.

Thus, during the first year of what would become the consumer loans division of the FI, the focus was on administrating the old, special kind of government loans as efficiently as possible. Consequently, when hiring the 30–40 employees needed for the customer support center being set up in Middletown in 1992, the focus was on hiring efficient administrators and bureaucrats. Team leader John, who had been working at the FI since that time, recalled:

> . . . this centralization ended up in Middletown. At the beginning, the work was all administrative, so we weren't lending any money then; on the contrary, we were looking after the about . . . half a million customers with those old government loans. That was quite a lot of customers. There had to be payment notices, people can't pay and have to be reminded that now's the time to renegotiate their loans, that all adds up to quite a lot of administration.
>
> (Team leader John)

Two of the FLEs that were hired in 1992 hold similar positions concerning the nature of the work: 'Then, in 1992, when we started up, there were loads and loads of problems with payments. Sweden was in chaos. It was called the banking crisis. There were lots of questions concerning the obtaining of time extensions and other normal administration such as notifications, renegotiations of loans, answering detailed questions etc.'. Her colleague elaborates. 'The FI was formed in 1985, but we took over the administrative bit of these special loans on 1 January 93, here in Middletown, from the 24 Regional Housing Boards and there were supposed to be 30–40 of us to do the work they did then . . . There was no lending when we started, our task was to administer the Regional Housing Board loans'.

The nature of the tasks and the decision to employ administrators shaped the subjectivity of the FLEs in a particular way. In addition, this had implications for changing the subjectivity of the FLEs when the demands shifted later on, as alluded to by team leader John, when I interviewed him in 2006 and 2007: 'we are still in the midst of a major change. Many of the employees we hired between 1993 and 1996 were administrators. Now the focus is on selling and customer service. It isn't self-evident that it's possible to convert each and every one painlessly'. One of the FLEs who was also hired early on (1992) holds a similar position:

> Answer: The major change, if we summarize it, was when I started off at the FI in 1993, it was only a matter of answering the phone and replying to the questions that were asked, nothing more. Later on . . . when we were starting to nick loans from others and making sure that they [the customers] borrowed from us instead, then it was more a question of starting to do business, quite simply. You had to be better, be read up, know your onions.
>
> Question: That's what you think the major change was?
>
> Answer: Yes, it was. For me it was . . . It was a fierce change from just being an administrator, just sitting [and answering the questions of the customers]: 'what's the interest on my loan? 6.5. Good, now I know, bye'. We don't treat customers quite like that now. . . . if you get that question now: 'what's my rate of interest on this loan', of course you answer the question but now it's more a matter of course to think: 'why is she wondering about that'? Then you have to find out. Is she selling or does she want to renegotiate [the loan] or has she talked to another bank or does she want to borrow more money? [It is important] to try to grasp what the customer really wants to do . . . I think that a lot of the time we're still struggling to this day with that change of attitude, in some situations.
>
> (FLE)

The Reactive and the Proactive Subject

According to the FLE and team leader John quoted above, the biggest change pertaining to the subjectivity of the FLEs, from 1992 when they were hired up until I conducted the interviews with them in 2006 and 2007, is away from *reacting* to the information given by the customers and toward *proactively* acting on that information and taking initiatives based on it. As will be suggested in Chapters 5 and 6, the power/knowledge of the SMM practices contributed both to determining that the FLEs needed to be more proactive and to making the FLEs' subjectivity more proactive.

The word reactive is defined by the *Merriam-Webster online dictionary* as 'readily responsive to a stimulus' and by *thedictionary.com* as 'actions pertaining to or characterized by reaction'. The *American Heritage Dictionary* offers the following definition: 'Tending to be responsive or to react to a stimulus'. A reactive approach thus implies that a person reacts to a stimulus, but nothing more than that. When a reactive subject is asked a question, he or she answers that question, but nothing more than that. The reactive FLE neither associates the question with other issues connected with the customer being dealt with nor gives the asking customer any advice that he or she can make use of. Thus, when a customer asks a reactive FLE about the interest rate of his or her mortgage, the FLE will simply respond by giving the customer the interest rate and, if the customer does not have any more questions, the conversation will end. Because the FLEs working at the FI during the initial years of the customer support center were given the role of solely administrating the old government loans, and were not supposed to change anything concerning these loans simply because not much could be changed, they had little incentive to do anything other than act reactively.

A proactive approach, on the other hand, entails a person not only reacting to stimuli but also taking the initiative during an interaction with another person by means of trying to anticipate the other person's needs and underlying reasons for asking questions. *Thedictionary.com* defines proactive action as 'serving to prepare for, intervene in, or control an expected occurrence or situation, especially a negative or difficult one; anticipatory'. The *Merriam-Webster online dictionary* defines proactive as 'acting in anticipation of future problems, needs, or changes'. The *Oxford American Dictionary of Current English* has a similar definition, defining proactive action as 'creating or controlling a situation by taking the initiative'. When asked a question, for instance, the proactive subject may choose not to answer directly, instead posing a counter-question in order to take control of the conversation. Thus, when a customer asks a proactive FLE what interest rates apply to his or her mortgage, the FLE will immediately start to think why the customer is asking that question. Is the customer interested solely in wanting to know the interest rate? Or is the customer comparing interest rates between mortgage lenders and perhaps calculating which lender is offering the best deal? Or does the customer want to take out another loan? The proactive FLE is eager to know why the customer is asking this question, and when he or she knows why the customer is doing so, the FLE will be able to start controlling the situation in accordance with a specific set of intentions, e.g. customer retention.

ON THE MARKET

It might have been expected that the focus on administration would shift toward direct customer contact and selling during the late 1990s when the FI started to compete, just like a commercial company, on the Swedish home loans market. Indeed, the major formal goal of the FI was profitability, as measured in terms of a high yield on equity, which was supposed to be realized via an organization that was efficient and customer oriented. However, the low-price strategy that the government had ordered the FI to adopt was leading to rapid growth and an influx of loan applications, forcing the FI to focus on administrating applications as efficiently as possible. At this point in time, the major task of the FLEs was to accept or reject loans. Communication with the customer often consisted only of a notification letter. As team leader Alice put it, when reflecting on this period of time retrospectively: 'previously, the customers flooded in so we didn't really need to put a lot of effort into caring for them'. One of the FLEs agrees: 'We were barely able to deal with the loan applications coming in. Customer service was given a very low priority'. One of the team leaders put it like this: 'Eight, nine years ago, applications came flooding in. They were piled high and low. We worked and we approved loans and that was all there was to it . . . you were hired to be an administrator'. Sales manager David explains the implications of this situation thus: 'what we've worked very hard with is streamlining the loan process—from application to payment'. Efficiency was thus given priority over customer orientation and proactive customer communication. The formal goal of having a customer oriented organization was loosely coupled to the activities of the organization.

Management reinforced efficiency by putting a lot of effort into developing measurement systems and a computerized credit review system. The present section suggests that these systems encourage the FLEs to act as administrative officials who rely on bureaucratic procedures, retrospectively referring to themselves as "loan administrators" and being referred to by managers as "order clerks". When inquiring about the systems, it is not doable to ask the employees to remember exactly how these systems were designed at different points in time during the latter part of the 1990s. Rather, when describing them in what follows, I base my description mainly on their descriptions of the systems in use when I conducted the study. The systems had been developed over time between the late 1990s and the early 2000s. The important thing here is to describe, in principal, what type of organizing they produced and reproduced, not their different versions.

Measuring Results and the Credit Review System

The profitability goal was translated into specific formal goals and rules pertaining to the FLEs. In order to foster efficiency, management started to measure the results of each individual employee in relation to these goals and to give him or her feedback concerning the outcome of these measurements on a weekly basis. Examples of measures include the number of calls taken, the total value of loans issued, and the number of home insurance policies sold. Quantification is, thus, greatly emphasized when checking goal fulfillment. When it comes to measurement, most of the FLEs agree that, 'at the end of the day, the total amount of [home] loans approved, in monetary terms, is what counts'. This is also emphasized by the team leaders and exemplified by one of them thus: 'in order to obtain new volumes, new customers, sales [of mortgages] are very, very much in focus'. That was corroborated by team leader John thus: 'the most obvious thing [to measure], of course, is how much money they [the FLEs] have lent . . . based on that, it's very easy to know what the company gets back'. Given that home loans are FI's core service and source of revenue, the emphasis on issuing as many loans as possible makes sense, given the profitability goal.

Some FLEs found the measurement and feedback they obtained from their respective team leaders stimulating, 'to me, my figures are a tool, they spur me on to do a better job' said one FLE. That was corroborated by two colleagues thus, 'I'm competitive. My numbers spur me on to do even better' and 'If . . . my sales increase, I know that I'm on the right track'. Others found the measurement of results stressful. One FLE said: 'All these sales statistics . . . I find them stressful. I'm tired of them'. One of her colleagues made a similar point: 'I could do without this measurement [of sales]. At one point, I found it really stressful, but I've learnt to live with it'. Others had mixed feelings: 'Sometimes, there's just too much measurement. It forces you to work at several things simultaneously and that's stressful. . . . on the other hand, you need a carrot. It's nice to have your sales figures in black and white'. Even though not all the FLEs liked to receive measurement and feedback concerning their sales, it still affected them. It made them work more efficiently; they 'pushed harder', as one FLE put it, because they all knew that there was a direct link between sales and salary.

The computerized credit review system (CRS) was referred to by several FLEs as 'our tool', and used to investigate whether or not customers were eligible for loans. Important improvements to the CRS have been made over the last ten years: 'Previously, reviewing applications was more of a craft. Today, we have the CRS, which you feed the necessary information into and then you get a green, amber, or red light' (FLE). As several FLEs pointed out, the formal 'instructions [or rules for reviewing loan applications are built into the system', regulating what information is needed from customers and ensuring that the handling process is dealt with efficiently by the FLEs. As one of the interviewees put it, 'previously, you were supposed to have all the rules in your head . . . now the system remembers the rules for you' (FLE).

All the FLEs and managers interviewed argue that the CRS has increased the efficiency of the work they do, as exemplified by one employee who had advanced from FLE to team leader: 'The speed of the handling process has increased enormously'. Several FLEs believed that the increased level of efficiency had led to increased control. One FLE said: 'When I started working here [in 1996], you had rules for how loan reviews were to be done . . . but you were not under the control of the CRS system so much'. The CRS can be perceived as a form of 'equipment' or a 'tool', as several of the FLEs put it. As such, it controls efficiency, both input-wise—by regulating what information to obtain from the customers—and output-wise—by means of the decisions that the CRS makes, which form the basis for the feedback given to the customers by the FLEs: i.e. a 'red, green, or amber light'.

Technical and Bureaucratic Control

The measurement system and the CRS can be analyzed as forms of control and, more particularly, as forms of the technical and bureaucratic control notions associated with the works of Edwards (1979), which are central to Labor Process Theory (LPT). Departing from Marx, a key concept of LPT is the view that capitalism is characterized by the opposition between capitalists and workers (Braverman 1974). Furthermore, labor power is seen as a commodity; however, 'that commodity is unique in that it is indeterminate—labor power is a potential for work that has to be converted into profitable labor' (Warhurst et al. 2009: 98). Even though the labor process requires some degree of consent between capitalist and worker (Burrawoy 1979), the work behavior that the capitalist wants to obtain from the worker is not always in the interests of the worker. A key concept of LPT is, thus, that 'there is a control imperative arising from the need to reduce indeterminacy' (Warhurst et al. 2009: 98). Accordingly, Edwards (1979: 17), in his ground-breaking work, defined control as 'the ability of capitalists and/or managers to obtain desired work behavior from workers'.[3]

Edwards differentiated between two types of 'structural' control: 'technical control' and 'bureaucratic control'[4]. '*Technical control* involves designing machinery and planning the flow of work to minimize the problem of transforming labor power into labor' (Edwards 1979: 112). As an effect of the physical design of the work, technical control influences work behavior. Technical control is of obvious relevance to manufacturing work, but it is also relevant to service work. The work of, for instance, the FLEs of service firms is often controlled through technology, e.g. computer programs, which often sets boundaries for what actions to take and not to take (see, for instance, Callaghan and Thompson 2001; Taylor and Bain 1999; 2001). The CRS presented above is one example of such a computer program providing technical control. The FLEs are forced to carry out the credit reviews they have to make for each and every loan application using the CRS. Previously, when there was no CRS, every FLE, as one of the FLEs put it, was supposed to know the work rules 'by heart', implying that the FLEs all had slightly different work rules in their respective 'hearts', and that they made individual interpretations of these work rules and needed to spend some time figuring out which rules applied in specific cases. 'Now [when] the systems know the rules for you', the FLE continues, the credit review process is more standardized and controlled—there is simply no other way of carrying out the necessary operations than that prescribed by the CRS. This has ensured increased efficiency during the credit review process.

Whereas technical control is an effect of the physical or technological structure of the organization, *bureaucratic control* is embedded in the formal social structure. Scott (2003: 20) defines a formal social structure as 'one in which the social positions and the relationships among them have been explicitly specified and are defined independently of the personal characteristics and relations of the participants occupying these positions'. Accordingly, Edwards (1979: 131) argues that 'Bureaucratic control establishes the impersonal force of "company rules" or "company policy" as the basis for control'. Systems of bureaucratic control 'institutionalize values and give supervisors specific criteria against which to evaluate workers' (Callaghan and Thompson 2001: 24). However, 'it is not obvious that bureaucratic control is sufficient in itself to handle the complexities of the process' (Callaghan and Thompson 2001: 26). Formal social structures do not always affect values and behaviors in the intended ways (Gouldner 1954). At the FI, bureaucratic control is exercised by means of the measurement of goals and the feedback given to the FLEs. The major goal against which workers are evaluated is the number of home loans approved which, as the section on the measurement of goals and feedback above suggests, makes the FLEs work more efficiently. However, the data does not suggest that bureaucratic control fosters customer orientation by affecting the norms and values of the FLEs.

In conclusion, I would like to suggest that the technical and bureaucratic control imposed upon the FLEs by the CRS and the measurement systems fosters efficient work behaviors in the FLEs. The CRS and the measurement system produce and reproduce the administrative reactive subjectivity of the FLEs.

CHALLENGING THE ORDINARY BANKS

In addition to developing a distinct formal organization associated with the above described forms of technical and bureaucratic control over the years, a distinct corporate culture associated with a collective subjectivity has also evolved. Central to the latter was the FI's position as an underdog vis-à-vis the banks. When the FI seriously started competing on the home loans market, during the latter part of the 1990s, the commercial banks did not take it seriously, which was one important reason, in addition to the general market situation, that the FI succeeded so well. Judging from interviews and newspaper reports, the FI was seen by its competitors as the odd man out with little chance of succeeding. As FLE Anne puts it, 'during the early years, the banks thought that they'd be able to take us in their stride'. Another FLE corroborated this: 'Right from the start, we heard the banks: "that little FI won't last long"'. Accordingly, the banks were initially reluctant to compete on prices—they wanted to retain their margins.

The Challenging Spirit

From interviews with managers and FLEs, I discovered that being a 'challenger' to what many employees referred to as 'the ordinary banks' had for a long time been a key part of the organizational members' enactment of reality. During interviews, many respondents started to speak spontaneously about how important it was for the FI to challenge the ordinary banks without my mentioning it. Others referred to this challenging spirit as a response to my question on what was special about the FI. All respondents took the challenging orientation of the FI for granted, as exemplified by FLE Anne—'The company embodies the challenging spirit'—and by Mary, a project leader—'We have been the challenger with the lowest prices'. It can be suggested that the challenging mentality originated from—as did the subjectivity of the administrator and the focus on fostering efficiency by measuring results and working with the CRS—the FI's government brief which stated that it was to compete with the banks via lower interest rate margins (see above). Important parts of the FI's corporate culture, and the employee subjectivity it fostered, were thus constituted as a mirror image of the ordinary banks—of 'the other'. This reminds one of Mead's idea that the self is at least partly constituted in relation to the other using this other as a mirror image (Mead 1934). Indeed, this resonates quite well with Foucault's idea that subjectivity is constituted as a mirror image of the abnormal (Foucault 1977); in this case the ordinary banks represent the abnormal.

According to the FI personnel I interviewed, the FI challenged the ordinary banks, or mirrored themselves in the 'abnormal', in at least three ways. The most important way is by being the 'market leader', as many of the employees put it: a position mainly expressed in terms of being the 'price dumper' on the Swedish home loans market. But the understanding of the FI as a challenger was also constructed through the FI, according to its staff, contributing toward breaking up what many respondents found to be an oligopolistic Swedish home loans market. In addition, the challenging spirit was constructed via FI changing the ways home loans traditionally had been offered and by introducing new products and services onto the home loans market.[5]

A Market Leader and a Price Dumper

The broadest understanding of being a 'market leader', for FI staff, implies that the FI has made the banks follow its lead in the most general way: The FI has been the leader and the banks have followed. According to one of the FLEs: 'We've kind of been ahead the whole time and it feels like the banks have been tagging along the whole time . . . we've also made sure that the banks have changed by being there as an alternative'. Another FLE expresses a similar view: 'Yeah sure, we've done a lot for the private individual in any case. One thing's for sure. We've been a challenger. We've ruffled their [the banks'] feathers good and proper over the years, I have to say. Because the banks have been behind'.

The bulk of the respondents, however, prefer to qualify more precisely in what way the FI has been a market leader, arguing that the banks have 'followed the leader' in terms of forcing them to lower their interest rates and thus in terms of being a 'price dumper'. To many of my respondents, this constituted the core meaning of the verb 'to challenge'. One FLE, for example, argues: 'If we hadn't entered the market, the interest rate today would've been much higher'. Another FLE puts it like this: 'We've forced a lot of banks to offer these low interest rates because we've made things easier and quicker'. Thus, the FI has challenged the banks by being more efficient, something which has given the FI the possibility of offering lower rates. One of the back office staff takes a similar position: 'If we go back to 1999, it was like the banks thought then, yes that lot can keep at it, but nothing will come of it [the FI]. But we've been gaining market share the whole time. Now that we're up to 9–10% and beginning to get too big, the banks have lowered their rates too. Before, we were always the ones with the lowest rates, but now the banks are on more or less the same level'. This low price strategy, in combination with a challenging attitude toward the banks, is also something that the FI alludes to in its market communications. 'Sorry big banks' is an example of an advertising slogan. The 'sorry' implies that the FI is 'sorry' for offering low rates and for taking customers away from the banks.

The FI's low-price strategy has not only been of benefit to its customers, but also to general banking customers, and indeed to society at large, if we are to believe the FI staff. Two of the FLEs explain: 'Thanks to us, our customers get a lower interest rate and thanks to us the ordinary bank customer gets lower interest rates by referring to our interest rates'. Her colleague makes a similar statement: 'We've been of benefit to society. You see, we're good for all customers, including those with loans with the [ordinary] banks because the banks were forced to dump their prices due to us popping up and kind of challenging and nibbling away at market shares . . . a lot of customers use our rates to put pressure on their own banks to reduce rates'. Given the importance that its staff attaches to the FI, one could perhaps argue that it has played out its role as a 'price dumper' because it has succeeded in lowering the interest rates of the ordinary banks. However, this is not the position taken by the employees who argue that the FI still has an important role to play in this respect. 'If we didn't exist as a price dumper, the interest rates would shoot up directly. We play that part despite the banks having crept down and reduced their margins and come down to our level. So indirectly, we're still the price dumper and we're always just as low' says one FLE.

In addition, some employees argue that not only has the FI been a market leader, it has also created, or at least radically changed, the Swedish home loans market. This is a theme that is implicitly present in the discussion above concerning 'price dumping'—i.e. that lowering margins means creating a new market situation. However, this is more explicitly addressed in some of the interviews where there is talk of breaking up what the interviewees perceived to be an oligopolic home loans market in Sweden. This standpoint was explicitly avowed by, for instance, the marketing manager:

> We at the FI are fostered in this challenging spirit. It's the case that we've broken in [to the market]. The whole idea behind the FI's business concept is challenging the major banks with better offers, better distribution methods, better prices, simpler and quicker service. It's quite simply about changing the mortgage market. That's really what we're passionate about. This is an oligopolic market on which 90% are customers of the major banks—not because they have the best prices and the best service—but because it's about time-honored custom and tradition'.
>
> (Marketing manager)

According to the FI staff, the FI had succeeded in breaking up the alleged oligopolic mortgage market, as indicated by the following statements made by two FLEs: 'We were supposed to contribute toward competition and multiplicity on the mortgage market, and that we've succeeded with' says one. 'We've made competition on the market stiffer . . . [This] has benefited everyone' says the other. Thus, the FI, according to its employees, has contributed toward constructing a more prefect market. It has done this by being a 'price dumper', but also by changing the traditional home loans service offering. Says one FLE:

> We have stirred things up quite considerably. We have a uniform price level for detached houses and condominiums. We introduced that a few years back. The major banks followed our lead, after a few months. And then the big bit that we did away with was the final mortgage here a year or so ago and now offer the same interest level up to 95%. These are major things we've introduced, no trifling matters.
>
> (FLE)

Many other employees emphasized that these two changes—the introduction of similar interest rates for detached houses and condominiums, and the abolishment of the final mortgage / introduction of an initial mortgage at 95 percent of the market value[6]—re-constructed the market, as exemplified by one FLE: 'We were the first on the market with a reduction of the interest rate for condominiums to normal mortgage rates. The banks tagged along, you know, and we removed the final mortgage and then they [the banks] were forced to follow our lead. These are quite tricky matters that have made an impression on the market, I believe'.

Customer Friendliness and Fairness

The shared identity of being a challenger to the banks also expressed itself via two other themes, apart from being a market leader, i.e. customer friendliness and fairness. Most of the interviewees argued that FI staff interacted with their customers in a better way than bank staff did. One of the FLEs said: 'When the customers call us, they expect a good rate of interest as well as to be treated with friendliness. I think we probably give them what they want. I think that we're probably very customer-friendly and easy to deal with and upbeat on the phone and so on. I don't think you'll get the same reception from a bank'. The allegedly superior customer service of the FI was expressed, according to the interviewees, via a higher degree of availability. One of the FLEs said: 'At the bank, you often have to make an appointment and it's difficult to get anywhere by phone but my phone is always on and if I'm not in my office, I'm careful to call back as soon as possible'. Another FLE had a similar view: 'We're very accessible. You don't need to make an appointment 3 weeks ahead; instead, when you need help—you get it. We help our customers directly by phone if possible. It takes longer to get hold of a personal banking advisor at a bank'. The head of the consumer division held a similar position: 'You can't spontaneously visit a bank today as your personal advisor is always sitting in another meeting, if you have a good personal advisor who arranges a lot of meetings. But as we haven't had an office, we've been forced to be very available to our customers. You can always reach us and we are able, actually, to arrange a loan within 24 hours if there's a crisis.'

In addition, customer friendliness, according to the FLEs of the FI, was expressed through a more simple style and use of language during customer interaction, compared with the banks. Several of the FLEs had previously worked at banks and could compare: 'I've seen the banking side too . . . and I recognize a lot of what the banks do . . . It's supposed to be this traditional bank way of doing things, very formal, right' (FLE). Indeed, many associated the more formal and protracted methods of the banks with the expression 'the bank way of doing things'. Talking about a specific bank team leader, John says: 'They work in the "bankey" way. You see, they receive their customers and talk to them and have coffee with them and check how their kids are and all that stuff'. One of the FLEs elaborates on the informal ways of working practiced by the FI and sheds light on the 'bank way of doing things' by referring to the language use:

> A lot of our work is based on making the customer leave the bank and come to us instead. It's the case that, in contrast to the banks, we want

to convey to our customers when we talk to them that we're on their side, that's what we want to convey . . . [The banks] talk a certain language which is difficult to understand for those who don't know about mortgages . . . too technical and complicated: you take some papers home with you to sign but you never really understood what had been said or what you were about to sign perhaps . . . I believe our customers feel that, that we're, sort of, normal people sitting here, not suits.

(FLE)

Thus, by being customer friendly in its language and style and by means of a high degree of availability, the FI, according to its staff, sets itself apart from the ordinary banks, challenging them by offering better services and lower prices.

Finally, the boundary which the FI employees constructed between the banks and themselves, and which led them to see themselves as challengers, was based on the belief that the FI was fair whereas the banks were unfair. The fair-unfair argument is immanent in the above discussion and citations concerning being a price leader. Charging too high a price is, of course, unfair, whereas trying to offer one's customers as low a price as possible, as the FI has done, according to its employees, is fair. In a similar manner, operating on an oligopolistic market, and reproducing such markets, is unfair, whereas trying to break up such markets is fair. One FLE, who had worked in a bank before starting at the FI, refers to the 'banking crisis' at the beginning of the 1990s, when some Swedish banks made major losses on loans and had to be bailed out by the government 'We [as opposed to the banks] has no skeletons in our closet. "Fight the banks" was something the newspapers wrote frequently. We didn't catch any of that flack'.

In addition to this type of general critique, the fair-unfair dichotomy was addressed more directly by the FI staff in several ways. One way of doing this related to the fact that the FI offered each and every costumer the same interest rates, whereas the banks were willing to negotiate with some of their customers and to offer their most profitable customers better rates than those who were less so. The bulk of the employees agreed that offering everyone the same interest rates was a good thing to do, as exemplified by one FLE thus: 'No, I think it's a good concept that we have the same rate for all. It's fair'. The fairness argument is also something that has been played out against the banks in marketing communications concerning their interest rates policies: 'We've had slogans like you won't need to have a brother-in-law working at the bank to get a good price or a fair price. Everybody gets the same price regardless of whether they are low or high earners. Regardless of where you live, you'll get the same price' (sales manager David). But fairness was also referred to by many employees in relation to the normal working situation, expressed thus by one FLE: 'We can't squeeze the interest rate any further. That's something the banks can do for their real "gold customers". But what's nice about the FI, in my opinion, is that we give all our customers the same interest rate'.[7] The reason that the banks are able to bargain with their most profitable customers, according to the FI employees, is that the banks have sources of income that the FI lacks: 'We have no other sources of income [than mortgages and certain secondary services]. We don't get any money in from anywhere. [Question: So the banks get it back in other ways?] Yes of course, they have to do that . . . What have you got in a salary account today? What's your interest rate there?' Thus, what the banks give to some of their privileged customers, they take from their unprivileged customers.

In addition to the differences in interest rate policy, the FLEs believed that the alleged unfair approach of the banks emerged when they called the banks up to resolve loans for customers switching from the banks to the FI. When doing this, the FLEs had experienced all possible kinds of strategies on the part of the banks which were aimed at delaying and preventing switches: 'Oh, it could be anything, gosh. They [the bank clerks] could quite simply say that the system has gone down or that they can't talk now . . . Just saying that you are calling from the FI makes them take another tone with you. That's how it is. Not all of them, but many. Absolutely'. Another FLE elaborated: 'Yes, there's a lot of stuff about the system being down, we can't answer the question, you'll have to come back tomorrow—in order to give them time to ply their customer . . . They start quenching when things start to smolder, that's what they do'. Thus, in order to keep customers, the bank staff, according to the FLEs of the FI, invented problems that prevented them from resolving a loan which then gave them the time to work on those who were about to switch in order to keep their business. This type of behavior is unacceptable to many of the FLEs of the FI, one of whom says: 'When answering a bank, you have to bear in mind not to be unpleasant and answer them similarly to how you would've done if it'd been a customer who'd called. We don't retaliate the same way as the banks'.

THE BUREAUCRACY AND THE LOAN ADMINISTRATOR

The implications of the empirical analysis in the present chapter will be discussed in relation to Korczynski's (2002) notion of the customer oriented bureaucracy; an ideal typical organizational form articulated in order to describe the basic nature of service firms.[8] The customer oriented bureaucracy is 'a form of work organization in which there are dual, and potentially contradictory, logics at play. The logics are those of routinization and efficiency on the one hand, and those of customer and customer orientation on the other' (Korczynski 2002: 4). Customer oriented bureaucracies combine customeristic and bureaucratic ideals in a number of areas. In customer oriented bureaucracies, HRM fosters efficient and customer oriented worker behavior; the labor process has both a quantity and quality focus; the basis of the division of labor combines efficient task completion and caring for customer relationships; authority emerges from rational legal rules and customer relationships; and bureaucratic demands for internal stability are balanced with customer variability.

The main impression given by the analysis in this chapter is that the FI, prior to the introduction of SMM practices in 2002, should be described as a bureaucracy and its FLEs as bureaucrats with a reactive subjectivity. The focus has been on creating efficient work processes through standardization and routinization. As the chapter shows, the origins of the FI as an organization designed to administrate the special kind of home loans being offered to Swedish citizens in the 1980s and early 1990s made the FI focus on efficiency and hiring FLEs with administrative qualities. When the organization started to compete in the marketplace, its low-price strategy resulted in applications pouring in, thus emphasizing the focus on efficiency and the importance of hiring administrators able to carry out the handling process as efficiently as possible. The measurement systems and credit review system employed fostered bureaucratic and technical control, quantification, efficient task completion, internal stability, and based authority on formal rules in order to streamline the handling process. It can also be argued that the most salient themes of what was referred to as the corporate culture or the collective subjectivity of the FI—its challenging spirit and being a market leader and price dumper—contributed toward producing and reproducing the bureaucratic nature of the organization. When challenging the banks with low prices, an efficient work process is pivotal.

However, the chapter also shows that the formal strategy was geared toward both efficiency and customer orientation. In addition, the analysis suggests that other aspects of the culture—customer friendliness and fairness—are more closely related to the customeristic side of the customer oriented bureaucracy. This might be the reason why managers departed from the culture when seeking to develop the FI into a service and market oriented organization, a topic that will be dealt with in the next chapter.

4 'I Want To Help You'
The Power of Market and Service Orientation

In the previous chapter I argued that the organization of the FI, up until the introduction of the SMM practices in 2002, could be described as a classic bureaucracy which had been fostering reactive rather than proactive FLEs. In this chapter, as well as in Chapters 5 and 6, we turn our attention toward the SMM practices. The conceptual analysis in these chapters focuses on the SMM practices used at the FI, as presented in the academic marketing literature, whereas the empirical analysis focuses on the role of the SMM practices at the FI and how these order the subjectivity of the FLEs in particular. Compared with the previous chapter, the analysis draws more closely on the Foucauldian framework presented in the second chapter.

The present chapter analyses, in particular, strategic service and market orientation practices from the perspective of pastoral power. Whereas the conceptual analysis focuses on the articulation of these practices in the academic literature, the empirical analysis is devoted to the service and market orientation program at the FI, which was given the title 'I Want to Help You' (IWHY). When it comes to the conceptual analysis of the academic SMM literature in the present chapter and in Chapters 5 and 6, it is important to keep in mind that not every contribution to each respective stream of research can be reviewed. This would be too extensive a task for a single book. Rather, the most central contributions, or turning points, within the streams are taken into account (see Methods Appendix). I argue that this is sufficient for explicating the managerial rationality associated with the streams of research analyzed and how SMM practices shape subjectivity—key aims of the conceptual analysis.

The chapter opens with a section which, against the backdrop of the previous chapter, sheds light on why FI management chose to embark on the service and market orientation program. Then, our attention is turned toward the conceptual pastoral power analysis of the service and market orientation literature, followed by an extensive analysis of the IWHY program.

TOWARD A NEW STRATEGIC ORIENTATION:
THE IWHY PROGRAM

As explained in the previous chapter, the ordinary banks did not see the FI as a serious competitor when it started competing in the marketplace in the middle of the 1990s. But as the FI's market share steadily grew, the banks eventually started matching the low prices being offered by the FI: in some cases, competitors were even offering customers a better deal. According to the FI's employees, this change in attitude was due to the intervention of the FI on the Swedish home loans market. One of the FLEs put it like this: 'We're supposed to be adding to the competition and multiplicity [in the marketplace] and we've been successful'. One of her colleagues said: 'Now they [the ordinary banks] have realized that we won't be going away, so then they'll also have to do something'. During interviews, the FI managers said that they had predicted that their competitors would, at some point in time, match the low-price strategy of the FI. As team leader John puts it: 'It was predicted that we wouldn't have a difference of 30 to 40 basis points forever'. One of the FLEs agrees: 'Even when I started here [in 1998], there was talk of the banks eventually catching up with our interest rates'. This was also pointed out in the booklet that emerged from the IWHY program: 'If we don't change, we'll disappear in the long-run, something we all realize when we think about it'.

In order to counter a potential crisis, managers tried to prepare the organization for change early on—from a low-price strategy to a service and customer orientation strategy. However, it proved hard to change a rapidly growing and successful organization: the staff did not understand why they had to change when the company was doing so well. Neither was it easy to involve employees in change programs when they were so badly needed to keep the operation going. Sales manager David explains:

> I've been working here for nine years, and for eight years and eight months of these nine years, we've had too much to do. And this has hampered us—why fix something that's not broken? This is the classic problem of changing a business when your sole argument is that you think it will do badly in a couple of years' time. Changing a company in crisis is much easier because everyone realizes they are in trouble. Then, the co-workers look up and say: 'please change this company for me otherwise I won't have a job'.
>
> (David, sales manager)

However, in 2002, it became obvious to the FLEs that the market position for the FI started to change. At that time competitors started to call the FLEs up asking them to dissolve loans more frequently—now customers wanted to switch from the FI to a bank because the banks were offering lower interest rates, a completely new situation. In David's words, everyone was 'in trouble' and almost all the employees started to realize it, as suggested by interview statements made by the FLEs, such as, 'the competition is much harder now' and 'the inflow of loan applications is much lower now'.

When competitors started offering similar, or lower, interest rates, the employees interpreted this as if the FI had achieved its goal of lowering interest rates for the average customer. 'Mission accomplished' was the actual expression many employees used. But the subject position of being a challenger to the ordinary banks still made sense to the FI managers and many FLEs, but for other reasons. As explained in the previous chapter, many FI employees were convinced that, if the FI were to withdraw from the market, then the alleged oligopolic nature of the home loans market would make the 'ordinary banks' revert to their previous high interest rates. In addition, most FI employees, as we also saw in the previous chapter, thought that the ordinary banks were not offering their customers a good level of service. To use Grönroos' (1982; 1984) vocabulary, the 'what' of the bank offering—the interest rates and the efficiency of the handling process—was customer oriented and had been like this due to the intervention of the FI on the market. However, just 'how' the staff, especially the FLEs, were offering services to their customers was still not customer oriented. Thus, it was still possible to challenge the 'big banks' by offering a better level of service by improving the how or the interpersonal part of the service offering.

Service in the Champions' League

Informed by these images of the customer service being offered by the banks and by extracting 'change energy'—as one manager put it—from the stiffer market situation, management embarked, in 2002, upon a strategic service and market orientation program—IWHY—aimed at emphasizing and strengthening the customeristic side of the organization. In the booklet summarizing the IWHY program it is stated that the FI already offered a good level of service but that it needed to be a company offering services in the champions' league. 'There is rather widespread dissatisfaction with the level of service provided by the banks, and you can read in surveys that a million bank customers are dissatisfied with their banks. The FI's level of service is well known and here we saw our opportunity to become a lot better than the banks at providing service—to quite simply become a company in the champions' league' (IWHY booklet). Thus, offering services in the 'champions' league' was the main aim of the program and the way in which the FI was supposed to challenge the ordinary banks in the future. Indeed, it can be argued that this program marks a change in the overall strategy of the FI—from a low-price strategy (low interest rate strategy) to a customer, market, and service orientation strategy, something which was expressed like this by sales manager David who was the project leader of IWHY: 'We understood some years ago [i.e. before competition increased, see preceding] that having low prices wasn't something we would have a monopoly on forever. In the future, we understood it would be more important to treat our customers in a service minded way, to develop our interaction with them, and to change our behaviors accordingly'. The change of strategy is even more explicitly stated in the IWHY booklet:

> The FI needs its proportion of consumer credits to grow at a greater pace than previously. In total, we need a greater lending stock in order to be able to utilize benefits of scale . . . The solution is not simply cheap mortgages via the Internet—this is an all too simple business concept to copy. Our competitive advantage—low interest rates—can be eliminated by any bank using targeted promotions or a changed "list price". The banks have hitherto used the interest rate weapon selectively and defended individual customers, but now we are seeing that the major banks are also changing their interest rate policies and others may follow them. We ourselves remain stuck in the argument we often hear from our customers—"the banks provide the same rate of interest so why should I choose you?". We have few arguments of our own, or none at all, regarding why the customer should choose us if we do not have the lowest rate of interest . . . The goal is to create, care of our co-workers, an improved customer encounter, seen from the customer's point of view—experiencing service in the champions' league on a daily basis.
>
> (IWHY booklet)

This statement dismisses the previous low-price strategy. Or, formulated differently, low prices constitute a hygiene factor but not something to compete on. Indeed, the IWHY booklet puts forward the argument that the FI is stuck in its old strategy. The low-price strategy, implies the quote, had made the FLEs accustomed to purely selling home loans based on low interest rates but had not prepared them to argue that customers should do business with the FI rather than the regular banks for other reasons. The previous low-price strategy is thus portrayed as being in contrast to a service and customer orientation strategy. The latter is seen as the solution to the FI's problems. It is also interesting to note the relationship between corporate culture and strategy described in the extract from the booklet. The IWHY program presupposes that a service and customer orientation strategy has to be driven and supported by a service oriented and customeristic culture. This resonates well with the arguments put forward in the academic service and market orientation literature which we turn to next.

ACADEMIC SERVICE AND MARKET ORIENTATION DISCOURSE

This section reviews and conceptually analyses the service and market orientation literature. As will be evident these two strands of research share some important commonalities. Vargo and Lusch (2004), for instance, argued that the literature on market orientation constitutes one of the founding bodies of knowledge for the service-dominant logic.

Roots in the Marketing Concept

An archeological investigation (see Methods Appendix) of the notions of service and market orientation needs to take its point of departure in the articulation of the marketing concept during the late 1950s / early 1960s (see, for instance, Aldersson 1957; Borsch 1957; Keith 1960; Levitt 1960; McKitterick 1957) and the associated establishment of customerism as the managerial rationality of academic marketing discourse described in Chapter 2. After the initial boost which the articulation of the marketing concept gave the discipline and which the broadening of it fuelled in the early parts of the 1970s (see Kotler and Levy 1969; Kotler and Zaltman 1971; Kotler 1972), many researchers who studied the implementation of the marketing concept in the 1980s produced quite disappointing results. Even though some studies found that some organizations had implemented the marketing concept, the primary message was that most organizations had not. 'In general, the conclusion was that the marketing concept was easy to articulate but hard to implement in practice' (Webster 2002: 71). There were several explanations for the lack of implementation, including battles between functional silos; the domination of the 'production concept' in many organizations, giving engineers rather than marketers power; as well as a lack of information and knowledge within organizations regarding what the customers wanted and needed (see, for instance, Anderson 1982; Hayes and Abernathy 1980; Webster 1981).[1]

In addition, there existed a bias against the marketing concept as a strategic framework within the literature on formal strategic planning which dominated the field of strategic management during the 1970s and early 1980s. Ansoff (1965), one of the leading names in the field of formal strategic planning, was critical of the idea that the marketing concept was to inform the overall strategic intentions of any organization and gave marketing an operational role (Webster 2002). According to Ansoff (1965), the focus of the strategic planning process should be the competitors, not the customers.

A Variable Perspective on Culture

However, during the early 1980s, when many marketing scholars were concluding that the marketing concept had not caught on to the degree that they had hoped and expected, other fields of management were starting to move in directions other than the one set out by the strategic planning school. Two trends are noteworthy. In the field of strategic management, the focus shifted from formal strategic planning to strategy implementation (see, for instance, Porter 1980; Schendel and Hofer 1979). The resulting 'shift from strategy formulation and its emphasis on competitor actions, to strategy implementation and the need to understand customers and how they will respond to the firm's product offering, brought marketing competency back into the strategic management process. Now, customer value is at the centre of most strategic management frameworks' (Webster 2002: 74–75). When marketing and strategic management became synchronized in this way, the standpoint that marketing and the marketing concept played a strategic rather than an operational role gained ground.

The second trend, which provided an opportunity to further the agenda of the marketing discipline, was that the notion of culture started to creep into general management discourse at the same point in time when the shift away from strategic planning toward strategy implementation was taking place in the strategic management literature. Several consultants wrote books selling millions of copies about the symbolic aspect of leadership and the importance of managing organizations through common values and beliefs (see, for instance, Deal and Kennedy 1982; Peters and Waterman 1982). On the research side, several scholars who were inspired by anthropology imported and started to use the notion of culture in order to understand the basic nature of organizations (see, for instance, Morgan 1986; Schein 1985; Smircich 1983; Van Maanen 1975). This provided opportunities for marketing; basically because the marketing concept had been articulated and described as a form of potential culture from an early stage, despite the fact that the notion of culture had not been used explicitly. Keith (1960), for instance, writes that the implementation of the marketing concept implies a 'mental revolution' within the organization. Levitt (1960: 56) argued that the marketing concept implies that 'the entire corporation must be viewed as a customer-creating and customer-satisfying organism'. The marketing concept can indeed be seen as a potential form of corporate culture which companies should try to adopt and which some companies, e.g. Pillsbury focused upon by Keith (1960), have succeeded in doing. Marketing could thus draw conceptual strength from the notion of culture, and the entire discipline of marketing could be reinvigorated by surfing on the corporate cultural wave. This was an opportunity that was utilized first in the market orientation literature and later in the service orientation literature.

It was Deshpandé and Webster (1989) who imported the notion of organizational culture into marketing. Drawing on the five perspectives on culture outlined by Smircich (1983), Deshpandé and Webster argued that the organizational cognition perspective offered the richest research opportunities in marketing. Organizational culture was defined as 'the pattern of shared values and beliefs that help individuals understand organizational functioning and thus provide them norms for behavior in the organization' (Deshpandé and Webster 1989: 4). This is the understanding of culture that has dominated marketing research, in general, and market and service orientation research, in particular (see, for instance, Berry 1999; Edvardsson and Enquist 2002; Gebhart et al. 2006; Homburg and Pflesser 2000; Kholi and Jaworski 1990; Moorman 1995; Narver et al. 1998; Schneider and Bowen 1995). In marketing, culture is thus perceived as a variable possessed by organizations and not as a metaphor for the organization itself, i.e. that organizations are cultures (cf. Smircich 1983)—the latter being the most common perspective in organization studies and anthropology (Alvesson 2002; Geertz 1973; Martin 2002). When culture is treated as a variable possessed by organizations, it is something than can be acted upon, managed, and changed.

Culture as Governmentality

The variable perspective on culture, founded as it is on the idea that culture is made up of the values, norms, and beliefs residing in the person, is contingent upon a modernist understanding of identity. As explained in the second chapter, Foucault broke away from such an understanding of the person, arguing that identity, or subjectivity, is rooted in external discourse. However, Foucault took a reflexive view of modernity, arguing, on the one hand, that most people believe in the modernistic 'version' of the person and, on the other, that discourses addressing the person—e.g. contemporary psychology—are perceived by many as objective systems of truths. If this reflexive nature of modernity is paired with Foucault's notion of subjectivity, modernistic discourses addressing the person become regimes of power/knowledge or governmentalities (Foucault 1977; 2007). This has implications for the conceptual and empirical analysis of culture and cultural programs in the present chapter. In this book, the values promoted by service and market orientation discourse and programs are perceived neither as being internalized within the individual nor as the 'right' or 'best' fabric for a particular group of employees; rather, they are perceived as governmental bodies of power/knowledge external to the person. In line with the notion of governmentality, a service or customer oriented culture is a mentality of government, located in discourse, that operates on human conduct. Social domains regulated by such a mentality make customerism a guiding rule; an imperative that informs and frames action and thinking, not by being internalized within the individual but by ordering the social landscape or social ontology: the actual possibilities for action, thinking, and talk. Indeed, the key values associated with service and market orientation discourse and programs can be perceived as consisting of central *commandments* which organizations and their members orient themselves around.

By defining government in terms of regulating the 'conduct of conduct', Foucault (2007) wanted to imply that government is about managing, leading, directing, and guiding in a more or less deliberate way. However, more importantly, he gave the verb 'to conduct' a reflexive meaning which implies that government is not only about leading others, it is also about leading oneself in accordance with managerial rationalities such as customerism. Thus, the notion of government is closely connected with that of pastoral power (see Foucault 2007) which I thus draw upon in order to conduct the conceptual and empirical analysis of service and market orientation in the present chapter. As we recall from Chapter 2, the confession is the human practice associated with pastoral power. The confession is a governmental practice because the knowledge that the person is avowing about him- or herself during confessional sessions is drawn on by individuals serving as pastors and by the confessors themselves in order to orient the confessors / themselves toward the ethic that frames the situation. In relation to the present case, this means that the ethical imperative of customerism built into service and market orientation discourse, programs, and 'cultures', and the confessional practices such bodies of knowledge promote foster avowals colored by customerism. These avowals invite persons to orientate themselves toward the customeristic subject positions offered by marketing discourse and the pastors to support this reorientation.

Central Commandments

One year after Deshpandé and Webster (1989) introduced the notion of culture into marketing, two articles on market orientation were published in the *Journal of Marketing,* by Kholi and Jaworski (1990) and Narver and Slater (1990), which renewed interest in the marketing concept in a way that made it possible to connect it with the notion of culture. Drawing on an exploratory and qualitative research design, Kholi and Jaworski (1990) asked a cross sectional sample of managers the basic question of what marketing meant to them. The major theme that emerged in their material was that customer focus was the central element of marketing, or what they labeled market orientation. Kholi and Jaworski (1990: 6) defined market orientation as 'the organizationwide *generation* of market intelligence pertaining to current and future customer needs, *dissemination* of the intelligence across departments, and organization wide *responsivness* to it', a definition pointing to the fact that market orientation needs to have implications for the overall strategy of the organization. Based on their case study of one company's 140 business units, Narver and Slater (1990) adopted a broader definition of market orientation than that of Kholi and Jaworski, arguing that three factors—i.e. 'customer orientation', 'competitor orientation' and 'interfunctional coordination'—should be given equal importance. They also argued, and showed quantitatively, that market orientation was strongly correlated to the profitability of the studied organization. Thus, Narver and Slater also consider market orientation to be a strategic issue.

Even though Kholi and Jaworski (1990) did not draw on a cultural framework, and despite the fact that Narver and Slater (1990) did not utilize the literature on culture extensively, the way they defined and discussed market orientation was closely aligned with the notion of culture as imported into marketing by Deshpandé and Webster (1989). This is also true for the service orientation literature which emerged later on, but which has strong kinship with the market orientation literature. Lytle et al. (1998: 459), in a key paper, define 'service orientation as an organization-wide embracement of a basic set of relatively enduring organizational policies, practices and procedures intended to support and reward service giving behaviors that create and deliver "service excellence"'. A clear link between service orientation, service culture, and service strategy exist in the SMM literature as well. Edvardsson and Enquist (2002: 178) for instance, when investigating the relationship between service culture and strategy drawing on the case of IKEA, conclude that: 'The service culture in IKEA, with norms, values and beliefs, may be seen as on the one hand regulators for what is possible and not possible, on the other hand as a calling that gives energy and direction from within each employee and manager. This is the essence of strategy-making when it comes to intended service strategy and realized service strategy'.

According to Gebhart et al. (2006: 37) the focus of research into market orientation from the early 1990s up until now has been on 'developing measures of a firm's orientation and identifying antecedents and consequences of a greater market orientation'. Quantitative methods have thus ordered marketing research in this area too. Little knowledge has been generated about the basic nature or substance of market and service orientation as a form of culture. Gebhart et al. (2006) wanted to know more about this. They conducted a qualitative longitudinal empirical study of seven companies and used interviewing and participant observation as their data collection techniques. The paper that emerged from the study describes the basic nature of market oriented cultures. In the language of Gebhart et al. (2006), market oriented cultures are based on six values which are linked to certain assumptions and behavioral norms, as presented in Table 4:1. Because the study of Gebhart et al. (2006), in line with previous research in the field of market orientation, is managerially oriented, it is possible, from a pastoral power perspective, to read the paper as listing the central commandments that market oriented organizations need to be informed by.

Of these six values / commandments, Gebhart et al. (2006: 43) found 'the market as the raison d'être' to be the central cultural value providing a rationale for the other five values'. It needs to be noted that some of the five remaining values overlap each other, e.g. 'keeping promises' and 'trust' as well as 'collaboration' and 'openness'. Given the importance of proactivity as a managerial rationality at the FI (see subsequent chapters),

Table 4.1   Values, Assumptions, and Norms of Market-Oriented Firms

Value	Assumption	Behavioral norms
Markets as the *raison d'être*	We come together as an organization to serve the market and make a living.	Every decision and action must consider how it affects the market.
Collaboration	Working together we can achieve more, faster and better, than apart.	Work is done collaboratively by teams. Teams are jointly responsible for outcomes.
Respect/empathy/ perspective taking	People are basically good and have reasons for their actions.	Consider the perspectives, needs, training, expertise, and experiences of others when reacting to or interpreting their actions.
Keep promises	To succeed, everyone must do his or her part.	Each employee is responsible for following through on commitments to others.
Openness	Honestly sharing information, assumptions and motives allows others to understand and effectively collaborate with us.	Proactively and honestly share information, assumptions, and motives with others.
Trust	Everyone is committed to the same goal. Therefore, we can have positive expectations about their intentions and behaviors.	Trusting that your fellow employees are telling the truth and will follow through on commitments.

Source: Gebhart, G.F., Carpenter, G.S. and Sherry Jr., J.F. (2005) 'Creating a Market Orientation: A Longitudinal, Multifirm, Grounded Analysis of Cultural Transformation', *Journal of Marketing*, 70(4): 43.

it is also of interest to note that 'openness' is associated with proactive behavioral norms.

Investigating which values characterize market oriented companies has also been carried out in a few quantitative studies. Homburg and Pflesser (2000) found that the following eight values supported market orientation: 'success', 'innovativeness and flexibility', 'openness and external communication', 'quality and competency', 'speed', 'interfunctional cooperation', the 'responsibility of the employees', and the 'appreciation of the employees'. Even though the wording differs somewhat between Gebhart et al. (2006) and Homburg and Pflesser (2000), the content of several of the values / commandments overlaps to a great extent. 'Collaboration' has much in common with 'interfunctional cooperation', 'respect/empathy/perspective taking' has much in common with the 'responsibility of the employees', which is also the case with 'keeping promises' and 'openness' with 'openness and external communication'. In addition, Jaworski and Kholi (1993) found that 'connectedness among departments' promotes market orientation and that 'employee commitment' was an effect of market orientation. Furthermore, Moorman (1995) studied the role of culture in relation to organizational market information processes, which can be seen as an important part of market orientation (cf. Kholi and Jaworski 1990). She argued that clan cultures characterized by 'trust' and 'commitment' facilitate information sharing. Trust and commitment are also, according to Morgan and Hunt (1994), key intra-organizational mediators and facilitators of relationship marketing. Narver et al. (1998: 243) argued that 'A market orientation consists of one overriding value: the commitment by all members of the organization to continuously create superior customer value'. Commitment is not listed as one of the key values in the model of Gebhart et al. (2006) but is mentioned in the 'behavioral norms' connected to 'keeping promises' and 'trust'. In addition, if the organization is to work according to the schedule provided by Gebhart et al. (2006), this presupposes commitment to as well as identification with the firm amongst the employees.

In the service orientation literature, Berry (1999) argues, based on 250 interviews and 'visits' to 14 'successful' service companies, that seven values / commandments characterize service oriented service firms and their cultures: i.e. 'excellence', 'innovation', 'joy', 'respect', 'teamwork', 'social profit', and 'integrity', defining each value as in Table 4.2 (see next page).

Again, we have to note a great deal of overlap with the list provided by Gebhart et al. (2006). The value 'teamwork', emphasizing that employees collaborate in service oriented firms, has a lot in common with the value 'collaboration'; 'respect' has commonalities with 'respect/empathy/perspective taking'; 'social profit' with 'openness', emphasizing, as that dimension does, collaboration beyond the formal boundaries of the organization. There is also a blend of the customer being an important imperative or 'the market [being] the raison d'être' in Berry's work, which is the first value of Gebhart et al. (2006).

Toward Customerism

How does organizations and their members become service and market oriented? Gebhart et al. (2006) argued that the 'guiding coalition', the group of people spearheading the change in the organizations they studied, accomplished change in three ways:

> First, the guiding coalitions created change by explicitly modeling behaviors aligned with the desired values and norms. Second, they used rewards and recognition to encourage behaviors that were aligned with the desired values and norms and they penalized (including removal

Table 4.2 Key Service Orientation Values

Value	Definition
Excellence	'The word good is rarely used in the sample companies. Good isn't good enough. The pride of achievement comes from striving for excellence' (Berry 1999: 23).
Innovation	'The values of innovation and excellence are inextricably linked. Innovation—changing what exists into something better—is the primary tool of excellence. Great service companies . . . invent rather then imitate' (Berry 1999: 24–25).
Joy	'Sustainable successful service companies achieve their consistency by investing in that which brings satisfaction, pride, and joy to the service performers who, in turn, are more likely to bring satisfaction and pleasure to their customers' (Berry 1999: 26).
Teamwork	'Teamwork—individuals collaboratively pooling their resources in pursuit of a common purpose—is a core value of the sample companies and a primary way they enrich employees' quality of work life' (Berry 1999: 29).
Respect	'Fundamental respect is another core value in the sample companies. Respect for the customer. Respect for the employee. Respect for suppliers and other business partners. Respect for the community' (Berry 1999: 30).
Integrity	'[Excellent service] companies value honesty and fair play not only as the right way to compete but as the best way to compete. Integrity with stakeholders, it is believed, wins the day' (Berry 1999: 34).
Social profit	'Social profit is analogous to profit sharing, except the profits are not limited to financial profits, and the sharing is not confined to the organization' (Berry 1999: 36).

Source: Berry, L.L. (1999) *Discovering the Soul of Service: The Nine Drivers of Sustainable Business Success*, New York: The Free Press.

from the firm) failure to adhere to the desired values and norms. Finally, they inculcated desired values and norms in the organization members through participation in subsequent transformation activities.

(Gebhart et al. 2006: 43)

When it comes to the first way of accomplishing a change of culture—'modelling behaviors aligned with the desired values and norms'—Gebhart et al. (2006) argue that the behaviors and rituals of the guiding coalition played an important role in the companies studied. As an example, Harley-Davidson, one of the studied organizations, shared detailed financial information with the union when the company was bought out from another company in order to create 'trust' and stimulate 'openness' (cf. the key values of market orientation suggested by Gebhart et al. 2006, listed in Table 4:1). Harley-Davidson also eliminated dedicated parking for its executives at its headquarters in order to convey the thought that every employee is valuable, in this way trying to create 'respect' and 'collaboration'. The importance of 'modeling' values is also referred to by Berry (1999) as one of the important ways of making the culture of organizations service oriented. He writes: 'The primary way values-driven leaders articulate the dream and define organizational success is through their own behavior. They live out their values in their daily behavior . . . Values-driven leaders are visible, authentic leaders. They devote considerable time and effort to personally communicate the company's values in the workplace' (Berry 1999: 43). Edvardsson and Enquist (2002: 180) also note that the management of IKEA 'walks the talk and talks the walk'. Good leaders who contribute toward making organizations market and service oriented are thus the ones who live according to the service and market orientation commandments; they are role models or pastors who lead by example. In this way, according to Berry (1999: 40), they mobilize 'emotional and spiritual resources that so often lie dormant in other organizations' and show that 'people at work don't just have a job; they have a cause'. In accordance with the analysis of the view of leadership in the service-dominant logic literature in Chapter 2, the service orientation literature holds that leaders need to be supportive, focusing on positive reinforcement and very seldom giving negative feedback, if they are to manage to service orient their organizations.

This supportive type of leadership is also emphasized by Gebhart et al. (2006: 43) who argue, when describing the second way of changing culture, that: 'The guiding-coalition also used rewards and recognition to create cultural change. The most prevalent recognition was interpersonal, with the guiding coalition showing approval, support, or disapproval of particular employee comment or actions in various venues'. Gebhart et al. (2006: 44) also found that the guiding coalition in the companies they studied, which had accomplished market oriented cultural change, 'exhibited an almost evangelical passion and commitment to the change process and espoused cultural values'. Seen from the perspective of pastoral power, the guiding coalition is a group of pastors convinced that the central commandments will lead the organization (or shall we say the congregation) and its members (i.e. the flock of sheep) in the right way. On the other hand, when the guiding coalition consisted of consultants who did not really commit themselves to change, and did not function as true pastors, change was not effective. Thus, market oriented change requires convinced leaders / pastors who try to get their flock of sheep on the right track by using interpersonal communicative skills, referred to as coaching by Gebhart et al. (2006). Coaching is also mentioned by Berry as an important tool when describing the role of frontline managers: 'Managers at the scene must assume the mantle of leadership; they must be the ones to coach, teach and inspire, hour after hour, day after day, week after week' (Berry 1999: 45). This is important to remember. As will be evident from the following, coaching is one of the main practices used at the FI to make organizational members believe in the commandments of market and service orientation. Indeed, coaching can be perceived as a confessional practice that the pastors / managers use to make the employees declare how they perceive themselves as service workers. Based on this knowledge, the pastors / managers can decide whether or not the individual sheep / employees are living according to the central commandments. If the pastor / managers find that the sheep / employees deviate from the ethic of customerism given by the central commandments the former can take initiatives that encourage the latter to align themselves and their selves closer with the commandments associated with service and market orientation discourse. Thus, it is possible to perceive the literature on market and service orientation as promoting confessional practices, upon which pastoral power is dependent in order to be effective, and as positioning the employees as a group of sheep because they are the ones who are supposed to hear confessions and take pastoral care (Foucault 2007).

This is supported by the third way of accomplishing market orientation suggested by Gebhart et al. (2006): i.e. to involve employees in future change events that reproduce the market oriented culture, e.g. the strategy process. An executive of Motorola, one of the companies studied by Gebhart et al. (2006: 46) explained 'the change in developing strategy as paradoxical; there were more people involved than ever before, but it was more productive and definitive than pretransformation efforts'. True believers, i.e. believers that really believe in the commandments of the congregation, are easy to lead because they lead themselves in the right way. Drawing on the vocabulary of pastoral power, they have the ability to lead themselves reflexively toward the goal given by the common ethic: in the present case, customerism. The language used in the service and market orientation literature also suggests a close coupling with pastoral power. Edvardsson and Enquist (2002: 175) refer to the testament of the furniture dealer, which incorporates the central commandments of the IKEA ethic, as 'the bible for all IKEA' and argues that the '"words" are followed as virtues for all believers'. They claim, furthermore, to study 'holy documents' and suggest that the 'strong culture in IKEA can give IKEA an image as a religion' (pp. 166 and 167). Gebhart et al. (2006) also make use of Christian language, arguing that leaders show an 'evangelical passion' and that 'believers' should be hired and 'dissenters' fired. Berry is no exception, describing leaders as mobilizing 'spiritual resources' and service oriented organizations as being full of 'true believers' (Berry 1999: 40–41). It can thus be claimed that the scheme of pastoral power lurks beneath the argument made by the literature, giving advice about how service and market orientation should be established.

Accordingly, it seems possible and plausible to understand and analyze service and market orientation programs from the perspective of pastoral power. This is what I have set out to do with the FI's IWHY program in the next section.

THE 'I WANT TO HELP YOU' PROGRAM

As the reader may recall, the 'I Want to Help You' program changed the overall formal strategy of the FI from a price-leader focus to a service, market, and customer oriented focus. With the introduction of the IWHY program, the strategic intentions of the FI moved away from focusing on *what* the FI was offering to *how* they were offering their services, mainly home loans. With this move, it can be suggested that the strategy of the FI entered the domain of SMM, which, from Grönroos (1978; 1982; 1984) and Shostack (1977) onward (see, for instance, Vargo and Lusch 2004), has given priority to researching and understanding the social and interactive aspects of service production and prescribing to organizations how service production should be carried out, rather than which offerings should be produced.

As in most interactive service organizations, it is the FLEs at the FI who provide the customers with service. Therefore, they became the major target of the service orientation program. Indeed, it can be suggested that changing the subjectivity of the FLEs was the single most important aim of the program, as well as of the other SMM practices that were subsequently drawn on (see Chapters 5 and 6). However, as we will see in this chapter and the following, repositioning the subjectivity of the FLEs was not an easy task. As shown in Chapter 3, the FLEs were reactive in their orientation; they saw themselves as administrators and behaved, according to their managers, like order clerks. The IWHY booklet states that the FLEs need to be 'aggressive customer representatives'.

The Content of IWHY and the View of Culture

David retrospectively explains the specific background to, and major content of, IWHY thus:

> In 2001, we [the managers] started to discuss things like—how can a change in behavior be accomplished, how do we acquire new habits . . . There are different roads to take but then I met the previous Principal of the Disney University, Rick something [thinks for a while]—Johnson was his name, which had a very, very clear image and a very clear idea of how to build culture . . . When working with corporate culture, you have to start with values. The co-workers need to share the values of the company; the staff must have values they share with the company

and the company needs clear values. These values lead to attitudes. You create an attitude from the values you have. From attitudes follow behavior, which is how you are *de facto* when you have these values in the back of your mind. The right behavior creates some kind of habit . . . These habits, he [Rick Johnson] said, are the culture.

(Sales manager, David)

The IWHY booklet provides a similar view of culture and presents Rick Johnson as the father figure of it. As the former Principal of Disney University, he is introduced thus: 'Service and putting the customer at the centre is his field'.[2] The booklet presents the model of Rick Johnson as a service-cultural change model. According to the booklet, Rick Johnson sees service-cultural change processes as 'a chain of activities . . . This chain is a methodology which describes how a change process should be conducted. If you want to change a culture, you will have to take it step-by-step; that is, begin with the values and then gradually build on that. The FI has adopted the thought and has thus begun at the beginning and is working with the values' (IWHY booklet). The image depicted in Figure 4.1 of the service-cultural change chain is displayed in the IWHY booklet.

Rick Johnson's view of corporate culture, which inspired David and the other managers of the FI when designing IWHY, is similar to that inherent in the market and service orientation literature, which also links customer oriented values with norms and behaviors (see preceding). In line with the academic literature previously analyzed, the service orientation program of the FI will be analyzed as a governmental discourse and, more particularly,

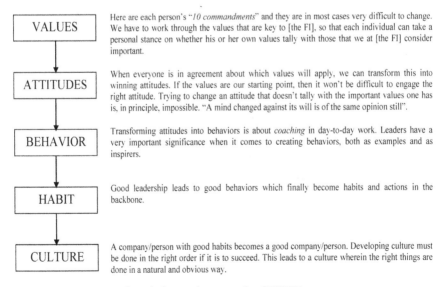

VALUES — Here are each person's "*10 commandments*" and they are in most cases very difficult to change. We have to work through the values that are key to [the FI], so that each individual can take a personal stance on whether his or her own values tally with those that we at [the FI] consider important.

ATTITUDES — When everyone is in agreement about which values will apply, we can transform this into winning attitudes. If the values are our starting point, then it won't be difficult to engage the right attitude. Trying to change an attitude that doesn't tally with the important values one has is, in principle, impossible. "A mind changed against its will is of the same opinion still".

BEHAVIOR — Transforming attitudes into behaviors is about *coaching* in day-to-day work. Leaders have a very important significance when it comes to creating behaviors, both as examples and as inspirers.

HABIT — Good leadership leads to good behaviors which finally become habits and actions in the backbone.

CULTURE — A company/person with good habits becomes a good company/person. Developing culture must be done in the right order if it is to succeed. This leads to a culture wherein the right things are done in a natural and obvious way.

Figure 4.1 Service cultural change framework of IWHY.

as a pastoral discourse in the subsequent sections. Three central pastoral power themes run through the program. Firstly, IWHY prescribes a customeristic ethic. The program thus relies on a transcendental truth (not on an objective positivistic truth, which is the case with disciplinary power), and the aim of the program is to color the subjectivity of the FLEs with the ethic given by this truth. Secondly, it has as its managerial object the subject. More importantly, IWHY envisions two major subject positions, that of the pastor (for the manager) and that of the sheep (for the FLEs)—the former guiding and leading the latter toward the subjectivity prescribed by the customeristic ethic of customer orientation. Thirdly, the program suggests confessional managerial practices that generate knowledge about the sheep which the pastors draw on to provide pastoral care for the sheep and which the sheep draw on to manage themselves in line with the customeristic ethic of the program.

THE CUSTOMERISTIC ETHIC AND THE SUBJECT

Let's start by analyzing the customeristic ethic and subject positions associated with the program. It is interesting to note that David makes a direct link between the service orientation program and subjectivity: the behavior (possibilities for actions) that follows from attitudes and values frames 'how you are de facto', he says. The connection between service orientation and subjectivity is also salient in the IWHY booklet which will be analyzed in depth here. The booklet aimed to support the controlling of the subjects in line with the values prescribed by the program which would foster a customeristic subjectivity. Indeed, the booklet can be thought of as the FI bible, providing the central commandments of the FI religion.

The FI Bible

David refers to the booklet thus: 'Instead of submitting a project report, we wrote a booklet . . . it's just as good each time I look at it . . . It's really ingenious. If you read it on one level, it's about you yourself and if you take a different level, it's about the group . . . It's about us and it's about you, your own stance and that of the group. And then there are exercises, issues to take a stance on' (sales manager, David). David's description of the booklet supports the interpretation that the subjectivity of the FLEs was a salient theme in the IWHY program. The latter is also supported by other key parts of the booklet. Subjectivity is addressed, for example, in connection with the presentation of the overall aim of the customeristic strategy—'*service in the champions' league*'—and, more particularly, when it is explained in the booklet, why the label 'I Want to Help You' was chosen for the program in the first place.

- 'I comes from the fact that it's about all of us . . . The commitment of the individual is crucial to success. As you know, no chain is stronger than its weakest link'. Everyone thus has to evolve and it is the I—the subjectivity of the employees—that has to evolve.

- 'Want is about the idea that the effort needs to come from the own undertaking. You can't order service in the champions' league to appear, it comes from one's own conviction that one's efforts are important. You have to want in order for it to be good'. Apart from that this formulation talks again to the individual and his or her subjectivity; it also alludes to other themes associated with pastoral power, which will be discussed later. We learn from the quote that service in the champions' league cannot be commanded to appear through sovereign power, instead being something that the employees have to feel that they really want to do, something which is attractive to them and makes them happy—not something that can be forced upon them. Will is about determination and is something that only the convinced believer is really able to mobilize. We also note the religious language— e.g. 'conviction'—which in line with the service and market orientation literature (see preceding) is a salient theme in the booklet.

- 'Help you stands for all of us being dependent on each other and that we make a bit more of an effort and help out. Of course, this matches the customer excellently, whereby the entire notion of service in the champions' league is based on us helping the customer out in a better way than our competitors'. Again, the subject is addressed, but this time in the form of the 'us'. However, let us not fool ourselves in any way: it is the employees, the FLEs in particular, that are supposed to provide the help—to each other and to the customers. That the employees, or the good sheep, not only shall help the customers they serve, but also their fellow sheep or congregation members, is a recurrent theme in the booklet; only then will 'the good company'— the label used in the booklet—be realized. As the SMM literature has pointed out, employees of service organizations have internal as well as external customers (Grönroos 2007b; Gummesson 1987). Internal and external customer service is also a theme pointed out when the question of how the FI should go about creating service in the champions' league is commented upon in the booklet: 'How do we then create service that's in the champions' league? Service is provided to people by people. We all provide service in some form, internally or externally, and we will never be better outwardly toward the customers than we are internally toward each other. Those who meet the customer are dependent on those who work in the background, and everyone is equally important'. Note also that employee subjectivity is addressed again. All employees have to work to their full potential if service in the champions' league is to become a reality.

Indeed, a recurrent theme throughout the booklet is formed by the subject and subjectivity being the main object of the program, and the subjectivity of the employees needing to be changed, if the service strategy is to be realized. The heading of one section, for instance, is: 'Use a mirror—not binoculars—when looking for faults: In your thoughts about others, there's a message to you about you'. In another part of the booklet, a similar message about self-reflection is conveyed.

> There are times in everyone's life when the best glasses are those with reflective glass. So that you can see yourself as you really are, accept reality and realize that you are you . . . It will not be until then that you see yourself without veiling and forgiving shells and you like the overall picture you see. It will not be until then that you have the prerequisites to dispassionately and respectfully look at others and be able to contribute to their growth. It's all about you—the choice is yours.
>
> (IWHY booklet)

The Five Commandments

Thus, the person has to confess to him- or herself who he or she really is and work on—empowered by that image—reaching full potential. But what is 'full potential'? What kind of subject is envisioned? It is the five values—or as I, in line with the booklet, which talks about the human beings 'ten commandments' (see Figure 4:1) and my pastoral power point of departure, prefer to call them: *the five commandments* of the program that is regulating who the subject should strive to become. The five commandments are:

- Comprehensive view: Be there for each other and help broaden the company's interface. How can you actively contribute? Catch balls that are in the air and be sensitive to various external activities. What's going on right now? See constantly different issues in a greater context. How can you contribute toward a greater holistic view?
- Innovation: Encourage and support new ideas. How can you do this in a more concrete way? Play down the issue of innovation. How can you, in your everyday life, see simple improvement measures which you yourself can grasp and which simplify your work? Tell us about your immediate surroundings. Exert an influence by being a good example yourself. The sum total of these numerous small steps entails a positive change for the customers. How can you and the group regularly gather up all the small ideas?
- Empathy: Take time to reflect on how others are. Care. How can you do this more often? Shape the thought *how*. Act, transform into action. Having a friendly week once a year isn't enough. How can you and your group do your bit?

- Trust: Don't have double diaries. How will you and your group contribute toward creating trust and respect, both for time and for the individual? Clarify your expectations. How can you be more clear vis-à-vis your surroundings as regards what you and your group stand for? Keep your promises and don't make promises you can't keep—when there are problems, get back to people in time. Talk to each other and not about each other. How can we jointly work toward reducing harmful gossip?
- Commitment: See the opportunities. The problem will not disappear but may, perhaps, become slightly visible from left field to help you discern a possible solution. Think positively and express yourself positively. Statements like "Can't be done" and "We've never done that" could, perhaps, be expressed a bit differently; "Exciting", "We haven't tried that—let's check it out!". How can you and the group contribute toward creating commitment? Don't waste strength and energy on negative experiences—they're rarely world-changing. How can you and the group support each other in seeing the right perspectives and putting things into their rightful context?

(IWHY booklet)

The overlap between the commandments of the IWHY program and the commandments promoted by the service and market orientation literature is striking (see preceding). It is almost as though FI made a synthesis of this literature as a point of departure for the IWHY program. The booklet also bears similarities to the 'testament of a furniture dealer', which Edvardsson and Enquist (2002) found to be central to the service strategy and culture of IKEA and which the two researchers referred to using the terms 'bible' and 'holy document', arguing that this plus other texts, as well as 'the strong culture of IKEA' which emerged, 'can give IKEA an image as a religion'. As suggested, the IWHY booklet can be described as the FI's 'bible' and its most 'holy document', providing the central 'commandments' in what can be referred to as the 'religion of the FI'. According to the booklet, the commandments can 'be difficult to put your finger on but still difficult to change'. The five commandments emerged during workshops attended by all staff and are, or have to become, of key importance to FI staff. The IWHY booklet again: 'Those of you who have not thought through which values are important now have that opportuntity by further exploring this book'.

CONFESSIONAL PRACTICES

The task of transforming the central commandments of the program into action was given to operative management, the team leaders in particular. David is very clear on this: 'We said this is a relay race. We've run the first leg. Now this has to work on a day-to-day basis, now you [as a team leader] have to take the baton and start talking about values day-to-day'. The booklet supported this task by suggesting what I refer to as confessional practices facilitating the operation of pastoral power. The booklet states, for example: 'The expectations that you as a co-worker have on yourself, your colleagues, and your leaders must be clarified in order for them [the leaders] to get the chance to encounter you'. Thus, in order to 'develop', the person must confess and avow who he or she is and who he or she would like to become. This presupposes the person adopting the position of the sheep. It also presupposes management acting as pastors who are ready to hear confessions and provide the pastoral care that this sheep so badly needs.

Dividing Questions

One resource that the managers can use for checking who the employees of the FI really are is the exercises and reflective questions that are interwoven with the body text of the booklet. These are confessional in their character, designed to get people to avow their beliefs, as well as what discourses, subject positions, and 'plug-ins' (see the second chapter) that constitute them: information which the pastor—in the case of the FI, the team leader in particular—draws on to check whether or not the individual represents the right discursive material. However, these questions and exercises can also be used by the employees themselves to check whether or not they are expressing, in the light of the five commandments, the right views and standpoints. Two important confessional questions in the booklet are:

> For you yourself to reflect upon:
> • How well do your values match those of the FI?
> • Can you, in a natural way, live these values?
>
> (IWHY booklet)

These questions are important because they serve as dividing practices, the notion that Foucault used for practices that distinguish different categories of people from each other (Foucault 1970; Townley 1994). The 'dividing questions' convey the following message to the employees: you are either in or out, you are either with us or against us. If the answer to the first question is 'not at all' or 'poorly', there would seem to be no hope for the person at the FI. As the booklet states: 'If the FI has values that do not match yours, then you will have to take the consequences. Neither the company nor you will change fundamentally'. From the perspective of the booklet, companies and people are similar. Both are rooted in distinctive imperatives that are either hard or impossible to change. In the booklet, individuals are defined thus: 'Individual = indivisible, separate being'.

However, confessing that one's personal values match the common values of the FI poorly cannot seriously be expected of any employee who wants to keep on working there. The reason for the latter is that the modern person is reflexive about what it means to be a person in the modernistic sense. The IWHY program presupposes this knowledge which every modern human being tacitly or explicitly has about self and self-formation and draws on that presupposition in order to govern the employees. The question thus serves as a reminder to the individual employees that they need to check themselves against the five commandments that are central to the ethic of the FI.

Giving a no answer to the second question—'can you, in a natural way, live these values?'—is not so dangerous because it says: 'I want to live the right way but I am not able to yet. Can someone help me please?'. Indeed, the very title of the program 'I Want to Help You' indicates that such an approach is alright, and even to a certain extent expected from the ordinary employee. Especially because, adjacent to the presentation of the overall goals of the program, it is stated that: 'We provide everybody with service in some form, internally or externally, and we will never be better toward our customers than we are internally toward each other'. Thus, the FLEs are not only expected to help their customers, but also their own co-workers. They are, according to the booklet, expected to serve as role models for each other.

> Are you conscious of the power you have to act as an example? What you do is just as important as what you don't do. You can do right, wrong, or nothing at all . . . when you yourself treat others with respect, because you want respect, you will be practicing what you preach in order to be correctly treated by others. You yourself will become an example regardless of your role in the company.
>
> (IWHY booklet)

The phrase 'practice what you preach' is repeated several times and is a central theme in the booklet, indicating that it is okay to be helped as well as to help. In fact, the second dividing question can be interpreted as serving the purpose of turning the employees into a flock of sheep, ready to take pastoral care, by the team leaders / pastors. According to this interpretation, the employees are almost expected, to some degree, to answer no to the second question. If not, the program will not really be needed, and the subject will be displaying an attitude that is unrealistic, positioning him- or herself above the flock of sheep.

The Personal Tender as a Pastoral Power Practice

What makes the confessional questions in the booklet so potentially powerful, in terms of ordering subjectivity, is their linkage with human practices, two of which are salient in the booklet: the *personal tender* and *coaching*. The personal tender is a performance appraisal evaluation practice based on a form that each employee is supposed to fill out once a year. It serves as input material for the annual progress interview and addresses the following areas: what the person has been doing over the last year, what the person is doing right now, what the person wants to do, and how he or she wants to be perceived by others. According to the IWHY booklet, the person when filling out the personal tender must also 'clarify [his or her] stance on the values in everyday actions . . . An aggressive supplier's tender contains clear parts which raise the things you are best at and can contribute to the group, in order for you to jointly solve the task'. The personal tender addresses the individual who is supposed to avow who he or she is and what he or she wants to become in relation to the group by filling out the form accompanying it.

The reflective confessional question connected with the presentation of the personal tender in the booklet: 'Would your tender look the same if your colleague had written it?', alludes to the notion that the individual employees need to see themselves as part of a collective. This is a typical trait of pastoral power, which subjectifies from the inside out and views the person in relation to the group—the flock of sheep. Thus, the personal tender locates the person as a part of the group, as one of the sheep constituting the congregation, and as a person who is in need of pastoral care and development. The subjects are instructed to reflect upon the development that they are in need of themselves by avowing who they are and who they want to become, by confessing divergences between actuality and possibility, between the actual situation and the ideal situation; then the distance that these people need to transcend in order to become a good organizational member becomes clear. Or, as it is expressed in the booklet: 'What you want is what you aspire to express in your personal tender—the more clearly this can be done, the better will be the prerequisites you create for making it a reality' and 'By respectfully and mutually working with the tender as a living expression of what you want and recurrently reconnecting with this, you will create prerequisites for the distance between how you want to be perceived and how you actually are perceived to shrink'. The person is also instructed to reflect upon in writing the distance transcended between the ideal and the norm since he or she filled out his or her last personal tender a year ago. 'It's important that you make visible how your everyday life looks [and] what has changed since the last tender'. Moreover, the subject also needs to focus on his or her present state, as addressed by the following reflective questions: 'What are you good at?'; 'What do you do to make yourself an aggressive supplier?'.

It is also here, in connection with the self-reflective confessional practices, that the common customeristic ethic enters the governmental equation of the IWHY with full force. The person is not advised to avow and confess his or her present and past actions in general, but in relation to the five commandments. As expressed in the section about the personal tender in the booklet, the person is supposed to 'clarify [his or her] stance on the values in everyday actions'. Or, as stated elsewhere in the booklet: 'We must all become and be committed aggressive suppliers and, on a daily basis, live the jointly developed values in all our actions'. To what degree does the person presently live these commandments? In which ways has the person been moving closer to a lifestyle in accordance with the ethic since the last time he or she filled out the personal tender? How would the person ideally behave if he or she were supposed to live life according to the commandments of the FI? These are questions that the personal tender urges the employees to consider. As such, the personal tender seeks to move the person from his or her present state to the ideal state, as defined by the commandments. As with pastoral practices in general, the personal tender can thus be perceived as a self-reflexive governmental practice. In other words, the personal tender is designed to encourage the person to lead him- or herself toward the common customeristic ethic.

However, these important questions and topics cannot be left solely to the sheep to ponder, incapable as they normally are of truly interpreting the real meaning of the FI ethic, or any other ethic for that matter. The pastor takes the stage in the form of the team leader. They are the ones who receive the personal tenders—the written confessions of the sheep—and who are appointed to interpret them and give feedback to the sheep. Based on the knowledge about the sheep, that the personal tender provide them the team leaders / pastors can guide and lead the individual sheep in relation to the customeristic ethic during the individual 30-minute progress interviews that the team leaders hold seven to ten times a year, as well as during the annual and more extensive progress interviews and during regular work. Because, based on the fixation of the employees / sheep in customeristic discourse which the personal tender seeks to accomplish, the team leader will be able to draw a lot of conclusions regarding how the sheep needs to change itself in order to live according to the five commandments, and whether or not the individual employee has the capability to become a good organizational member providing service in the champions' league. The pastors can, for instance, ask themselves the following fundamental question that pertains to each individual employee: Has the person understood the ethic? Does he or she have the possibility to regulate him- or herself toward the customeristic ethic? Has the person pointed out a relevant gap between the present and the ideal that will enable him or her to live according to the customeristic ethic of the commandments? What kind of correction to the fundamental insight is needed? What guidance and support does the person need in order to reach the goal? In what ways does the person help others in the group to reach the goal of service in the champions' league? Is the person a good or a bad sheep?

In addition, and as explained previously, set in a pastoral power framework, the person is not only expected to behave well for him- or herself, but also to set an example for the other employees: to serve as a role model. As stated in the IWHY booklet: 'You can inspire others by setting a good example! . . . The power of example is great and each and every one of us is an example for others—but we have to obtain the courage to dare to reveal what we do to inspire others'. Thus the good sheep not only has to perform the right actions in the right way, but also avow how he or she carries out those actions so that his or her co-workers can follow his or her example and learn from him or her. Indeed, the personal tender can serve this purpose by being avowed between the staff or throughout the whole company, as suggested by two of the reflective questions: 'Can you show each other your tenders? Can you publish all or parts of the tender on [the intranet] in order to inspire others, and put pressure on yourselves?' Moreover, based on the knowledge that the team leader receives and on the interpretations of that knowledge that he or she makes, the team leader can reflect upon what the person is worth to the company in financial terms. What salary should the FLE have? At the FI, the team leader has a major influence on what salary the FLEs have, something which the FLEs were very much aware of. Perhaps it's best to behave like a good sheep!

Thus, the personal tender can be perceived as a practice of pastoral power. It encourages confessions and subjectification, informed by the customeristic ethic built into the form, it promotes self-regulation and enables regulation by others in accordance with the five commandments, it positions employees as sheep and team leaders as pastors, and it encourages the managers and the employees to see both themselves and their own subjectivity in relation to the group and the customeristic ethic. In addition, it also governs, not through force or violence, but through kindness and gentle guidance, through developing and leading the employees toward the common and agreed upon ethic and the good life that this ethic promises.

Coaching as a Pastoral Power Practice

The practice of coaching, and the theme of coaching that runs throughout the entire booklet, is the second important confessional pastoral power/ knowledge practice associated with the IWHY program. In the service-culture change scheme previously discused (see Figure 4:1), coaching is related to behavior and is perceived to be the most important practice for transforming 'attitudes into behaviors'. Again, we have to note the overlap between the IWHY program and the service and market orientation literature which, as the preceding review in this chapter of this literature showed, also recommends coaching as a practice for turning the commandments / values that it prescribes into practice. According to the booklet, it is the managers who need to take the responsibility for coaching the rest of the employees, in particular the FLEs. 'On your home turf, you as a leader need to bring out behaviors by coaching on a daily basis in order for them to become a habit . . . which . . . creates . . . a natural corporate culture. How you as a leader act in your role as a leader must be in harmony with our values in order to achieve our shared goals'. The same message is conveyed elsewhere in the booklet: 'In order to change an attitude into behavior, coaching is required in day-to-day work over a long period. Management has a key role to play, both as an example and in order for the change to last'. The practice of coaching positions the managers as pastors. The managers are supposed to take care of the employees, to listen to their confessions, and, based on that information, guide and lead them toward the common ethic. The managers are expected to act as role models living in accordance with the five common commandments of the FI. As a pastor, the manager sets an example.

> Very clear demands are made of the leaders to be culture-bearing examples . . . How senior executives live the idea and work with their leadership, as well as monitor normal operations day-to-day, is . . . a crucial success factor for the work of change. Change at the FI will not be credible if senior executives do not lead by example. You as a co-worker have probably at some point experienced a gap between what is said and what you see being done in practice. It is little motivating for you as a co-worker to try to make an effort to work on a daily basis with values, attitudes, and habits if this is not felt to be important by your manager, your example, or your colleague.
>
> (IWHY booklet)

Thus, the pastors / managers need to be true believers. They can never doubt their calling. If they do, they will not be able to lead and guide the employees in the right way.

But what is coaching more exactly? It is a little fuzzily expressed in the booklet, and I will return to the question in the next chapter when discussing the measurement of service quality at the FI, which directed the substance of the coaching toward fostering proactivity and provided the use of the confessional practice with impetus. However, according to the IWHY booklet: 'Coaching at the FI is about you [as a manager] wishing the other person well' or, as it is stated in the heading for the section on coaching by managers: 'Encouragement gives stamina'. A similar description of coaching is given in another part of the booklet: 'At the FI, our coaching culture must be about wishing each other well and that the other person must grow. Coaching entails listening, supporting, encouraging, and being behind your colleagues. Any remarks made must be in a positive spirit. Criticism with any other intention than helping the other person is not what we define as coaching'. Encouraging the members of the congregation, 'to wish the other person well', and make them happy, is the role given to managers by pastoral power. The pastor governs and controls, not through force or brutal strength, but by guiding and leading kindly (Foucault 2007). Coaching contributes toward turning the managers of the FI into pastors—their job is to provide pastoral care. The rest of the organizational members are turned into sheep who receive pastoral care.

Coaching, as described in the booklet, is also associated with self-regulation ordered by the common ethic, another key feature of pastoral power. As stated in the IWHY booklet: 'In order to be able to lead others, you as a leader have to be able to lead yourself. Management's ultimate aim is to get others, both management colleagues and co-workers, to lead themselves'. Elsewhere in the booklet: 'As a co-worker, you must have the capacity to be able to lead yourself. As a manager and leader, you must also be good at leading others.' As with pastoral power and care in general, the goal of the pastoral power in the service orientation program at the FI is to turn each and every one into a pastor, in relation to the self. The sheep that provide themselves with pastoral care, guided by the shared ethic surrounding the governmental situation, have the capacity to lead themselves toward salvation. But they will also serve as role models for others, even for the real pastors, by setting a good example. This is what is meant by economic government, i.e. government that requires very little in terms of resources because it is conducted by the self on the self, and by a subject that is not formally a manager. One of the confessional questions associated with the coaching theme encourages this type of management: 'How can you coach each other, including managers and specialists, so that the whole group develops so that you jointly rise?'. Thus, even though the employees have no formal management position, the good sheep is expected to serve as a good example to others and, in this way, contribute more informally to the coaching effort. 'The most important thing anyway is . . . [that] we are examples to each other, both co-workers and managers. On both a grand and a small scale to coach, support, and encourage each other to live our values'.

As pointed out, such economic government is ordered by the shared commandments of the group, but can also be facilitated by identifying sheep that deviate from the shared ethic and which can serve as examples about how not to behave. The following confessional question: 'How do you feel that the group's results are affected by a member of the group not sharing the group's ambitions?' encourages the group to identify the infidels who are setting examples of how not to behave. Indeed, in the IWHY booklet, two subject positions are given regarding who the infidels are: the 'conscious' and 'unconscious' 'anti workers'. The question: 'Are you a conscious or an unconscious anti worker?' is given one page in the booklet.

What, then, is an anti worker? The terms says that you are against something and, in this case, you are against the FI, the task, and the group's aspirations to achieve the vision. We can see two types of anti workers; those who do not want to because they do not understand and those who do not want to even when they understand. The former are unconscious of what consequences their actions entail. The latter are fully aware and are indifferent or, putting it bluntly, anti workers against all change.

(IWHY booklet)

It is important, the text implies, when the group is considering whether or not someone in the group does not share its common objectives, to identify and distinguish between the conscious anti worker and the unconscious anti worker. The former is the dangerous type, the real infidel that needs to be burned at the stake, excluded from the congregation permanently or at the very least sent to a monastery until he or she betters his or her ways. He or she is also mimicking how a sheep should not be, serving as a mirror image role model for the good sheep in the same way as the big banks constitute the mirror image of a good organization for the FI. The bad sheep provides the aspiring sheep with a learning opportunity. The second type of anti worker—the unconscious—can be thought of as a savage who is invited to do things the right way if he or she, in action and thought, shows that he or she will try, and try hard, to live in accordance with the customeristic commandments. As stated in the booklet: ' . . . most people have it in them. It's more a matter of extracting the thoughts, conveying them to your colleagues, holding a dialog and, on the basis of this, reaching agreement about what is required of you and the group'.

Thus, most people can become believers. All it takes is to confess and avow to the work group one's innermost thoughts, which should not just be restricted to working life but to all parts of life. As stated in the booklet, it is important to strike the right balance between work, family, and free time in order to become a good person. Furthermore, this balance should be dwelt upon collectively: 'You and your colleagues in your group may need to discuss how things are with everyone's balance, which measures everyone is working with, for instance in areas like keeping fit, culture, and knowledge. You will surely be able to find shared activities which contribute toward a healthier life, better care of your own self, and which augment the group's own relations and identity'. Several confessional questions also address the topic of work life balance: 'Balance in life, how well do you divide up your time between work, family, and your personal self?', 'Do you do activities which augment your own self—that is, which create time for caring for and looking after your self?'. If everybody in the work group takes part in a sincere dialog about all aspects of themselves, the group, under the guidance of the pastor, will reach consensus regarding how to live a life in accordance with the commandments. In the section on coaching, in the booklet addressing the individual co-worker, several confessional questions are provided that are intended to encourage what could be referred to as a confessional and pastoral climate: 'What does good coaching look like? Are you a good coach? Do you coach others? Do you think you should be coaching? Do you give praise? Do you get praise? Are there obstacles to giving encouragement and praise?'.

Another group of confessional questions, included in the section on coaching, addresses the repositioning of subjectivity: 'Is there an ideal image of a leader? Do we have the right demands and expectations? How do we shrink the gap between demands and expectations?'. Elsewhere in the booklet, questions pertaining to a similar theme are provided: 'What do you want to change? What do you dislike about yourself, can you change it?'. One interpretation might suggest that the questions invite a giving and taking kind of exercise, e.g. a collective modification of the shared rules of the game within the group—this interpretation is supported by another question associated with coaching: 'What rules of play are you going to have in the group?'. An alternative interpretation, which has a great affinity with the notion of power/knowledge, suggests that the questions are about closing the gaps between the present subjectivity and the ideal state, as given by the common ethic. The first group of questions, addressing the coach and coaching, is particularly interesting because it checks what type of leader the sheep imagine. Is it the pastor or the sovereign? If it is the latter, this is a problem that needs to be addressed, a gap that needs to be transcended, an image that needs to be corrected. Because, at the FI, the IWHY booklet states 'no one is needed to point with all fingers in order to indicate what is required'. No sovereign is needed, rather the pastor acting as a role model, who encourages the co-workers to confess, and who, based on these confessions, leads and guides the sheep and the flock of sheep toward the subject positions provided by the commandments. The second group of questions concerning demands and their appropriateness checks whether or not the sheep have the right substance. Do they subscribe to the shared ethic? Can they articulate it? If not, do the really believe in it?

In conclusion, this section suggests that coaching can be perceived as a confessional practice fostering subjectification in line with the notion of pastoral power. Coaching, as expressed in the IWHY booklet, positions managers as pastors who hear confessions and provide pastoral care based on these confessions and employees as sheep who are supposed to confess their sins to the pastor, but also to themselves, regulating both themselves and their colleagues. It is the five commandments of the FI that order the actions and behaviors of the pastors and the sheep, as well as the confessional talk and the subjectification processes aimed at. A sheep who follows this scheme will be a happy sheep and a true believer.

THE SERMONS OF THE HIGH PRIESTS

It is also interesting to analyze and position the two forewords to the booklet, written by the project leader, sales manager David, and the CEO of the entire FI, in relation to the pastoral power framework. The forewords are written, as they usually are, in such a way that the following text should be read as the words of David and the CEO. Put another way, and given that the substance of the rest of the text is so ethically loaded, David and the CEO take the position of the pastor, or maybe better, the high priest who puts in writing to the pastors and members of the church their central sermon—the notion of the holy scripture or the bible comes to mind again when thinking about the booklet. Indeed, in the forewords, we find many of the themes of pastoral power. David addresses the individual subject directly by emphasizing how pivotal it is that the individual develops him- or herself, phrasing it like this: 'It's about you', ' . . . don't be afraid of changing yourself—maybe you're wiser today than you were yesterday', and 'With the project, we wanted to arouse, inspire, and emphasize each individual's opportunity to grow by him- or herself or to grow with the FI'. The individual employees are thus the target of the sermon; it is they who are given the possibility of developing their subjectivity in line with the opportunities; and the central commandments and the practices associated with them. Or, as David puts it in his final phrase: 'Good luck on your own journey!'. Not travelling, not changing themselves, is out of the question for the employees. As an example of self-development, David refers to his own experiences as a project leader for IWHY. 'As project leader, I have been given a personal opportunity to work full-time both with myself and with many of you'. In this way, David demonstrates that he is a good pastor capable of renewing himself.

The CEO focuses on the individual employee in relation to the work group, something which is also very much in line with the pastoral power framework which holds that the sheep needs to see him- or herself as part of the flock and contribute toward achieving the common goals of that flock. The CEO writes: 'I have a very strong belief in you as individuals. And it won't be until we make a joint effort that the company becomes a vigorous organism with all its parts in harmony', and 'At a good company, the people are the soul of that company . . . There, you will also find the insight that the individual's consciousness decides the company's development opportunities'. The person in relation to the flock is also something that is alluded to by David: 'The power of one is a motto that doesn't fully work in reality . . . the work has to be done together', and 'You as a person and a co-worker are the most important resource that we have. In collaboration with the team, your group, we can tackle the task and become the obvious choice for the customer and the obvious choice as a workplace'.

Another pastoral power/knowledge theme in the forewords is that of self-management. In order to achieve the goal, says David, not only are committed co-workers needed, but also 'co-workers who assume responsibility for the FI's and their own development', positioning the subject as a responsible agent who is ready to take care of him- or herself and his or her own self-development. The CEO puts it like this: 'We must all assume responsibility for the development of both ourselves and our operations'. However, both David and the CEO emphasize that this self-regulation needs to be coordinated: It cannot be self-regulation in accordance with each individual's potentially disparate preferences. Rather, they argue, it needs to be in line with the shared ethic as given by the five commandments. For instance, the CEO points out: 'The inner work must be characterized by vision, value and goal management, as well as a corporate culture based on the fundamental values; trust, empathy, innovation, a comprehensive view, and commitment'. David argues for a similar position. At least two of the preceding quotes taken from David's foreword, concerning self-development, communicate the notion that self-development has to be governed by the shared FI ethic. This suggests that the CEO and David both embrace a pastoral view of leadership, positioning themselves as high priests of the FI congregation and arguing that other managers at the FI also need to perceive themselves as and act like pastors. The CEO is very clear about this: 'To achieve power and conjure up energy, it is also a requirement that every leader complies with the FI's management philosophy . . . All co-workers, especially managers and leaders, must see themselves as examples who involve and stimulate their co-workers into working committedly and customer-centrically'. Not mentioning the managers of the FI *per se,* David alludes more to another side of pastoral power, care, and leadership: its supportive function. As has been explained previously, pastoral power manages through kindness and by supporting self-development, not through force. David puts it like this: 'The booklet you're holding in your hand is primarily envisaged to help you move forward' and 'The reflective questions you encounter support you'.

In conclusion, it can be suggested that the type of change which the strategic service and market orientation program at the FI promotes can be understood against the backdrop of pastoral power. This is something the program shares with the service and market orientation literature.

ACTUAL ORDERING EFFECT OF IWHY

Did IWHY order the FI and the subjectivity of the FLEs in the intended ways? Answering this question requires, in addition to the empirical material I have following completion of the program, data collected prior to the program being launched. However, it is possible, based on the empirical material I have, to analyze whether or not the five commandments of the IWHY are characteristic of the FI and the subjectivity of the employees. Because, if the analysis in this section finds that one or more of the five commandments are not salient following the IWHY program when I made my interviews, this would indicate that they were not salient before the program either.

Innovation

Let's start with innovation which seems to be the most salient of the five commandments. When asked during the interviews what they believed was characteristic of the FI, many employees referred spontaneously to innovation. One of the FLEs, for example, answered the question thus: 'Innovation. We're not afraid of new endeavors. We dare to make new endeavors and fail, kind of thing'. One of her colleagues said: 'If I compare with friends working in the same business as me, the FI is a company that is characterized by innovation'. Another FLE corroborated this: 'The company wants to move forward, there's been a lot of fresh ideas and innovation'. Yet another said: 'We [the FI] have always been this spearhead, you could say, that has been responsible for these fresh ideas'. Other FLEs did not mention the word innovation explicitly when asked the question of what they thought was characteristic of the FI, nevertheless alluding to innovation quite clearly. One of the FLEs said: 'The FI is a hungry company that wants to move forward, which pushes forward'. One of her colleagues said: 'The FI is a company that dares to believe in a new idea . . . you can hardly keep up at times because of all the new stuff we do and all the new routes we take'. When relating her thoughts about what is so special about the FI, one of the back office staff said: 'That there's always something new happening, that it's almost never routine, kind of thing . . . There's always something new for you to get hold of, new things going on, fun things. I think a lot happens here'. An FLE corroborated, referring to the fact that the FI has innovated by means of the changes that have been made to the market offering: 'We've introduced a lot of new stuff. We removed the surcharge on condos'.

Empathy

The interviews also suggest that empathy is a feature of the FI, and the subjectivity of its employees, even though it seems to be less salient than innovation. No one mentioned the word empathy explicitly when asked about what characterized the FI, but several employees believed that the co-workers of the FI cared for others, and especially their fellow employees, with the latter being an aspect of empathy emphasized in the IWHY booklet. One FLE said, for instance: 'We help each other and support each other. I really feel that we do'. Another FLE held a similar position, saying: 'We help out across boundaries, that's what I feel'. One of the back office staff who had previously held a position as an FLE said: 'We help each other and we don't work against each other, which people sometimes do in other places'. The HRM manager said: 'There's an incredibly warm and cordial atmosphere. Nothing's stiff, you can notice it and feel it. That's probably the most characteristic thing [about the FI]'. Some FLEs attributed this to IWHY: 'IWHY was a very good project. It taught us to help each other across the boundaries'. Others alluded to empathy, arguing that it was a salient theme, but they did not perceive it to be a purely good thing. One of the back office staff said: 'It's an incredibly cozy company where everybody's happy. One of our core values has been showing each other empathy. There's a risk that there's so much empathy that the company will keel over due to there being so much empathy'. The coziness was also referred to as a salient feature of the FI, but also as a risk, by the HRM manager and the manager of the customer support center. The HRM manager said: 'It's become a bit too cozy. It's supposed to be very nice . . . we need to make demands, too . . . now we're going to make more demands, not everything is ok'. The customer support center manager corroborated this: 'Yes, it's a bit too cozy . . . Some coziness we'd like to keep but I really don't want cookie managers, because that's simple, offer cookies and never make any demands'. In addition, several of the employees argued that the FI staff are helpful to their customers, at least in comparison with the banks. FLE Anne, for instance, said: 'In contrast to the banks, we're on the customer's side. We want to live up to that image when we talk to our customers . . . we want to talk to them in a language they understand . . . many customers tell me that the banks use a language they don't understand'.

Trust

Trust was not mentioned as a characteristic of the FI by any of the employees when asked the direct question of what they thought characterized the FI and its employees. Team leader Alice, however, argues that frequent communication with the customer 'creates a relationship with the customer, which makes him or her feel a sense of trust in us'. Some link trust with simplicity, which resonates quite well with the definition of trust in the IWHY booklet, where trust is talked about in the following way: 'Clarify your expectations. How can you be more clear toward your surroundings as regards what you and your group stand for?'. The marketing manager, for instance, is one of the people who makes the coupling between trust and simplicity: 'Of course, if you can work in a simple way, transfer your knowledge to a customer who doesn't know anything, then of course that will create a lot of trust I think'. Simplicity was a common theme among the employees when describing the basic characteristics of the FI. One FLE argued 'We're easy to deal with'. Another FLE said: 'People expect things to be easy'. 'That we're quick and handy' was what another FLE believed the customers expected from the FI. David has a position similar to the FLEs: 'We've always been focusing on making mortgages simple and transparent and as cheap as we are able to make them'. The marketing manager has a similar position: 'It's actually one of the FI's sharpest competitive advantages, besides price and distribution, that it's simple'. One of the back office staff corroborates this: 'Our FLEs work a lot on making the business simple. I think that's what people need, getting one [a mortgage] must be simple and uncomplicated'. Thus, if we agree that there is a coupling between simplicity and trust, or that trust is driven by simplicity, one could argue that the employees thought of the FI as a company characterized by trust when they were asked to describe its characteristics. If that connection is contested, which seems plausible, the employees do not seem to think of the FI as a company characterized by trust.

Commitment

When it comes to commitment, none of the FLEs described themselves explicitly as committed, and none referred to the FI as an organization characterized by commitment. However, the FLEs, and the employees in general, were described by managers as committed. The head of the consumer division said, for instance: 'There is fantastic commitment, knowledge of the earnings trend of the company, which is simply enormous. Despite the fact that many have not been educated in economics, there is such a genuine interest in these economic issues'. The HRM manager made a similar point:

> What strikes me, after having worked here for a while, is that my co-workers are so into the earnings trend and have such good knowledge, involve themselves, and care. It is also incredibly characteristic of the FI, that level of commitment, the interest. On the basis of where I worked before, I think it's fantastic how it's interconnected, how committed my co-workers are to where we're going, why, questioning like mad whether that vision really is good, what's the point of it. My point is that all of them know about the vision and the business concept, the business plan—when we get going with that there's an enormous level of participation'.
>
> (HRM manager)

When I interviewed the head of the consumer division and the HRM manager, they had not been working for the FI for long—the former for about three months and the latter for about a year. Maybe this was the reason why they could 'see' the commitment. As newcomers, they could mirror the FI in other organizations. The impression I get from interpreting the interviews is that the personnel are very committed; perhaps they take this for granted themselves, and do not mention it when asked about it. With the exception of the HRM manager, and the head of the consumer division, only one of the back office employees describes the staff as committed, saying: 'They're very committed actually, our FLEs'. Other things that support my interpretation include expressions such as: 'I put my body and soul into it', as uttered by one FLE and 'it's important for me to give the customer a piece of myself so that he feels comfortable' uttered by another. Similar statements were not uncommon during interviews.

Comprehensive View

Judging from the interviews, it is hard to find support for the last of the commandments, comprehensive view, being a key characteristic of the FI. No one mentions comprehensive view when asked what they feel characterizes the FI. However, many FLEs felt that their professional role had changed, with some attributing this change explicitly to the general change in orientation and some connecting this change to IWHY. Anne, for example, who started working at the FI in 2002 (the same year that IWHY was introduced), argued that 'the entire organizational culture has changed. We [the FLEs] have moved from merely being administrators, if I put it like that, to being customer representatives, as we call it. Everything the customers ask you about you should know about. Your role consists of so much more now than it did previously. The role has expanded'. Anne's way of defining her role has a lot in common with the IWHY value *comprehensive view*. When I ask Anne to describe the difference between the 'old' role and the 'new' one more particularly, she exemplifies this with a customer buying a house.

> Previously they [the customers] contacted us in order to take out a loan and we paid the realtor. Now, the typical customer contacts us before even starting to look at houses. And from the first phone call, you stay in contact with them as long as they have their loan. In this situation, it's not only about paying the money on the right day, we're also involved in how they insure their houses, what insurance to take out to cover them during unemployment, how they pay their bills to us, etc. We have moved from helping our customers to get house loans to helping them with all their housing matters.

Only a few FLEs discussed the changed role in a way which resonated with the value of comprehensive view. One reason for many not alluding to comprehensive view might be that there seems to be a contradiction between simplicity—which some interviewees argued was a salient feature of the FI (see preceding) driving trust—and comprehensive view. Perhaps this indicates a movement away from simplicity toward a more complex service offering. Just before I started my empirical study, and during it, the FI introduced a lot of add-on services in addition to the core business of home loans, such as different forms of insurances, house alarms, deposits, and the services of Anticimex, indicating that the service offering could not be described as that simple any longer. In particular, the focus on relationship marketing, which will be discussed in Chapter 6, supports this claim. Relationship marketing at the FI seems to cater to getting the FLEs to take a comprehensive view of the customer relationship in order to know which service to sell them. In their new role as sales staff, this is important.

In conclusion, it thus seems as if two of the commandments—innovation and empathy—are key features of the FI and its employees. For two of the commandments—commitment and trust—arguments can be put forward which both support and oppose them being key characteristics of the FI. Lastly, the analysis pertaining to comprehensive view suggests that this is not a major feature of the FI or its staff, at least not yet.

THE SUBJECT: AN AGENT?

One key aim of the present study is to analyze how SMM practices facilitate customer orientation and the role of marketing in organizations more broadly defined. In this chapter, I have begun to describe the introduction and to analyze the role of SMM discourse and its associated practices at the FI. Whereas I argued, in the previous chapter, that the organization of the FI, prior to the introduction of the SMM practices, had much in common with a classic bureaucracy, the present chapter suggests that the marketing and service orientation program contributes toward moving the organization in the direction of a customer oriented bureaucracy: an organization combining customerism with efficiency and routinization (Korczynski 2002). This seems to be the case, at least, as regards what could be referred to as the rhetorical, textual, or formal level of the organization. When it comes to the actual ordering effect of the activities carried out, the results are more ambiguous. Although some commandments of the service and market orientation strategy seem to reflect how the employees perceive both themselves and the organization, others seem not to. However, with the introduction of the service and market orientation program, it must be considered undisputed that SMM discourse has entered the organization and that the management of the FI intends to manage the organization by drawing on that body of knowledge.

The analysis suggests that these managerial intentions can be understood against the backdrop of the notion of pastoral power. Indeed, the pastoral power analysis of service and market orientation carried out in the chapter suggests that such programs and forms of knowledge can be seen: firstly, as a common customer oriented ethic, or even as a religion revolving around central commandments; secondly, as contributing to the repositioning of managers as pastors and the employees as a flock of sheep; and thirdly as promoting certain confessional practices that managers can draw upon to work the common ethic of service and customer orientation into the employees and suggest ways for the employees to work this ethic into themselves. Thus, the chapter suggests that subject positions colored by customerism are introduced into the organization even though it is hard to say to what degree these subject positions order the actual subjectivity of the staff of the FI.

It is also interesting to note, in the light of the previous chapter where it was argued that the bureaucratic nature of the FI organization has contributed toward shaping reactive and passive FLEs, that the present chapter suggests that the subject positions associated with the service and market orientation program presupposes and promotes *responsible* and *active* subjects. Responsible and active subjects are able to take their own initiatives and responsibilities, not least when it comes to themselves and their own self-formation, something that the IWHY program spurs the employees to do. Rather than relying on rules and procedures that someone else has developed, the good sheep, at least to some degree, are expected to re-create themselves in line with the ethic that service and market orientation promotes. Such a responsibilization of the subject is closely associated with the notion of the active self that neo-liberal regimes of government, such as marketing, promote (Skålén et al. 2006; 2008; see also Dean 1995; 1999; O'Malley 1992; Rose 1996; 1999). It is also one step toward the subject position of the proactive self, a theme that will be central to the next chapter.

5 The Power/Knowledge of Service Quality and Coaching

The previous chapter suggests that the managerial rationality of customerism embedded in the service and market orientation program has informed the strategic intentions of the FI. But the chapter also suggests that managers were operating with a very general understanding of customerism. Even though they had the impression that the customers of the FI, on a general level, were satisfied with the services they received, they did not know exactly how those customers perceived the services, whether or not they were satisfied with how the FLEs offered the services to them, and whether or not they wanted to change anything in the service offering of the FI. In order to grasp these issues and, formulated in the analytical language drawn on here, to embed deeper into the organization and the employees the power/knowledge of SMM, the management of the FI decided to systematically measure customer-perceived service quality, known to be one of the major research fields of SMM (see, for instance, Berry and Parasuraman 1993; Brown et al. 1994; Schneider and White 2004). To help them, the managers had consultants and researchers acting as consultants specializing in service quality measurement and closely related fields, e.g. customer satisfaction measurement. The coupling with academia and academic knowledge was thus tight.

The present chapter opens with a conceptual analysis that positions customer-perceived service quality theories and knowledge as disciplinary power. I then turn to the empirical analysis focusing on the disciplinary power effect of the service quality surveys used by the FI. The results of these surveys convinced the managers that the FLEs were reactive but needed to be more proactive in the customer interface (compare Chapter 3). In order to accomplish this, the managers decided to adopt coaching as a management practice, something that is promoted by the service quality literature in order to align employees with the subject positions generated by service quality surveys (Zeithaml et al. 1990). In the conceptual analysis, coaching, in line with the analysis in the previous chapter, is positioned as a pastoral practice. The empirical analysis focuses on how and to what extent the pastoral power of coaching makes the subjectivity of the FLEs more proactive. The chapter ends by discussing to what extent the service quality practices and the associated coaching practices have been effective in working the managerial rationality of proactivity into the FLEs.

SERVICE QUALITY AND DISCIPLINARY POWER

In this section, theories and knowledge concerning customer-perceived service quality are seen through the lens of power/knowledge, particularly the notion of disciplinary power. I track the roots of service quality discourse to the very emergence of SMM research and analyze the most central development within this stream of research by drawing on the work of Christian Grönroos, one of the founders of both SMM and service quality research. I then analyze the gap model of A. Parasuraman, Valerie Zeithmal, and Leonard Berry, which is the single most important service quality measurement and management technology outlined thus far. Indeed, Schneider and White (2004) in their review of service quality research argue that the debate on service quality in marketing has revolved around the gap model. Focusing on the gap model makes sense because it embodies the more general managerial rationality of service quality discourse (Skålén and Fougère 2007).

The Archeology of Service Quality Discourse

Service quality is one of the central research fields of SMM (Berry and Parasuraman 1993; Brown et al. 1994; Schneider and White 2004). It is also a research field with one of the longest intellectual histories in the field of SMM, emerging as it did right out of Lynn Shostack's and Christian Grönroos' presupposition, put forward in the late 1970s, that the human resources—the staff—of a service firm are an integrated part of the service offering. As suggested in the first and second chapters, this presupposition implies that the actions of the staff largely impact on the perceptions of the service and the service firm held by the customers (Grönroos 1978; Shostack 1977). The power/knowledge of service quality discourse, as will be more evident in the following analysis, is thus contingent on human beings in SMM discourse being turned into objects of and subjected to the managerial customeristic rationality of marketing (cf. Heskett et al. 1997; Schneider and White 2004). As Grönroos (1978: 593) puts it: 'the manner in which the bank manager, the bank clerk, the travel agency representative, the telephone receptionist, the tour guide, the barber, or the waiter treats the customers, what he says, and how he behaves are very critical to the view of the service which the consumers get'. In line with general marketing discourse, service quality is thus seen and measured from the perspective of the customer. What Schneider and White (2004: 10–11) call, in their review of the service quality literature, 'the user-based perspective' has 'become the main approach to assessing quality in the service literature . . . This definition of quality takes the view that quality is subjective and hinges on the individual perceptions of customers'.

However, in Shostack's and Grönroos' earliest work (see Shostack 1977; Grönroos 1978), the notion of service quality is not central. It was the latter of these two who brought quality into SMM discourse by basing the notion of service quality on the novel idea that the behaviors of the staff influence customers' perceptions of a service and service firms. By drawing on the critique of marketing management, delivered by himself and Shostack a few years earlier, Grönroos did this in two *European Journal of Marketing* papers published 1982 and 1984. In the first of these papers, Grönroos argues that services differ from products in three ways. The service is 'physically intangible, it is an activity rather than a thing, and production and consumption are, at least to some extent, simultaneous activities (Grönroos 1982: 31). These three 'basic characteristics of services make the marketing situation and the customer relation of service firms fundamentally different from that of a consumer goods company. The customers of the latter kind of business normally see only the product itself and the marketing mix activities—place, price and promotion—of the firm and of the distribution channels' (Grönroos 1982: 31). The customer of a 'service firm faces an entirely different situation' (Grönroos 1982: 32). It is not just that the customers 'will be influenced by what happens in the simultaneous consumption and production process', which the customer 'certainly' will be. Grönroos goes as far as to suggest that the customer of a service firm 'enters the production process of the service firm' and will 'by his behaviour, have an impact on the production process itself' (Grönroos 1982: 32)! By opening up the discursive articulation of the organization to the environment, which had remained closed in the marketing management school of thought due to its focusing on products (see Chapter 2), Grönroos not only rearticulates the subject positions referring to the employee, but also those referring to the customer. The latter is no longer, as in marketing management, positioned in the 'market' 'outside' of the organization but also 'inside' the organization as a kind of production staff member producing the services s/he consumes (for a critique, see Bonso and Darmody 2008). That customers co-produce or co-create the services they consume in collaboration with the seller and its personnel is also a central trait of the recent influential service-dominant logic literature (see, for instance, Lusch et al. 2007; Vargo and Lusch 2004; 2008b;).

As radical as Grönroos' rearticulation of the subject position of the customer in marketing discourse might be, it is the repositioning of the subject positions and the 'plug-ins' (see Latour 2005 and Chapter 2), relating to the service firm employee and the very role of marketing 'inside' service firms, that is Grönroos' most drastic move (see, for instance, Lusch et al. 2007; Vargo and Lusch 2004; Vargo and Morgan 2005). 'The objective of marketing', argued Grönroos (1982: 32), 'should be to manage all resources that influence the market's preference toward products and services on the market'. At a 'consumer goods company', marketing manages the flow of 'resources' between production and consumption by utilizing technologies such as segmentation and the marketing mix. Due to the specific nature of service firms described previously, the role of marketing in these is quite different. Drawing on Rathmell (1974), Grönroos maintains that:

> There are separate marketing activities, for example, advertising and other non-interactive means of promotion, in service marketing, too. These are, however, only part of the company's total marketing function because the consumer's opinion of the service firm and its services and his future buying behaviour are also determined by what happens in the buyer-seller interactions of the simultaneous production and consumption. Therefore, managing these interactions is also part of the total marketing function.
>
> Grönroos (1982: 32)

The conclusion of this rearticulation of marketing for service firms is that 'the service company has two marketing functions, which are quite different from each other in nature: the traditional marketing function and the *interactive marketing function*, where the latter function is concerned with what happens in the interface between production and consumption' (Grönroos 1982: 32–33, emphasis added). With the introduction of the notion of 'interactive marketing', marketing becomes indistinguishable from management. Marketing no longer concerns itself only with designing products from the perspective of the customers' needs and wants as in marketing management; it is also about coloring human beings and their subjectivity by the managerial rationality of customerism. Thus, even though Grönroos prefers to use the term service marketing in his 1982 paper, it is clear that he is also concerned with service management: a term that zips more readily into his vocabulary in his 1984 paper. Making the managerial rationality of marketing target humans in addition to products, which was also central to Shostack's 1977 paper, is an extremely important redirection of marketing discourse, from a power/knowledge perspective. From now on, marketing discourse has as its direct and primary object the thinking, actions, and behaviors of human beings. The founders of SMM intervention in marketing research diffused the managerial rationality of marketing deeper into the discursive understanding of the organization. Indeed, the very implicit and explicit notion of the organization in marketing discourse as an effect of their intervention was redefined and broadened.

The Emergence of Service Quality Discourse and Its Power/Knowledge

Quality was not invented as a managerial imperative by SMM scholars. Rather, at the point in time when service quality was emerging as a notion in SMM discourse the notion of Total Quality Management (TQM) had been around for a while. However, it was not until the early 1980s that the idea that quality and quality management was a solution central to the problems of mass production entered into mainstream management thinking, resulting in research and consultancy activities in the quality sector increasing in importance (Cole 1999; Zbaracki 1998). The practices associated with TQM were, at least at the time, mostly concerned with the quality of the products—not people. From the perspective of SMM, 'the product' in TQM discourse, in a similar way as 'the product' in marketing management discourse, was standing in the way of articulating a theory; but this time, a quality theory that was suitable for service firms. However, the focus on products in quality management discourse also opened up opportunities and spaces for SMM scholars to redo, in the field of quality management, what they had already done—or tried to do—with general marketing only a few years earlier, e.g. argue that existing notions of quality were inappropriate for service firms and that the development of a notion of service quality was needed. Again, the product constituted the key for opening up and rearticulating the discourse.

Even though Grönroos does not refer to TQM explicitly, he was the first person within the SMM stream of research to skillfully utilize the possibility created by the TQM movement. Departing from the general idea that people, in addition to products, need to be customer oriented, Grönroos turned his attention toward quality. Grönroos' (1982: 33) general argument was that, because a 'consumer of a service can and will evaluate a vast number of different resources and activities in connection with the production resources and the production process when formulating his opinion of the service, the quality of a service will be complicated in nature'. He argued that the different 'resources and activities' could be divided into three groups jointly making up the total service quality, as shown in Figure 5.1.

Grönroos (1982) argues that it is essential that the service has technical quality—referred to as the result of the service. 'On the other hand it is also important how the technical quality is transferred to the consumer. The service must have functional quality . . . in many cases the functional quality may be the more important one' (Grönroos 1982: 33). In addition to technical and functional quality, and due to 'the intangible nature of services, corporate image is also vital to the service firm' (Grönroos 1982: 33). The notion of image is somewhat vague in the 1982 paper. It seems to be about the organization's 'outward appearance': 'the service business must not only be good, it must look good' (Bessom 1973 quoted in Grönroos 1982: 33). 'Looking good' seem to be associated with image. 'Technical quality' corresponds with the focus on customer orienting products in marketing management discourse. 'Functional quality' and 'image' correspond with the broadening of the managerialism of marketing in SMM discourse to also account for the customer orienting of human beings, in addition to

Figure 5.1   A model of service quality.
Source: Grönroos, C. (1982) 'An Applied Service Marketing Theory', *European Journal of Marketing*, 16(7): 30–41.

products. What Grönroos thus did was to infuse this 'new' managerialism of marketing discourse into the field of quality management. According to Schneider and White (2004), the emphasis in service quality research has been on functional quality. Employee characteristics and behaviors toward customers have thus been seen as the single most important driver of service quality (cf. Heskett et al. 1997).

From a Foucauldian perspective, Grönroos' service quality model can be perceived as a human practice (cf. Rose 1996). It transferred the somewhat abstract managerial rationality of SMM, prescribing the customer-istic management of products and employees in general, to a much more concrete framework summarizing the relationships between the elements of SMM discourse. As such, it contributed to the closure of SMM discourse (cf. Laclau and Mouffe 1985). The power/knowledge of the service quality model provided managers with a framework, or a lens, for viewing service firms, inviting them to focus on the important and, from a managerial point of view, appropriate aspects. It contributes toward making visible the aspects of service firms which had previously been invisible. However, it is hard to see how the model could be used by organizations to generate more detailed knowledge of the level of service quality delivered by their employees. What functional quality, for example, would the customer of a particular service firm like to perceive? The model only accounts for this aspect in very general terms. Furthermore, exactly what total quality is, apart from being a function of image, and technical and functional quality, is far from clear. As a disciplinary practice, the model is thus somewhat indistinct, partly due to the somewhat indistinct treatment of its central concepts.

Refining the Disciplinary Power of Service Quality

Perhaps this is one of the reasons why Grönroos decided to write a sequential paper on service quality, published in 1984. In this paper, technical quality is defined as '*what* the consumer receives as a result of his interaction with a service firm' (Grönroos 1984: 38). Functional quality is defined as '*how he* [the consumer] gets it' (Grönroos 1984: 39), which makes it very clear that the definition of these two central terms is directly contingent upon the managerial rationality of SMM discourse. Corporate image is now defined as 'the result of how the consumers perceive the firm' (Grönroos 1984: 39). It is stated, furthermore, that 'the most important part of a firm, which its customers perceive, is its services. Therefore, the corporate image can be expected to be built up by the technical quality and the functional quality of its services' (Grönroos 1984: 39). Technical and functional quality, mediated by image, affect the customer's perceived service quality. Grönroos also acknowledges that other factors might influence the image of a service, differentiating between 'external factors'—e.g. 'ideology', 'tradition', 'word-of-mouth'—and 'traditional marketing activities'—e.g. 'advertising', 'pricing', and 'public relations'.

These other factors are handled by the most radical addition to the 1984 paper—the introduction of the so called 'disconfirmation paradigm' for conceptualizing service quality, from the consumer behavior literature, and, more particularly, from the satisfaction literature (see Fishbein and Ajzen 1975; Oliver 1977; 1996). Compared with the service quality model that was presented in the 1982 paper (see Figure 5.1) 'total quality' is replaced by the notion of 'perceived service quality', seen from a customer perspective. 'Perceived service quality' is a function of the service that the customers of a service firm expect—the 'expected service'—and the service they perceive—the 'perceived service'. This way of conceptualizing service quality, as a gap between the customer's expectations and perceptions, became the dominant one in the service quality field (Schneider and White 2004), even though models only measuring perceptions have also been put forward (see, for instance, Cronin and Taylor 1992). In Grönroos' 1984 model (see Figure 5.2), the 'expected service' is a function of the 'external factors' and 'traditional marketing activities' (see preceding).

The replacement of 'total quality' by the construct of 'perceived service quality' and the associated notions of 'perceived' and 'expected' service are extremely important because they incorporate more clearly into the model of service quality the customeristic managerial rationality of marketing discourse and explain that service quality is a relative construct. Service quality is an effect of the difference—the gap—between the level of service quality the customers expect and the level they perceive. This might vary a whole lot between different service firms. The service quality of a fast food restaurant is, for example, a completely different thing than the quality of a fine dining restaurant. The model thus makes it possible to contextualize service quality: that is, to adapt general service quality discourse to local practice. As such, the model can be understood as a disciplinary practice. Seen as a disciplinary practice, the quality model defines, from the perspective of the managerial rationality of SMM, the norms or ideals that should guide action and behavior—the service that the customer expects—and

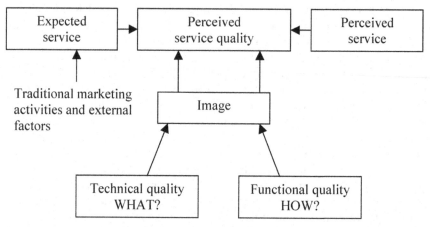

Figure 5.2   Grönroos' 1984 model of service quality.
Source: Slightly adapted from Grönroos, C. (1984) 'A Service Quality Model and its Marketing'.

what constitutes actual behavior—the service that the customers perceive. As such, it defines, from a managerial marketing perspective, the relevant gap between the actual and the ideal to focus upon. Eliciting such gaps is one of the chief functions of disciplinary power (Foucault 1977). The service quality model also explains variances in service quality and thus suggests actions for closing the gap between ideal and actuality. It suggests ways of balancing perceived and expected service. By turning functional and technical quality into explanation variables, gaps between perceived and expected service quality can be reduced by means of changing what the customers get or how they get it—the latter implies changing the personnel. This gap can be addressed, furthermore, from the perspective of 'traditional marketing activities' which might have made the wrong 'promises'— a word frequently utilized by Grönroos (1982) when discussing traditional marketing—to customers, thus creating expectations that are too high or by addressing the 'external factors'. According to one interpretation, an adequate or 'excellent' level of service quality, as the SMM scholars like to phrase it, does not lie in maximizing the customers' perceptions of a service delivery. It is more a case of placing the perceptions on an equal par with expectations, or changing the expectations so that they compare with perceptions. Excellent service quality can, in absolute terms, be constituted by very low service quality if the customer expects low quality. As such, service quality discourse seeks to normalize employee behavior within organizations (cf. Skålén and Fougère 2007), which is another central feature of disciplinary power (Foucault 1977).

Still however, the service quality model proposed by Grönroos lacks many of the features of a fully fledged disciplinary practice. Most importantly, the model has no inbuilt technologies for more precisely suggesting what actions to take to close service quality gaps. Clues about whether the gap is a function of technical or functional quality, or a combination of these, are not given. As an effect, exactly what aspect of functional quality, for instance, that causes the gap cannot be specified by using the model. In addition, it is limited when it comes to generating knowledge of service quality. The model conceptualizes service quality as a gap between customer expectations and perceptions but does not provide any exact suggestions regarding how to gain knowledge of this gap, something which could have been done by coupling the model to a standardized survey, for instance. The model fails to quantify service quality. As Rose (1996) has shown, quantification is a powerful power/knowledge tool.

In Grönroos' (2007a) work, it is possible to see a bias against quantitative methods. Therefore, it can be presumed that he had taken his model of service quality as far as he wanted to take it in his 1984 paper. It was time for other more quantitative and positivistically orientated researchers to take over the relay race baton of service quality research. It was a trio of researchers who took the notion of service quality to the next, and perhaps final, stage in terms of power/knowledge. These were A. Parasuraman, Valerie Zeithaml, and Leonard Berry.

The Gap Model as a Disciplinary Technology

It is almost as if Parasuraman and his colleagues (Parasuraman et al. 1985; 1988) had studied the works of Foucault as a point of departure for their work on service quality. Not only did they bring quantitative methodology and positivism into research on service quality and developed a survey for measuring service quality, they also labeled their service quality model *the gap model*—detecting and reducing gaps being one of the chief ways in which disciplinary power operates, according to Foucault (1977). However, contrary to Foucauldian analysis, they did not reflect sociologically upon how gaps order the world. Their objective was, rather, to prescribe what type of 'quality gaps' managers ought to focus on, how to detect them, and most importantly, how to close them. Parasuraman et al. (1985; 1988) developed the types of managerial technologies that Foucault made the object of research and critique. Thus, it seems that the trio of researchers did not take Foucault as their point of departure after all.

Drawing on the 'disconfirmation paradigm' when conceptualizing service quality, Parasuraman et al. (1985) followed in the footsteps of Grönroos, referring to his 1978 and 1982 (but not his 1984) papers discussed previously. Unlike Grönroos, however, they utilized more explicitly the 'discursive space' that the TQM literature had created in order to legitimize their research arguing, referring to this literature, that their focus on quality is managerially relevant: 'Its importance to firms and consumers is unequivocal' (Parasuraman et al. 1985: 41). But they also claim that knowledge of goods quality is insufficient to understand service quality because 'the characteristics of services . . . have to be acknowledged for a full understanding of service quality' (Parasuraman et al. 1985:42). In order to gain such knowledge of service quality, and to create their model, they used an exploratory research design. Four service categories were chosen for their investigation: retail banking, credit cards, securities brokerage, and product repair and maintenance. A single firm represented each service category. In-depth open-ended personal interviews were conducted with fourteen executives (three or four from each firm), and twelve focus group interviews were carried out with customers of the firms. The main conclusion from the executive interviews was that 'a set of key discrepancies or gaps exists regarding executive perceptions of service quality and the tasks associated with service delivery to consumers. These gaps can be major hurdles in attempting to deliver a service which consumers would perceive as being of high quality' (Parasuraman et al. 1985: 44). The gaps that Parasuraman et al. (1985) detected are:

1. Between what customers expect from a service and managers' perceptions of customer expectations.
2. Between management's perceptions of customer expectations and service quality specifications.
3. Between service quality specifications and the actual service delivery.
4. Between service delivery and external communications.

(Parasuraman et al. 1985: 44–46)

The analysis of the focus group interviews also provided strong support for the conceptualization of service quality as a comparison between customer expectations and customer perceptions: referred to as gap five. According to Parasuraman (et al. 1985), a customer's perception of a service is dependent on the size and direction of gaps one to four, and customer expectations are a function of 'past experience with the service', 'word of mouth communication' regarding the service, and 'personal needs'. The perception-expectation construct—gap number five—thus takes a heuristic position in the gap model, because it brings together the customer and organization sides of the model (see Figure 5.3).

Compared to Grönroos' 1984 model, the gap model suggests more precisely how the power/knowledge of customerism can regulate organizations and their members at the micro level. It breaks down the expectation-perception gap into the four internal gaps specifying the 'intra-organizational reasons' for a particular level of service quality. Addressing managers (gaps 1–2) and FLEs who are usually involved in service delivery (gaps 3–4), the scheme promotes a disciplinary technology detailing which intra-organizational gaps that needs to be closed if the customers are to perceive the level of quality they expect. The four internal gaps bring impetus to how to

Customer

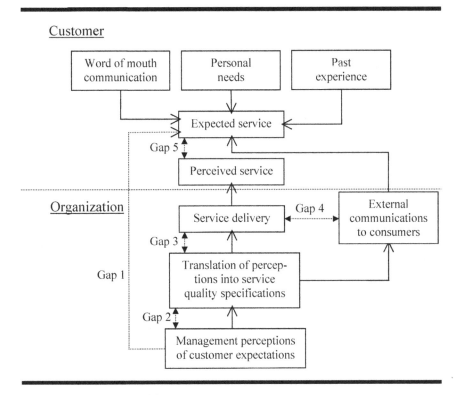

Figure 5.3 The gap model.
Source: Adapted from Parasuraman, A., Zeithaml, V.A. and Berry, L.L. (1985) 'A Conceptual Model of Service Quality and its Implications for Future Research', *Journal of Marketing*, 49(4): 253–268.

regulate the staff in accordance with the managerial rationality of SMM by pointing to which gaps to close.

When interpreting the focus group interviews, Parasuraman (et al. 1985: 46) also found that 'regardless of the type of service, consumers used basically similar criteria in evaluating service quality. These criteria seem to fall into ten key categories which are labelled "service quality determinants"'. Using factor analysis, these service quality determinants were reduced, in later versions of the model, to five and eventually to three. The gap model is most often presented with five determinants (see Brady and Cronin 2001; Parasuraman et al. 1988; Schneider and White 2004):

- Reliability: Ability to perform the promised service dependably and accurately.
- Responsiveness: Willingness to help the customers and provide prompt service.

- Empathy: Caring, the individualized attention the firm provides to its customers.
- Assurance: Knowledge and courtesy of employees and their ability to inspire trust and confidence.
- Tangibles: Physical facilities, equipment, and appearance of personnel.
(Parasuraman et al. 1988: 23)

In line with the emphasis on functional quality in the service quality literature (see Schneider and White 2004), all five of the service quality determinants address human capabilities. Empathy, assurance, and tangibles (the latter including the appearance of the staff) are human characteristics, whereas the reliability and responsiveness delivered by a service firm is largely contingent upon human abilities. Alternative service quality models are also based on quality determinants addressing human characteristics. Professionalism and skills, attitudes, behaviors, expertise, and flexibility are examples of service quality determinants put forward in the literature (see Brady and Cronin 2001; Schneider and White 2004). Accordingly, the disciplinary power of the gap model, as well as other models of service quality, has as its main object the human resources of organizations. More particularly, if the five gaps of the gap model give advice on how to regulate the staff, the five quality determinants give advice on what to regulate. The quality determinants bring clarity to the 'what' of disciplinary power, revealing which aspects of human beings have to be changed in order to close service quality gaps. It is important, however, to understand that a gap conceptualization of quality, as pointed out previously, is a relative construct. According to its logic, service firms should not focus on making their staff express as much empathy or assurance as possible. Rather, the level of empathy and assurance that should be expressed should be on a par with the level of empathy and assurance that the customers want to perceive—i.e. the customers' expectations.

The service quality determinants gave increasing precision to the perceived service quality construct and provided a foundation enabling the creation of a standardized scale for measuring service quality. The 22-item instrument or questionnaire that Parasuraman et al. (1988) developed is labeled 'Servqual', and operationalizes the five quality determinants. Following the logic of the 'disconfirmation paradigm', the same 22 questions are used to examine the customer's expectations and perceptions regarding service delivery. The invention of Servqual made it possible to measure service quality systematically for the first time. It also turned the gap model into a fully fledged disciplinary technology as the gap model with this key addition can work as an examination, the technology of the self which, according Foucault, is typical of disciplinary power practices. By using Servqual, managers are able to check up on how each individual employee is doing in terms of service quality, locating gaps in relation to the service quality determinants, and reducing them by addressing the relevant human characteristics pointed at by the gap model.

The presentation of Servqual gave rise to a debate about service quality in prestigious marketing journals. The debate centered on the measurement of perceived service quality (e.g. Cronin and Taylor 1992; 1994; Parasuraman et al. 1994; Teas 1993; 1994), but also on applications of (Brown and Swartz 1989) and elaborations on (Brady and Cronin 2001) the gap model, as well as presentations of alternative models (Dabholkar et al. 1996; Rust and Oliver 1994). Rather than reviewing the somewhat technical research into customer-perceived service quality, which the gap model gave rise to and which could be, and in fact has been, the topic of a book in its own right (see Schneider and White 2004), the aim here is to explicate how service quality practices generally work as disciplinary technologies and to bring to the surface the managerial rationality they embed. Because the gap model encapsulates and represents many of the general features of service quality measurement technologies (Skålén and Fougère 2007), the disciplinary power analysis of the gap model, together with the preceding review of Grönroos' works, has fulfilled this aim.

THE DISCIPLINARY POWER OF THE
FI SERVICE QUALITY SURVEYS

The conceptual analysis suggests that models for understanding and measuring service quality can be perceived as disciplinary power practices and technologies. However, to what extent and how this disciplinary power order organizational practice remains to be empirically studied. In this section, the service quality surveys used at the FI, and their ordering effects, are the empirical focus of the analysis. The aim is to see if service quality practices foster the discipline that they are designed to do, and thus if they in practice work the customerism embedded in the service quality discourse into the subjectivity of the FI employees.

Comparing FI Service Quality Measurement
Instruments with Servqual

The FI uses several surveys to measure service quality. Three of these surveys have been developed in collaboration with the consultancy firm QuestBack, and in close collaboration with service quality researchers and consultants based on Questback's common platform, to suit the individual needs of the FI. Questback's website (retrieved from http://www.questback.se on 2008–03–24) states that the company's surveys can be used to measure customer satisfaction, an area of research closely related to service quality research, and promoting a similar form of managerial rationality. As stated previously, service quality researchers have drawn on customer satisfaction research quite a lot. It was, for example, from the quarters of customer satisfaction that the 'disconfirmation paradigm' for measuring and conceptualizing service quality was imported into SMM. One of the FI surveys which was developed on the basis of Questback's platform is sent out to the customers three months after they have taken out a home loan with the FI and is referred to as 'Welcome to the FI' survey. The 'Thank you and goodbye' survey is sent to customers who have left the FI. This is, as one of the respondents put it, 'more a way of saying goodbye and not so much of a survey'. It only contains a few, mostly open, questions. The 'customer barometer' is sent to all customers nine months after they take out a home loan with the FI and, together with 'Welcome to the FI' survey, constitutes the major survey by which the FI measures service quality.

In addition to measuring service quality by drawing on its own surveys, the FI also takes part in more general measurements of service quality conducted by consultancy firms which sell the information gathered to the organizations taking part in the survey. Major external measurements like these that the FI has taken part in are the 'Swedish Quality Index' and the Swedish 'Web Service Award'. The 'Swedish Quality Index' is the Swedish branch of the 'European Performance Satisfaction Index' which measures customer satisfaction for different businesses in up to 20 European countries. The organization behind the Swedish Quality Index measures quality in many sectors of the economy and makes the figures for the organizations participating in each sector public. The FI has been referred to the banking category and has ranked among the highest there in terms of quality. The 'Web Service Award', according to the website of the consultancy company in charge of the survey, 'has developed a way of measuring service quality for your website' (retrieved from http://www.webserviceaward.com on 2008–03–24). The 'Web Service Award' is awarded in three categories. The FI has won the 'Information and Service Category' once. Besides the honor, the FI has received, through the 'Web Service Award', a lot of suggestions for improving the service quality of its website. Since the staff do not interact with the customers face-to-face the website is very important for the FI.

In order to relate the service quality measurement initiatives of the FI to the academic service quality discourse, I compare the statements in the FI's own surveys with the questionnaire associated with the gap model, i.e. Servqual. Servqual consists of 22 items in the form of statements that operationalize the five service quality determinants that the gap model is based upon (see Parasuraman et al. 1988). Four or five statements operationalize each service quality determinant in the following way: tangibles (statements 1–4), reliability (statements 5–9), responsiveness (statements 10–13), assurance (statements 14–17), and empathy (statements 18–22). Servqual uses similar, but semantically slightly reformulated, statements to measure both customer expectations and perceptions. In the language of disciplinary power, the customer's expectations constitute the norm that the focal organization and its members should live up to whereas the customer perceptions represent the current situation. The difference between them is the gap that needs to be transcended if the potential disciplinary power inherent in the gap model is to be realized. With the exception of the 'Swedish Quality Index', none of the surveys used at the FI—neither their own nor the external ones—measure expectations and perceptions on separate scales. It must be kept in mind that Servqual accounts for a scientifically rigorous way of measuring quality—and not the most practical way of doing it. Perhaps it is not realistic, in practice, to ask the customers fairly similar questions twice and expect a high response rate. In addition: 'From the very first, Parasuraman, Zeithaml and Berry (1988) recognized that Servqual would not be adequate to measure services in all organizations and all industries without some modification' (Schneider and White 2004: 38).

Most of the surveys used by the FI only measure customer perceptions which, as we saw previously, were suggested as a main alternative to measuring both expectations and perceptions in the academic literature (see also Cronin and Taylor 1992). However, some of the questions have expectations built into them. The 'Web Service Award' survey, for instance, has one question formulated thus: 'When I've sent an email, I got an answer within the time I expected' (Retrieved from http://www.webserviceaward. com on 2008–03–24). Furthermore, many of the open questions in the FI's own surveys ask the customers to compare the expected service with that delivered. 'How do you think we can improve communications with our customers?' (taken from the customer barometer), is one example of such a question. 'The FI wants to be the obvious choice when you take out a mortgage! Write down what you consider to be important and how the FI can be even better' (taken from 'Welcome to the FI' survey) is another.[1] Servqual and the FI questionnaires use similar scales for measuring service quality. The Servqual uses a seven point Lickert scale where seven equals 'strongly agree', and one signifies 'strongly disagree'. The FI's own questionnaires use a five point Lickert scale where the customers are asked to say to what extent they agree with the actual statement, from 'not at all' to a 'very high degree'.

Despite the slight differences in formulation between the Servqual and the FI surveys, it is possible to maintain, by comparing the statements in the Servqual and those included in the FI surveys, that the latter accounts for service quality by drawing on similar service quality determinants as the ones suggested by the gap model. This is central to the present analysis because it is these determinants that provide the nodal point of the managerial rationality and power/knowledge of service quality discourse. Table 5.1 links the FI survey statements with the Servqual statements and the service quality determinants of the gap model which the Servqual statements operationalizes.

It needs to be maintained that some of the statements in the FI survey link up better with the gap model quality determinants than others. The link with reliability, responsiveness, and assurance is quite clear. The FI presents its customers with similar questions to those compromising the

Table 5.1   A Comparison between the SERVQUAL and FI Customer Surveys

Service quality determinants	Servqual statements	FI survey statements
Tangibles	XYZ's physical facilities are visually appealing.*	The design of the webpage makes it easy for me to find the information I need.
Reliability	XYZ provides its services at the time it promises to do so.*	When I send an e-mail, I get an answer within the timeframe I expect to. Have we made home loans simple and easy?
Responsiveness	You do not receive prompt service from XYZ's employees.* Employees of XYZ are not always willing to help customers.*	Have you received prompt service from us in connection with your home loan? Are you satisfied with the level of service provided by your contact?
Assurance	Employees at XYZ are polite.*	Have you been dealt with satisfactorily?
Empathy	Employees of XYZ do not give you personal attention.*	Have you been treated nicely by your contact person?

Source: Parasuraman, A., Zeithaml, V.A. and Berry, L.L. (1988) 'SERVQUAL: A Multiple-Item Scale for Measuring Consumer Perceptions of Service Quality', *Journal of Retailing*, 64(1): 12–37.

Servqual for these determinants. The fit of the statements with tangibles and empathy is a little less distinct. At least three of the four statements accounting for tangibles in Servqual focus on the visual appeal of the facilities or the employees, presupposing that the customers have been physically inside the organization's buildings, which is never the case for the FI's customers due to the service being offered at a distance by phone, email, and the Internet, etc. Furthermore, the fourth statement in Servqual regarding tangibles, 'XYZ has up-to-date equipment', can also be hard for the customers to judge without having been to the premises of the organization. What the FI's customers mainly see is the website of the FI and the materials that are sent to their homes, e.g. letters and information packs, which I argue play a similar role, for the FI customers, to experiencing firsthand the actual physical organization. Consequently, the design or appeal of the website and the information materials can be seen as a part of the tangibles of the FI. Empathy is a different matter. The word empathy, or a synonym for it, is never used in the FI's surveys. However, it can be argued that the empathy the customers have perceived informs the answers given to other questions such as the example given in

Table 5.1. Furthermore, it is possible that empathy is also accounted for by more general questions regarding service quality included in the FI's surveys, such as the following: 'Have you received good service from us as regards your mortgages?'.

In conclusion, it is thus possible to say that there is a relatively strong link between the surveys used at the FI and the customer-perceived service quality measurement models promoted by the academic SMM discourse, of which the gap model is the most prominent example. A perfect link between 'theory' and 'practice' is hard to come by, so empirical examinations of the impact of marketing 'theory' will always suffer, to some degree, from such inconsistencies.

Proactivity as a Managerial Rationality

All the managers I interviewed had a good understanding of the results of the service quality measurement. They all believed that the overall results of the surveys revealed that the customers were very satisfied with the level of service quality being provided by the FI. Team leader John said: 'In the quality surveys, the customers most often say: "Mark is very good. He helped us a lot when we bought our house". That is the information we get. "Mark is crap. He didn't really help us at all." We never get that kind of information'. Sales manager David made a similar remark when asked about the results of the service quality measurement: 'The customer surveys show that the vast majority of our customers are very happy with the service we provide'. The FLEs also believed, based on the quality surveys, that the service delivered by both the FI and themselves was of high quality. They were able to make that judgment because they were continuously receiving information about the general results of the service quality measurement. In addition, they also received, at least for a time, the survey response given by the customers they had served, thus providing them with an overview of how the customers perceived their customer interaction in terms of service quality. About the general result of the service quality measurement, one of the FLEs said: 'It's really been very positive actually. Then there are minor issues, specific issues that the customers remarked on, but nothing major'. Another of the FLEs revealed: 'It's great fun. I think it's really good. You get good, positive feedback from your customers'. One of her colleagues corroborated that: 'You see, it's mostly positive stuff, so it's just a matter of licking it up, it's really nice'. Thus, the managers and the FLEs I interviewed believed that the service quality surveys made it clear that the FI offered high quality service: that is, service in line with the expectations of the customers. Therefore, argued David, not that many changes had been initiated as an effect of the service quality measurement. 'Very much of it is confirmation of what we know already. The consequence can be consolidating one method of working more than, maybe, changing things a hell of a lot. Basically, our business is successful and we have to take care of it.

No, in concrete terms, we probably haven't changed so much as a result of the quality measurements'.

There was only one point of criticism that all the managers I interviewed agreed had been made explicit to them by the service quality surveys. Mary, a project leader, who had systematically analyzed the results of all the customer surveys, said: 'The only general criticism we've had in the quality surveys is that we're not *proactive* enough. On the whole, the customers think that we should make more proposals for improvements. That, really, is what they want. They always want us to check whether it's possible to borrow at a better interest rate by changing last mortgages to first mortgages, for instance'. David expressed it like this: 'What the customers generally tell us in the surveys is that we're too passive. We must be more *proactive*'. The five team leaders I interviewed interpreted the results in a similar way. One of them said: 'We were very passive before. We've done the deal and then we haven't followed it up, we've left the customers in peace because they pay up, you see. Sure, we send out some newsletters and stuff, but we don't do anything active to strengthen the relationship. It's stuff like that which has always emerged in the quality surveys, that we're too passive and that we have to be more *proactive*' (team leader). One of the back office staff made a similar point when I asked her about the source of proactivity:

Question: The proactivity then, where did that come from? How did you find out it was something to aspire to?

Answer: It was the quality surveys. It was the customers who thought that we . . . were good at carrying out what they wanted us to do, but that we weren't so good at taking the initiative ourselves.

(Back office staff member)

As shown in Chapter 3, dictionaries define proactive action as anticipatory action: that is, a form of action which, based on anticipation of a future situation, takes the initiative in the current situation. This is very much in line with the organizational behavioral literature on proactive behavior in organizations. Crant (2000), for example, defined proactive behavior as taking the initiative in order to improve current circumstances, or create new ones. But it is also very much in line with the meaning attached to the word by the FI personnel. An HRM manager argued that proactivity means 'Taking the initiative. For me it refers to the one who takes the initiative'. Some of the FLEs attached a similar meaning to the word. Anne, for example, argued that proactive means 'Anticipating the customer. You realize the customers have a need before they realize it themselves and then you act on that knowledge'. Another FLE did not give a formal definition of the word but exemplified proactivity thus: 'We call the customer and establish contact, we think it's proactive to establish contact instead of the other way round—that it's just the customers who do that'. However, not all of the FLEs I interviewed had heard the word.

Proactivity, from a Foucauldian perspective, needs to be treated as a managerial rationality. Proactivity is a way of knowing and a way of being known that furthers certain mentalities or ways of thinking that inform the calculated management of human conduct (Rose 1999). At the FI, this rationality is directed toward the FLEs. The 'we' that the managers refer to in the preceding quotes is not 'we' as in the whole FI but 'we' as in the FLEs. Even though the managers were responsible for helping the FLEs to become more proactive, it is the FLEs that need to embody and perform proactivity in the customer interface. My interpretation is supported by the following statement from an HRM official: 'You see, we want to have a more selling structure among our customer representatives [FLEs], a more aggressive, proactive mentality that makes them dare and want to take the initiative in order to close the deal in all possible situations'. The managerial rationality of proactivity can thus be seen as a nexus of subject positions that the subjectification of the FLEs is informed by. The role of the managers, as we will see, is to support proactive behavior by creating systems and by pursuing a particular management style.

Proactivity is not only central to the managerial rationality of the FI. Rather, the notion has been commonly referred to both in theory and in practice. When it comes to the theoretical level, proactivity was introduced into the organizational behavior literature in the early 1990s. An important contribution to the conceptualization of proactivity is Bateman and Crant's (1993) Proactive Personality Scale (PPS). The organizational behavior literature does not argue that all forms of proactive behavior contribute toward an organization's performance but that the right form of proactivity contributes toward fulfilling managerial ends. The goal is not to promote as much proactivity as possible in organizations but to find out—by drawing on the disciplinary power inherent in the examinations, e.g. the PPS developed to investigate proactive behavior—the right level of proactivity and to adjust organizations and their members accordingly. The goal is thus to normalize proactivity. As the next chapter will reveal, proactivity has also been discussed in the relationship marketing literature. Kotler (1992), for example, argued that an organization whose employees express proactivity demonstrates a high level of relationship marketing orientation. Dibb and Meadows (2001), based on a study of relationship marketing in financial organizations, argue in favor of making proactivity the central yardstick of relationship marketing orientation. Furthermore, sociologically oriented empirical studies of financial service firms, some of which have focused on traditional marketing management practices and practices loosely related to relationship marketing discourse, have concluded that proactivity has been a salient managerial rationality within these firms (see Hodgson 2000; 2002; Morgan and Sturdy 2000; Peccei and Rosenthal 2000; 2001). Indeed, a proactive rationality resonates with the claim, made in critical management studies, that organizational members are perceived by management, and perceive themselves, as active and entrepreneurial selves who take the initiative in the light of customer demands (Dean 1995; du Gay 1996; du Gay and Salaman 1992; Rose 1996; 1999). Drawing on a Foucauldian framework, Hodgson (2002) analyzed relationship marketing initiatives in the banking sector in relation to the notion of the active self.

In addition, some of the staff I interviewed at the FI, who had job experience at other service firms, argued that proactivity had been a popular approach at these firms too. One HRM official, who had experience working at the telecommunications service provider Comviq, made the following observation. 'It was really very easy for the customer to choose Comviq at the beginning because we were cheaper than Telia [denationalized Swedish telecoms operator]. We really didn't need to argue with the customers too much, they rang us and said that they wanted to leave Telia as they were so expensive. Ok then, come over to us was what we said.' This resembles the market situation of the FI at the point in time when it had a price-leading position in relation to the ordinary banks and was attracting a lot of customers. As we learned in Chapter 3, at this point in time, the managerial focus of the FI was on having FLEs who worked efficiently. Accordingly, the FLEs were perceived as order clerks by management and perceived themselves as administrators. I argued that they were reactive rather than proactive in their orientation. The HRM official argues that proactivity became a central managerial rationality at Comviq when the competition stiffened, something which also seems to be well in line with the FI case. According to the HRM official, a market situation involving stiff price competition, many alternatives, and a range of services to choose from—which is a market situation where it can be expected that the bulk of service firms operate—creates a demand for proactive employees in order for the focal organization to be competitive. All in all, this suggests that proactivity is a managerial rationality that has influenced the management of a broad range of service firms on the field level. Proactivity seem to be an institutional phenomenon that is not limited solely to the FI (DiMaggio and Powell 1983).

The Truth Effect of Service Quality: Proactivity as a Subject Position

Proactivity is not, however, purely a managerial rationality. From the perspective of the power/knowledge framework, being proactive also needs to be seen as a way of being an FLE; it is a possible and, according to FI managers, a preferable subject position for the FLEs. The research conducted in organizational behavior is straightforward in this respect, arguing for and creating measurement technologies that foster 'proactive personalities' (Bateman and Crant 1993). However, as was suggested in Chapter 3, the bulk of the FLEs perceived themselves, and were perceived by managers and back office staff, as administrators: a subject position which most of the managers associated with a reactive subjectivity, the antithesis of a pro-active FLE. This is exemplified by project leader Mary who argued that the FLEs 'needed to shift from being reactive order clerks to being proactive customer representatives' implying, as one HRM official suggested, that 'They're supposed to dare to ring the customer and suggest add-on products . . . and not be afraid to do that. Those who have been working here for many years, who have this previous banking experience, they're a bit more cautious. They're from the old school. To the bank, you [as a customer] go or call them up to ask for a loan'.

The results of the service quality surveys—or more exactly, the managers' interpretations of the survey results—were taken as fact by the managers, meaning that they had a huge effect on the strategic orientation of the FI. As David puts it: 'Since they [the customers] say in the surveys that we are too passive and reactive, we [the FLEs] have to become more proactive'. This 'truth' or power/knowledge effect of service quality surveys is consistent with the conceptual review of service quality research mentioned previously: Service quality measurement technologies emerge as a form of disciplinary power ordering reality and, in particular, subjectivity through the production of truths. As we recall from the second chapter, Foucault (1977), based on his general understanding of power/knowledge, argued that examinations such as service quality surveys make people visible, detectable, and known objectively—they establish 'truths' about people, e.g. that the FI's FLEs are reactive. Examinations also embody norms of appropriate behavior which are labeled, in the positivistic language of marketing research, 'service quality determinants' (see preceding). One such norm / determinant is 'responsiveness', which 'concerns the willingness or readiness of employees to provide service' (Parasuraman et al. 1985: 47). Responsiveness was, perhaps, the most clearly manifested quality determinant in the service quality measurement surveys conducted at the FI. Table 5.1 shows a striking resemblance between the Servqual statements operationalizing responsiveness and some of the statements included in the surveys used at the FI. Based upon how the concept is qualified, it can be suggested that FLE proactivity is a prerequisite for 'responsiveness'. Parasuraman et al. (1985: 47), for example, argue that responsiveness implies 'calling the customer back quickly'. Thus, being responsive not only implies responding to customer demands, but also taking initiatives in order to satisfy the customers.

Consistent with Foucault's understanding of disciplinary power, the FI service quality surveys—in addition to knowing the present state of the person or a group of people—also produced knowledge guiding action, e.g. that FLEs should be more proactive. In line with the notion of disciplinary power, quality surveys reveal gaps between the person's present state and the norm, between the present subjectivity and the subject positions ascribed to them: in the case of the FI, between the reactive subjectivity and the subject position of being a proactive FLE. In closing the gaps between the actual and the ideal self, between a reactive and proactive subjectivity, FLEs are managed and controlled through disciplinary power (Skålén and Fougère 2007). Thus, the analysis here suggests that service quality measurement models should be conceptualized as disciplinary practices and technologies on a conceptual level, but also that they function as disciplinary technologies in practice. They objectify the employees, particularly the FLEs, in the light of SMM discourse, they make visible the gap between the ideals the SMM discourse prescribes and the current situation at the focal organization, and they suggest to the organization a plausible direction in which it needs to move the subjectivity of its employees. By drawing on the Foucauldian framework, it thus becomes possible to understand how marketing technologies and practices affect fundamental internal organizational processes within an organization.

Closing the Subjectivity Gap

The quality survey used at the FI was effective in detecting a gap between the present reactive FLE subjectivity and the subject position of being proactive, but not in closing it. Management tried to accomplish the latter by presenting the results to the FLEs. Because it was possible to link individual FLEs both with the customers they had served and the quality surveys their customers had returned, presenting the surveys to the FLEs seemed like a powerful change tool. But this was not the case. The FLEs did not understand that they were being criticized by their customers for not being proactive enough. When asked about the feedback they had received from the service quality surveys, none of them interpreted the feedback in such a way that they themselves had been lacking proactivity. If the results of the service quality surveys affected the FLEs at all, it was in terms of reproducing rather than changing their behavior. The following is a representative interview statement from one FLE: 'No, I don't think I'm doing anything differently [as a result of the quality measurements], but maybe I'm focusing more on being bright and cheery, and helpful. It's probably not something that would change, kind of thing, my entire behavior, I can't say that'. One of the FLEs that was influenced the most by the results of the service quality surveys said:

> Answer: If I see a recurrent pattern, for example that the customers say that they didn't understand the arrangement of the down payment loan. Then maybe I'll sort of rethink it. How can I make things clearer for the customer? It's mostly that which I think is interesting, to see if there's anything which recurs the whole time that I need to work on.
>
> Question: Can you provide an example of a pattern that has been recurrent?

Answer: [long pause for thought] It's rare that anything recurs. I can't actually think of anything right now.

(FLE)

To some extent, the critique pertaining to proactivity was probably swamped by the positive feedback that dominated the survey results, making the FLEs reproduce and consolidate their reactive ways of working. In addition, the critique pertaining to proactivity was probably not interpreted as negative feedback by the FLEs because behaving reactively, for an administrator, is not necessarily a bad thing. It may even be likely that the FLEs did not see that they were being critiqued for not being as proactive as the customer wanted them to be, by reading the survey results, because the FLEs are not trained to interpret service quality survey results from the perspective of customerismn. As Zeithaml et al. (1990) suggest, it is the managers, and particularly senior managers, who are responsible for setting up the right quality standards in accordance with customer expectations; in the vocabulary of the gap model, they are responsible for gap 2—the difference between the service quality specifications and management perceptions of customer expectations. Thus, the managers at the FI, and particularly senior managers such as sales manager David, who argued that the FLEs at the FI had to be more proactive because the customers had said so were the ones who were really affected by the survey results. They adopted the subject position that the gap model gives to them. Similar to a doctor examining a patient informed by medical discourse and prescribing a cure based on that examination, the FI managers interpreted the customer's expectations in relation to SMM discourse and then prescribed a 'cure'—i.e. they formulated service quality specifications—based on that interpretation. Accordingly, their actions were ordered by the disciplinary power of the gap model and the SMM discourse more generally.

It soon became evident to the managers that the FLEs were in need of direct guidance in order to change. Framed by the power/knowledge of the results of the service quality measurement, the managers therefore adopted coaching and relationship marketing in order to produce something which has to be described, from the perspective of the FI management in the light of the truth or power/knowledge effect of the quality surveys, as the truly customer oriented FLE: i.e. the proactive FLE.

THE PASTORAL POWER OF COACHING

This section is devoted to the coaching practices initiated by FI management as an effect of the power/knowledge effect associated with quality measurement—the topic throughout the next chapter is relationship marketing. Coaching is an increasingly popular management practice (see Downey 1999; Hargrove 2000), being applied in many fields. It is also a management or leadership style that researchers of service quality pre-scribe in order to turn the prerogatives of service quality discourse and the disciplinary effects of quality measurement into reality. In this section, I position coaching as a confessional pastoral power practice that turns man-agers and leaders into pastors and the employees into a flock of sheep.

Coaching, Proactivity, and the Subject Position of the Pastor

Coaching, as perceived by FI management, is a leadership style empha-sizing social interaction and communication with the FLEs, something which, as team leader Alice puts it, aspires to lead in a 'help-to-self-help' way. At the FI, coaching is a strategic kind of social interaction between the coach and the FLEs whereby the former tries to support the latter so that they behave in a customer oriented and proactive way. As FLE Anne puts it: 'The bulk of the feedback we get from the boss deals with the extent to which we have been proactive during the conversation'. The approach to coaching used by the FI is consistent with the recommendations given in *Delivering Quality Service*, a book written by the trio of researchers behind the gap model (Zeithaml et al. 1990), about how to close the 'ser-vice quality gaps' detected by service quality surveys, particularly the gap model. Zeithaml et al. (1990) emphasizes the importance of leadership in accomplishing change in line with the prescriptions of service quality discourse. Toward the end of the book, Zeithaml et al. (1990: 154) reflect on their text thus: 'Getting started on the service quality journey—and then keeping going—is, in the final analysis, a result of leadership. Lead-ership is the only engine that can transform organizations from service mediocrity to service excellence—a point that we have not been shy about making'. They argue in favor of what they call an 'in-the-field leadership style'. This type of leadership implies that 'excellent . . . service leaders lead in the field . . . They are visible to their people, endlessly *coaching*, praising, correcting, cajoling, sermonizing, observing, questioning, and listening. They emphasize two-way, personal communications' (Zeithaml et al. 1990: 7, emphasis added).

As was shown in the previous chapter, the service and market orienta-tion literature (see Berry 1999; Gebhart et al. 2006) also recommends a similar leadership style and suggests coaching as a management practice in order to make the employees more customeristic. The analysis of the IWHY program in the same chapter suggests that this type of leadership style, and coaching in particular, can be seen as a form of pastoral leadership. The manager / pastor is supposed to listen to the confessions and avowals of the employees / sheep whom they are in charge of. This is the case because the interaction between managers and employees which coaching fosters can be seen as a form of avowal whereby the employees are supposed to talk about their work, how they think about it, and what they want to change. Based on that knowledge about 'the sheep', the managers / pastors will be able to lead the employees toward an explicit or implicit normative system, by persuading them to behave differently, by questioning their current way of working in the light of the ethic, and by praising the co-workers', or some of the co-workers', way of working that is already well in line with the prerogatives. As pastors, the managers of service firms are even supposed to hold sermons with the objective of getting their sheep to behave properly, in the case of the FI: proactively. This implies that the service manager is not a manager who forces employees to do things against their will. Rather, it is the kind of manager who does for the staff what is 'best' for them. This is very much in line with the notion of pastoral power. It is, furthermore, also in line with the type of management practiced at the FI. In all the interviews with the managers of the FI, sovereign forms of power were only alluded to a few times. On the other hand, the managers often argued that they managed by helping and supporting people to develop by means of coaching. One of the team leaders argued: 'Coaching entails gaining understanding of the company. Why does it look like this today? That's development. But I don't think there have been any major difficulties [for the staff]. Some we've had to help more than others in understanding the wider world and how it affects their work situation'. Another one of the team leaders makes a more specific statement explaining how she, by means of coaching, has helped the FLEs to sell more add-ons.

> There's been a lot of focus now on selling add-on products as hardly anyone [of the FLEs] delivers on target. I began by taking in some phrases from those . . . in the building who things were going very well for . . . I started talking to them [FLEs] about it: "What do you think the others are doing to make things go so well for them?", "What makes them so successful?". Sometimes they had the answers themselves, even though they hadn't started trying it in reality. In other cases, I started guiding . . . "how do you think it would feel if you said this?" "Does it feel right to try that?" Then, nobody says no, they most frequently think that it feels right to try it. Then, you build things up that way.
>
> (Team leader)

This is hardly an example of the classical sovereign manager but an example of the pastoral manager devoted to helping his or her 'sheep' improve by guiding them along the right track. This management subjectivity is neatly captured in the phrase that Alice uses to describe coaching, quoted previously as leading in a way that entails 'help-to-self-help'.

The Pastoral Role of the Middle Manager

Even though it seems that the 'in-the-field leadership style' (as Zeithaml et al. 1990 refer to it) is suited to both top and middle managers, it seems, judging from the service quality literature, to be extra important that middle managers lead this way. When Zeithaml et al. (1990) discuss the roles of—or shall we say that they outline appropriate subject positions for—top and middle managers more exactly (on pp. 137–40), the role of top managers is to 'build an organization's value system on the pillars of satisfying customers . . . ' (p. 137). This is consistent with Schneider and White (2004: 118) who argue that the role of top management in facilitating the delivery of quality services is: '(a) to espouse serviceoriented values to employees, (b) to design organizational policies, practices, and procedures that are consistent with these values, and (c) to ensure reward and recognition go to those who most fully implement the policies and procedures to achieve the service vision'. As we saw in Chapter 4, these were duties that David and the other top managers of the FI preoccupied themselves with during the IWHY program. Thus, rather than primarily interact directly with the operative staff, which is the primary role of middle managers, top managers should devote themselves to strategy and policy formulation. In the language of pastoral power, the top manager can be conceived of as being the high priest who is more involved in codifying the scripture and developing the appropriate liturgy, rather than providing pastoral care.

Zeithaml et al. (1990: 138–39) believe that 'middle' in the term middle manager is appropriate because 'middle managers are right smack in the middle—of everything . . . Middle managers represent the linkage between the top and the bottom of the organization'. In a similar manner, the pastors represent the linkage between the high priest—the top manager—and the common people—the FLEs—trying to guide the latter in accordance with the word of God: the latter, within the somewhat mundane but nevertheless spiritual world of SMM, needing to be the customer. Interpreting the subject position of the top manager by means of drawing on the metaphor of the high priest is also consistent with the gap model, which makes top managers responsible for setting up the right quality standards in accordance with customer expectations, expressed as gap 2 in the vocabulary of the gap model. This also seems to be consistent with the role adopted by top management at the FI. This tier of management is not very involved in the day-to-day coaching of the FLEs, such as walking around and interacting with them, for instance. Many top managers are even located in a different city than the customer service part of the FI, some 250 kilometers away (see Chapter 3). Even though some top managers visit the customer service center as much as once a week, these visits are usually devoted to meetings with middle managers. In addition, the lower strata of top management or the top strata of middle management (the level above the team leaders, directly involved in interaction with the employees), who are located in the same office building as the customer service staff, do not coach either the team leaders or the FLEs. Several team leaders were frustrated by the lack of coaching. Team leader Alice, for instance, said: 'The FI wants to be a coaching company, but it starts with me . . . but I feel that I need coaching too. My boss doesn't have time for that and things get very strange . . . I also want to develop and know what I do well and what I can improve for this company so that we can flourish even more than we do today . . . I've put that across in many different contexts, that I think it's equally important for me and equally important for my boss to coach and be coached'. Thus, the top managers at the FI seem to be playing a role similar to that given to them by the service quality leadership literature. They are high priests involved in interpreting knowledge of the customers into bureaucratic rules and quality standards, or shall we say commandments.

It is, thus, the middle manager who most readily matches the subject position of the pastor, interpreting the commandments from above and guiding those below—this is also an image of organizations which is much in line with the one in the works of Zeithaml et al. (1990), arguing that middle managers are the link between the 'top' and 'bottom' of organizations. As mentioned previously, Zeithaml et al. (1990) believe that 'middle' in the term middle manager is appropriate. 'Manager', however, is less satisfactory. 'For an organization to truly pursue service excellence, it needs people in the middle who go beyond managing and lead; it needs people in the middle who reinforce the service vision . . . and act as *role models* that show *the way* and remove service obstacles from *the path* of subordinates' (Zeithaml et al. 1990: 139, emphasis added). Or, in the words of Schneider and White (2004: 118–19, emphasis added): 'the major job for a leader is to clarify the behaviors (*paths*) required by *followers* for them to attain goals or outcomes that are valent (valued) to them . . . With regard to service . . . the challenge of the leader is . . . to clarify and facilitate *the paths* most likely to promote service quality experiences for customers'. Pastors are also 'role models' who show their sheep (the 'followers') 'the way' or 'the path' leading toward the ethic governing the situation: 'the service vision' in the words of Zeithaml et al. (1990) and Schneider and White (2004). Middle managers of service firms, in a similar manner as pastors, embody the virtues of SMM discourse and lead by example—by being true believers. Middle managers who are in doubt about their calling and do not speak from conviction are less effective than true believers. In the words of Zeithaml et al. (1990), 'middle managers are often ill equipped to be effective service leaders. They may have been promoted to management positions because of their success in technical roles or sales roles . . . once in these [middle] management positions, they may not be held accountable for their willingness or ability to *coach*, communicate, or model a service ethic' (Zeithaml et al. 1990: 139, emphasis added). Middle managers need to be true pastors guiding and coaching their sheep toward the 'right' ethic— the 'service ethic'. Middle managers also need to behave in a particular way: 'the how of management is crucial to improving service firms; how superiors relate to subordinates can be the difference between awful service and excellent service' (Zeithaml et al. 1990: 139). This is much in line with Foucault's notion of power, which localizes power to the relationships between people rather than to powerful people. According to this notion, power can be both a negative and a positive force. Again, it needs to be emphasized that middle service managers are not managers who manage by means of force, or other forms of sovereign power. In order to succeed with service quality within an organization, middle managers need to be 'service champions' (cf. the expression 'service in the champions' league' from the IWHY program discussed in Chapter 4) rather than 'service stranglers', in the terminology of Zeithaml (et al. 1990: 139). In order to make their point, Zeithaml and her co-researchers (1990) affirmatively quote James Houghton who, at the time of their study, was the CEO of Corning Glass.

> Instead of saying, 'Do this, do that', firstline supervisors are now being asked to be *coaches*, to be part of a team, and to listen to their employees on how things could be done better. That takes away some of their management prerogative, which is very hard to deal with. It's very hard for someone who's been doing things the same way for 30 years to be told 'you are still the boss, but you're a different boss'
>
> (Interview with James Houghton, quoted in
> Zeithaml et al. 1990: 141, emphasis added)

Coaching, Proactivity, and Pastoral Power

Being a coach thus takes away the firstline manager's sovereign power, replacing it with power/knowledge and, more particularly, pastoral power. Rather than forcing employees to do things against their will, the firstline manager becomes a coach, i.e. a pastor who is part of a team but who also leads it. This entails 'listening' to the confessions of the members of the team, and informing them about 'how things could be done better'. In addition, it is an important middle management task to decide or interpret what is better; this task cannot be left entirely to either the FLEs or to top managers because it is only the middle managers who simultaneously know the scripture and have access to the confessions of the FLEs. They are the only ones who can be true pastors, i.e. 'still the boss' but a 'different boss'. Being a coach thus resembles being a pastor. The FI team leaders saw themselves as coaches and can thus be positioned as pastors, which the following quote exemplifies.

> Question: If you were to describe your duties, your work as team leader, what you do during your days, how would you describe them?
>
> Answer: Well, there's a lot of coaching, walking around and talking a lot to your co-workers, asking them how things are going, how things are and sensing the situation. Then there's tele coaching, as we call it. We sit beside them and listen in when they [the FLEs] talk on the phone. . . . But coaching, I don't know what to make of that word. Tele coaching is a major part of coaching. But then, of course, it's also a matter of

noticing someone if he or she has done something that's good and getting hold of him or her if there's someone who's done something that's not so good, something I don't appreciate or that the group doesn't appreciate, or which can be a problem for someone else. The customer may have been given the wrong information. There might be a customer who calls me and isn't satisfied at all with the way he or she was treated. Then it's a matter of talking to the employee in question. That's also a form of coaching, getting to know what can be improved.

(Team leader)

Alice was frank in her corroboration: 'I'm a coaching leader'! Another one of the team leaders argued that 'The FI is a coaching corporation'. As we will see from what follows, many of the FLEs referred to the team leader either using the word coach or describing them as coaches.

At the FI, the pastoral power of coaching manifests itself in several confessional coaching practices, including monthly personal progress interviews, weekly group discussions, annual salary reviews, and telecoaching. All this involves the team leader interacting with individual FLEs, with regard to their work, and the FLEs confessing their thoughts about work to the team leaders. The coaching practices thus turn the team leaders into pastors and the FLEs into sheep. As a team leader, Alice is one of the FI's pastors. The following quote suggests that Alice is a facilitator of pastoral power. 'Conveying images to my co-workers [meaning the FLEs] as regards how they should be can be done in several ways. My successful approach has been to ask them questions aimed at making them reach the same conclusion, as regards how they should be, that I have in mind'. By asking the 'right' questions, Alice makes the FLEs avow who they are. Based on this knowledge about the FLEs, Alice can apply appropriate measures in order to coach them so they become more proactive. The interpretation that the team leaders are facilitators of pastoral power is also supported by many of the FLEs. Anne, for example, pointed out that 'the feedback we get from the team leaders centers on how we have treated the customers and particularly how proactive you have been'. Another FLE put it like this: 'They [the team leaders] are coaches . . . [their coaching] focuses on how you should talk to the customer. It all ends up with us selling more, they're going to develop us in that direction, we'll become more proactive in everything we do'. The quotes suggest that the coaching conducted by the team leaders can be interpreted as being aimed at making the FLEs present a more proactive aspect of themselves which might entail 'selling a bigger part of myself in order to create extra value for the customer', as one of the FLEs put it.

Telecoaching as a Confessional Practice

Telecoaching is the most prominent confessional practice employed at the FI. Telecoaching involves the team leaders sitting and listening in on the

FLEs while these talk to their customers by phone, and then giving them instant feedback afterwards or, alternatively, as one FLE put it, 'we tape record my interactions with the customers which I and the team leader then listen to and evaluate together'. Several of the team leaders attempt to get the FLEs to ask requirement-oriented questions, which is one way of presenting oneself proactively to the customer. Anne explains: 'Most of us work by putting requirement-oriented questions to the customer. Right from the beginning of the call, you take charge and ensure that it's not only the customer who talks'. Anne makes a direct link between the telecoaching that her team leader, who happened to be Alice, has provided here and the practice of using requirement-oriented questions. 'Alice does a lot of telecoaching with us and she has pushed hard to get us to work with requirement-oriented questions'. Several FLEs on Alice's team emphasized this. One of them said: 'the telecoaching I got from my boss [Alice] made me use requirement-oriented questions'. In the two interviews I conducted with Alice, she confirmed that this was indeed the case. She also explained more fully what a requirement-oriented question was and why such questions were so useful when fostering a proactive subjectivity:

> What I call requirement-oriented questions are questions about what we can help the customer with . . . A customer makes a phone call. A co-worker, let's call her Sophie, says: "Welcome to the FI, my name's Sophie". "Hi, my name's Ian. I want to talk about home loans". Then Sophie says: "We have interest rates on such and such a level, we mortgage up to 95% of the market value of the property, our various contract periods are this, that, and the other, etc". This has taken about seven or eight minutes. All this is very good to know the customer thinks; "but I'm calling to inquire about a loan of SEK 100,000 [approx €9,000 (February 2009)] on a second home". Ten minutes have now elapsed. And then Sophie has to say: "we don't do mortgages on second homes with such a low market value" . . . If Sophie says this instead: "Welcome to the FI this is Sophie. Hi, my name's Ian. Hi Ian, how can I help you? I want a mortgage on a second home and I need 100,000". Sophie can then say: "I'm afraid we can't help you with that Ian" . . . Rule number one is, ascertain what the customer wants while rule number two is, do we want the customer?
>
> (Alice, team leader)

Taking charge of the phone call implies anticipating what the customer wants, apart from what he or she explicitly expresses that he or she wants. Accordingly, requirement-oriented questions drive proactivity. Closing the gap between the reactive subject and the proactive subject position, which the disciplinary power of the FI quality survey has detected, thus frames and provides the general direction of coaching at the FI, which is exemplified by telecoaching. Furthermore, by annually measuring customer-perceived service quality, and by linking measurements to individual FLEs, FI management can check whether a particular FLE is changing in a desirable way or not. This affects the substance of future coaching. As team leader John puts it: 'By means of the [quality] measurement, we can check whether the employees are making progress or not'. Because many of the FLEs, at least on Alice's team, use requirement-oriented questions, the pastoral power of the coaching seems to have been effective. Many FLEs outside of Alice's team confirmed this impression. One of them said: 'Without telecoaching, I wouldn't be talking to the customers the way I do now'. A colleague of hers agreed: 'Telecoaching has been great. It's helped me so much'.

But the FLEs also manage themselves without the direct support of their team leaders. When speaking about themselves during telecoaching, they reveal to themselves what type of people they are and if they are dissatisfied with who they are—a satisfaction that is contingent upon the customeristic proactive ethic—they will try to change themselves. As said previously pastoral power promotes and enables reflexive self-management (Clegg et al. 2002). Anne exemplifies this: 'You reflect a lot upon what you say to the customer during telecoaching. You go through your communication skills yourself'. Another FLE said: 'Telecoaching makes you think for yourself, it's an eye-opener, how you should be conducting the conversation', and thus how you should conduct yourself. Another FLE recalls a phone conversation with a man, which she tape recorded and listened to together with her team leader. 'I rambled on about evaluating houses for a long time and I said to my team leader: "I don't think he understands what I'm saying" . . . my team leader didn't need to make any suggestions about how I was supposed to act . . . I heard myself that I'd given too lengthy an explanation about something he hadn't asked for, and probably didn't need'. Because the customer did not need that information, the FLE was deviating from the proactive way of being because proactivity, as one FLE put it, entails 'knowing about the customers' needs before they do'.

But self-management is not restricted to formal, confessional telecoaching sessions. The FLEs continue to confess and confirm to themselves divergences from the ethic of proactivity during regular interactions with customers, creating opportunities for self-management. One FLE explains: 'During one telecoaching session, we recorded the conversation and listened to it afterward and it occurred to me that I talked too fast . . . After that, during conversations with customers, I often say to myself "calm down, talk slowly"'.

THE PROACTIVE SUBJECT

In this chapter, I have conceptually and empirically analyzed technologies and practices for measuring customer-perceived service quality and practices for conducting coaching associated with service quality discourse by drawing on the notions of disciplinary and pastoral power. The conceptual analysis of service quality discourse has positioned service quality practices and technologies as examinations promoting disciplinary power. The empirical analysis of the measurement of service quality has suggested that the surveys used by the FI, which had a lot in common with Servqual, connected with the gap model, have to some degree fostered disciplinary power. More particularly, it was claimed that the surveys generated proactivity as an ideal FLE subjectivity, making visible, to the managers, a gap between the institutionalized reactive subjectivity of the FLEs and the ideal subject position of proactivity. However, the result of the quality surveys *per se* did not achieve a closing of the gap between reactivity and proactivity. In order to do that, the managers introduced coaching, which is a management practice recommended by service quality researchers for closing service quality gaps. In the conceptual analysis, coaching was, in line with the discussion in Chapter 4, analyzed and positioned as a pastoral power practice. The empirical analysis suggested that coaching operated as a pastoral practice at the FI, working proactivity into the subjectivity of the FLEs. It was suggested that coaching turned the team leaders into pastors and the FLEs into sheep; that it made the team leaders lead their FLEs by being good pastors—e.g. supportive and kind; and that it encouraged the FLEs to confess to their respective team leaders how they worked, encouraged the team leaders to give the FLEs advice about how to work more proactively, and encouraged the FLEs to self-regulate themselves toward proactivity once they had understood the content of that rationality. Thus, coaching stimulated a form of manager-employee relationship that seems to be modeled on the notion of pastoral power.

The present chapter elaborates on the analysis in Chapter 4 describing the introduction of customerism as a managerial rationality for strategically reorienting the FI. More particularly, the previous chapter analyzed both the service and market orientation discourse as presented in academic texts, and as materialized in the IWHY program, by drawing on the notion of pastoral power. The present chapter makes at least three further important contributions to the analysis of the intra-organizational role of SMM. Firstly, the disciplinary power analysis of the service quality measurement suggests that it is the proactivity of the FLEs which was targeted at the FI, and not the customer or the service and market orientation of the FLEs in general. Secondly, the present chapter suggests that coaching is an effective managerial technology for working customerism, at least in the form of proactivity, into the subjectivity of the FLEs. Thirdly, the present chapter provides empirical support for the power/knowledge of customerism of SMM discourse materializing in organizations—that it exerts actual ordering effects on organizations—and that these ordering effects can be understood by drawing on the notions of pastoral and disciplinary power. This is something I will return to when discussing the relationship between academic marketing discourse and practice in the concluding chapter. However, before that, I will flesh the argument out by analyzing academic relationship marketing discourse through the lens of power/knowledge and by studying the introduction of relationship marketing into the FI.

6 The Managerial Rationality of Relationship Marketing

Coaching was one of the power/knowledge practices used to work the subject position of proactivity, generated by service quality measurement, into the employees and, in particular, the FLEs at the FI. Relationship marketing—the topic of this chapter—was the other regime of power/knowledge drawn on at the FI to make the FLEs more proactive. The present chapter opens with a conceptual power/knowledge analysis relating academic articulations of relationship marketing discourse to the notions of disciplinary and pastoral power. The conceptual analysis suggests that proactivity has been promoted as a managerial rationality by research into relationship marketing. In the next two sections, I return to the case of the FI, focusing on how relationship marketing has contributed toward making the subjectivity of the FLEs more proactive. The first of these two sections focuses on a relationship marketing project at the FI which involved the FLEs. The analysis especially focuses on how this project contributed toward making some of the FLEs more proactive by means of the pastoral power it fostered. The next section is devoted to analyzing how the disciplinary power of relationship marketing IT systems order the work and subjectivity of the FLEs. The chapter ends with a summary of the major conclusions which paves the way for a more general discussion concerning the contributions made by the book in the concluding chapter.

RELATIONSHIP MARKETING AND POWER/KNOWLEDGE

Creating and maintaining long-lasting and profitable relationships has a long history in business practice. Friedman (2005; see also Gummesson 2008; Parvatiyar and Sheth 2000), for instance, in his work on the history of salesmanship in the U.S. from 1840 up to the 1950s, shows how sales staff in sectors characterized by repeat sales valued and took good care of their customers, whereas sales staff operating in sectors characterized by single transactions were more interested in making a profit and generally did not care as much about the value obtained by the customer after the deal had been closed. It seems to be common sense for business practitioners to care for customer relationships in areas characterized by repeat sales, with historical work suggesting that it has been, implicitly or explicitly, a business strategy for quite some time. However, when rules of thumb are formalized, codified, and elaborated—when a discourse about an aspect of social life is articulated—it then becomes possible to refer to, talk about, rationalize, manage, and govern that area in a more precise, systematic, and explicit way (Laclau and Mouffe 1985). Furthermore, when a discourse about an aspect of social life is developed, it then becomes possible to 'export' the rationality associated with it to social domains previously untouched by the rationality using the rationality to governmentalize social domains which has previously been unaffected by it. For example, it becomes possible to export the rationality of caring for customer relationships from business areas characterized by repeat sales to areas traditionally dominated by single transactions. It is from this angle that we need to approach relationship marketing discourse. Despite the fact that a managerial rationality similar to the one promoted by academic relationship marketing discourse has been present for quite some time in business life, the researchers and consultants who founded the field of relationship marketing articulated a discourse of 'caring for customer relationships' which made it possible to spread more widely a relationship-oriented managerial rationality for governing business practice.

Besides acknowledging the fact that relationship marketing discourse has its roots in business practice, relationship marketing scholars also trace the roots of relationship marketing to other managerial discourses such as TQM, the network/interaction theory of industrial marketing and, not least, SMM. Gummesson (1997: 267), for instance, argues that 'My basic thinking on RM [relationship marketing] is a gradual extension of the "Nordic School" approach to service marketing and management, and the network approach to industrial marketing as developed by the IMP Group (Industrial Marketing and Purchasing Group) . . . More recent sources of inspiration are above all total quality management and the new theories on imaginary (virtual, network) organizations' (see also Gummesson 1987; 1991; 2008). In a similar manner, Grönroos (1997: 327) holds that 'the interaction and network approach of industrial marketing and modern service marketing approaches, especially the one by the Nordic School, clearly views marketing as an interactive process in a social context where relationship building and management are a vital cornerstone'. Another thing that suggests a close kinship between relationship marketing and SMM discourse is that the same scholars—Leonard Berry, Christian Grönroos, and Evert Gummesson, just to mention a few prominent ones—have been involved in developing both fields. Because the present book is devoted to studying SMM, I will focus on analyzing how academic relationship marketing grew out of SMM discourse, without denying that other research traditions, e.g. informatics, have also been pivotal in shaping relationship marketing discourse. Thus, the 'version' of relationship marketing presented here is primarily related to the general power/knowledge of SMM discourse.

The Archaeology of Relationship Marketing in SMM Discourse

Leonard Berry is usually credited with having coined the notion of relationship marketing (see Berry 1983). Yet, within the boundaries of SMM, relationship marketing should be traced back to the notion of interactive marketing, and thus to the selfsame notion that service quality research emanated from (see the previous chapter). Gummesson (1987: 13–14, emphasis added) is very clear about this: 'In services marketing interaction is a key word. . . . A distinction is made between interactive marketing (*sometimes called relationship marketing*) and non-interactive (mass) marketing'. Interactive aspects of marketing by service firms, and of services, were discussed by Rathmell (1974) and by Gummesson (1977) in his dissertation. As the section on the archaeology of service quality discourse in the previous chapter suggests, the notion was formalized by Grönroos (1982). As we recall, Grönroos (1982) makes a distinction between the traditional and the interactive marketing function. Traditional marketing has a lot in common with the marketing management approach to marketing and thus draws on practices such as the marketing mix, segmentation, and targeting. The activities of traditional marketing are carried out by the marketing department. Interactive marketing, on the other hand, is a form of marketing embedded in the interactions between the seller and the buyer, particularly between the FLEs and their customers. Thus, the employee's behaviors become a part of marketing and marketing becomes intertwined in the interaction between the employees and their customers. In interactive marketing, the interactions between the selling company and the buying customer become the object of the managerial rationality of marketing— the customer and market orientation of the firm, as prescribed by the marketing concept. In particular, this has implications for the relationship between the FLEs and their customers. As Gummesson (1991: 63) states: 'Interaction has become a key concept referring to the contact between the service provider's staff and the consumer. This creates another type of marketing than the traditional consumer product case where personal contact is handled by a salesperson and the impersonal contact by advertising'. In short interactive marketing creates relationship marketing.

Thus, there is not much of a leap between redirecting the power/knowledge of the marketing concept to the employees' customer interactions and systematically focusing on managing the relationships between the seller and the buyer. In this regard, it is indeed interesting to note that Grönroos (1982: 31, emphasis added) articulates the distinction between traditional and interactive marketing by arguing that the ' . . . basic characteristics of services make the marketing situation and the *customer relation* of service firms fundamentally different from that of a consumer goods company'.

Central to postulating a distinction between traditional and interactive marketing, thus, is the fact that the production of services calls for a different type of *relationship* with customers than does manufacturing. It is interesting that the signifier 'relationship' has provided one of the central provisions for articulating general SMM discourse. Therefore, it is indeed feasible to perceive relationship marketing to be a discourse ordered by the managerial rationality of SMM[1]. Relationship marketing offers subject positions associated with being a marketer to each and every employee: at least on part-time (cf. Gummesson 1991). However, as we have seen, and as will be even clearer in what follows, it is not the traditional subject position of the marketing mix type of marketer that relationship marketing prescribes. It is, rather, a marketer who, by means of his or her way of being human in the social world, embodies the managerial rationality of marketing. The power/knowledge of relationship marketing has social interactions as its object rather than products, as marketing management discourse had.

The Governmental Domain of Relationship Marketing

Parvatiyar and Sheth (2000) and Payne and Frow (2005) reviewed definitions of relationship marketing, making a distinction between narrow and wide definitions (cf. Boulding et al. 2005). The narrow definitions often stem from approaches focusing on the use of information technology and so-called Customer Relationship Management (CRM)[2] systems in relationship building. In this type of relationship marketing research, the focus is on 'individual and / or one-to-one relationships with customers that integrate database knowledge with long-term customer retention and growth strategy' (Parvatiyar and Sheth 2000: 5). Within the narrow approaches, the managerial rationality of relationship marketing, so to speak, orbits around a CRM system and the associated customer database that supports the FLEs' sales, marketing, and service activities, which are in turn supported by back office analysis and integration of customer data (Boulding et al. 2005; Greenberg 2001; Jayachandran et al. 2005).

Another category of scholar, which includes SMM scholars, has taken, according to Parvatiyar and Sheth (2000) and Payne and Frow (2005), a wider view of relationship marketing. These scholars do not deny that information technology is important, but they argue that CRM systems are not sufficient to enable the relationship marketing of an organization to succeed (cf. Day 2003; Speier and Venkatesh 2002). Berry (1983) argues that relationship marketing is about attracting, maintaining, and enhancing customer relationships. Morgan and Hunt's (1994: 22) definition is close to that of Berry, arguing that 'relationship marketing refers to all marketing activities directed toward establishing, developing and maintaining successful relational exchange'. Grönroos (1990: 138 quoted in Grönroos 2007a: 118) defines relationship marketing, and indeed every type of marketing, as aspiring 'to establish, maintain, and enhance . . . relationships with customers and other partners, at a profit, so that the objectives of the parties involved are met. This is achieved by a mutual exchange and fulfillment of promises'. Grönroos' definition is broad in the sense that it positions relationship marketing as a major alternative to marketing management, attempting to accomplish a hegemonic intervention in marketing discourse and rearticulate how the marketing concept should be realized. He shares this orientation with Gummesson, i.e. defining marketing as relationship marketing attacking the marketing concept directly:

> How then could the Old Marketing Concept be renewed. The key words are already found in the title of this article. At the end of the title, *relationship* is mentioned. Marketing can be seen as relationship management; creating, developing and maintaining a network in which the firm thrives. The next word is *interactive*, i.e. bilateral and multilateral supplier-customer activities to produce and deliver goods and services, primarily in a person-to-person communication with less left to mass communication. The last expression is *long term*, stressing that relationships need time to be built and need time to be maintained. They thus become central in strategic planning, both at the corporate and marketing level.
>
> (Gummesson 1987: 11)

Parvatiyar and Sheth (2000) as well as Payne and Frow (2005), in their respective overviews of definitions of relationship marketing, arrive at the following definitions. Parvatiyar and Sheth (2000: 9) hold that 'relationship marketing [is] the ongoing process of engaging in cooperative and collaborative activities and programs with immediate and end-user customers to create or enhance mutual economic value at reduced cost'. Payne and Frow suggest the following definition:

> CRM is a strategic approach that is concerned with creating improved shareholder value through the development of appropriate relationships with key customers and customer segments. CRM unites the potential of relationship marketing strategies and IT to create profitable, long-term relationships with customers and other key stakeholders. CRM provides enhanced opportunities to use data and information to both understand customers and cocreate value with them. This requires a cross-functional integration of processes, people, operations, and marketing capabilities that is enabled through information, technology, and applications.
>
> (Payne and Frow 2005: 168)

Providing a complete and comprehensive review of the definitions of relationship marketing is not the main aim of this book, which is, rather, analyzing the power/knowledge of relationship marketing discourse as well as what and who it targets. From the preceding definitions and discussion, it is clear that relationship marketing encourages the building of strong and long-lasting social relationships between buyer and seller. Furthermore, it gives the FLEs, supported by CRM technology, a key role in fostering and nourishing these relationships with the customers. In contrast to marketing management discourse, but in line with SMM discourse, it is thus not the products of the organization, but the employees, and particularly the FLEs, who are the main object or target of the customeristic managerial rationality promoted by relationship marketing. The locus of the power/knowledge of marketing is repositioned from the material world to the social domain. More particularly, the social domain that relationship marketing discourse targets is the interaction between the FLEs and the customers. Thus, if it can be suggested, based on the preceding review, that relationship building, maintenance, and initiation are central to the managerial rationality and that relationships can be positioned as a central nodal point of relationship marketing discourse, it is less clear which managerial rationality academic relationship marketing discourse more precisely fosters and what practices that is promoted in order to accomplish this rationality. This is the topic we will turn to in the following sections.

The Managerial Rationality of Proactivity in Relationship Marketing Discourse

The major problem with relationship marketing, from a management perspective, as with interactive marketing, is that marketing is embedded in interactions. Relationship creation, building, and maintenance seems to be everywhere—or, as expressed by Gummesson (1987: 17), 'customer relations are influenced by everybody'—which makes marketing hard to control. Gummesson's solution to the problem is the subject position of the part-time marketer who 'carry out marketing activities but, in contrast to the full-time marketers . . . they do not belong to the marketing or sales department' (Gummesson 1991: 60). According to Gummesson (1991; 2008), part-time marketers can be found in all departments of the organization: purchasing, finance, product development and design, manufacturing, and management. Part-time marketers can even be found outside the organization. Suppliers, customers and investors, media, and other stakeholders are all examples of part-time marketers who, by means of word-of-mouth communication, act as marketers for the company.

Gummesson (1991: 68) mentions four interactions between seller and customer that are important points of marketing, one of which is the 'interaction between the service provider's contact persons (the front line employees) and the customer'. In interactive service firms, such as the FI, this type of interaction seems to be the most salient type and thus the one that the managerial rationality of relationship marketing is primarily directed toward (cf. Korczynski 2002). This claim is supported by Sharma et al. (1999: 602) who studied the antecedents and consequences of relationship marketing, arguing that 'in examining the marketing strategies associated with long-term relationships, the activities of the salesperson as a boundary spanning agent are regarded as critical in enhancing long-term relationships' (see Dibb and Meadows 2001 for a similar point). More particularly, Sharma et al. (1999) suggested that one form of 'activity', which supported relationship market orientation, was proactive behavior on the part of the FLEs. They argue that: 'There is increasing research [suggesting] that proactive behaviours are critical in relationship management . . . [R]ather than customers seeking solutions to problems that they may have, service marketers need to anticipate problems and develop solutions for them . . . The rise of computers with increased graphical and statistical analysis has made proactive behaviours easier with increased productivity and profitability gains' (Sharma et al. 1999: 604). The FLEs of service firms need to be one step ahead of the customer, and CRM systems can help them accomplish this (cf. Jayachandran et al. 2005; Payne and Frow 2005). The conclusion that Sharma et al. (1999: 608) draw from their empirical study pertaining to proactivity is that 'salespeople feel that "proactive behaviour" is another key driver for effective relationships . . . [A]t the customer level, salespeople are continuously interacting with their customers to identify emerging needs. This allows salespeople to develop solutions for customers even before they are aware of the problems'. The approach of Sharma et al. (1999) is deductive and positivistic. Their agenda is managerial. They suggested that proactive behavior would have a positive effect on relationship maintenance, which their study showed to be true. In the analytical language drawn on here, they turn proactivity into a part of the power/ knowledge of relationship marketing discourse.

This interpretation is supported by a reading of the work of Dibb and Meadows (2001), which approached relationship marketing in retail banking from a managerial, but inductive, perspective, asking the general question of where relationship marketing in retail banking is today. They compared the results of their qualitative study with Kotler's (1992) five-step relationship marketing level model, which includes 'basic', 'reactive', 'accountability', 'proactive', and 'partnership'. Dibb and Meadows (2001: 186) conclude that: 'In terms of Kotler's relationship marketing model . . . it seems obvious that the case companies have reached the *proactive* level four . . . For the banks this *proactive* stance involves the bank contacting the customer and attempting to understand and satisfy their needs, even when the purchase of a product is not being discussed directly'. Based on their study, Dibb and Meadows (2001) level criticism at Kotler's scheme, arguing that it is too unsophisticated. More particularly, they claim that 'a scheme of finer levels is required which grasps the variability in [the] important *proactive* stage' (Dibb and Meadows 2001: 187). Dibb and Meadows like to turn proactivity into the central yardstick of relationship marketing orientation. From the perspective of the analytical lens employed in this book, Dibb and Meadows (2001) want to make the managerial rationality of proactivity central to the power/knowledge of relationship marketing discourse and to promote subject positions of proactivity to organizations and their members. According to them, the central quest of the relationship marketing project is to make organizations and their employees more proactive.

The Pastoral Power of Relationship Marketing

How, according to the academic literature, is the managerial rationality of relationship marketing accomplished? How do the employees of an organization become more proactive? In trying to answer these questions, our point of departure can be the distinction between the strategic and tactical/operational approaches to relationship marketing referred to in the literature—a distinction that resonates with the distinction between the broad and narrow definitions of relationship marketing referred to previously (see, in particular, Payne and Frow 2005). Whereas some researchers, especially in informatics, have emphasized the tactical/operational side of relationship marketing, and the fact that organizations should focus on developing customer databases and implementing CRM systems software, the marketing and, in particular, the SMM literature has emphasized that organizations need to have both a strategic and a tactical approach to relationship marketing in order to succeed (see, for instance, Boulding et al. 2005; Day 2003; Grönroos 2007b; Gummesson 2008; Payne and Frow 2005).

In the SMM literature, both the strategic and the tactical approaches to relationship marketing can be approached via the notion of internal marketing (Grönroos 2007b; Gummesson 2008). This notion holds that the management of an organization should consider the employees as their first customers—if the employees cannot be convinced about management initiatives such as marketing communication campaigns, then the (external) customers will not be convinced either, so the logic of the argument goes. Grönroos (2007b: 383) says: 'The term [internal marketing] was coined as an umbrella concept for a variety of internal activities and approaches that are not new but, focused upon in this way, offer a new approach to developing a service orientation and an interest in customers and marketing among an organization's personnel'. As the quote suggests, the notion of internal marketing is closely associated with the notion of service orientation which, as we know from Chapter 4, is closely associated with market orientation. In the relationship marketing literature, the term relationship orientation, which has a similar meaning, is sometimes used. From Chapter 4, we also know that service and market orientation is closely associated with developing a service and market oriented culture by adopting a service or market oriented strategy. Indeed, at the strategic level, internal marketing, seen from a relationship marketing perspective, can be understood as an approach to developing or maintaining a service culture by turning the employees of the organization into proactive part-time marketers who live and breathe the marketing concept (Gummesson 2008).

The conceptual analysis of the academic marketing literature in Chapter 4 was devoted to understanding how service and market oriented cultures are developed and maintained, from a power/knowledge perspective. I will not go deeper into a similar analysis again but will repeat the main points from the analysis in Chapter 4. One of the key points was that the academic literature on service and market orientation was perceived as promoting pastoral power. The review suggested that several central values, or commandments, were put forward as a point of departure for service and market orientation change programs. Furthermore, the analysis positioned managers as pastors whose main responsibility was: (i) ensuring that the employees confessed their innermost thoughts, (ii) listening to these avowals, (iii) comparing them with the commandments, and whether or not the employees were deviating from the ethic as proposed by the commandments, and (iv) trying to work the preferred ethic into the employees and their subjectivity. The employees were thus perceived as a flock of sheep that was supposed to confess to the managers / pastors and to receive pastoral care from them. However, the conceptual analysis also suggested that the subject position of the employee, as articulated in the service and market orientation literature, encouraged the employees to become good sheep: i.e. responsible sheep with the ability to regulate themselves toward the ethic of service and market orientation. This resonates well with the research into relationship marketing which indicates how important it is for the staff to be involved in the planning, decision-making, and execution of relationship marketing projects, if the aims of such projects are to be realized (Grönroos 2007b; Gummesson 2008; Payne and Frow 2005)—the sheep need to feel that they are a part of the congregation. The analysis of the service and market orientation program at the FI—IWHY—contextualized and illustrated empirically the conceptual analysis of the marketing and service orientation literature. Thus, from the standpoint of the relationship marketing literature, we can expect that the managerial rationality of proactivity, which the relationship marketing initiatives carried out at the FI aimed to foster, is accomplished, at least partly, through the operation of pastoral power.

The Disciplinary Power of Relationship Marketing

However, the rationality of relationship marketing cannot only be realized through service and market orientation. Apart from the strategic initiatives, 'tactical / operational' initiatives, particularly CRM systems, are also needed (Boulding et al. 2005; Day 2003; Payne and Frow 2005). As stated by Sisodia and Wolfe (2000: 559): 'When a business gets redefined around customer relationships, and when the process of managing those relationships gets thoroughly reengineered, companies need to make significant changes in how they organize their activities . . . A vital component of success in this arena is the provision of cutting edge information technology to sales, customer service and other frontline personnel'. In addition to CRM systems, the SMM and relationship marketing literature suggests several other initiatives for working the strategic intentions into the FLEs, including human resource management, internal service recovery, market research, and market segmentation (see Grönroos 2007b; Gummesson 2008). However, I will focus on information technology for two reasons. Firstly, for many consultancy organizations, e.g. Oracle/Siebel systems, the Gartner Group, and SAP, selling and adapting CRM systems and customer database systems to individual organizations represents important business (Payne and Frow 2005; Speier and Venkatesh 2002), indicating a widespread implementation of such systems in service firms and that analyzing the role of such systems is of general interest. Secondly, one of the main goals of the FI's relationship marketing project was to develop a CRM system and a customer database.

Vavra (1994, see also Sisodia and Wolfe 2000) argues that customer databases emerged as a tool for re-creating the long-lasting and personal relationships that salespeople according to Vavra had with customers prior to the 1960s, and the form of 'relationship' marketing this implied (see above and Friedman 2005). Vavra (1994) also argues that marketing, during the period 1960–1990, drifted toward focusing on achieving greater distribution by establishing dealer networks and retail chains. Vavra (1994: 46) maintains that the resulting 'complexity of the market combined with marketers' isolation from their end-use customers made focusing on customer needs difficult'. Together with the right strategies, databases might offer the solution: 'Marketers who implement marketing strategies with well designed databases . . . will be able to interact with their customers in as personal a way as their sales counterparts did in the '40s and '50s' (Vavra 1994: 46–48). For Vavra (1994) and other relationship marketing scholars, such as Boulding et al. (2005) and Jayachandran et al. (2005), customer databases and CRM systems are thus a tool for accomplishing the kind of long-lasting and tight customer relationship, between the FLEs and their customers, implied by the realization of relationship marketing. This understanding of CRM systems is well in line with the role that they are supposed to play, according to SMM scholars (Gummesson 2008). More importantly, Vavra's paper gives support to the idea that CRM systems and customer databases support the employees in acting and thinking like proactive subjects vis-à-vis the customer, despite the fact that the word proactivity is not mentioned. Vavra (1994: 50) claims, for instance, that one of the great benefits of customer databases is the fact that 'marketing efforts become more efficient and effective by virtue of the marketer being able to identify her most important customers and present them with the right offer, product, or service at the right time'. Proactivity is also alluded to by

Sisodia and Wolfe (2000: 557), who argue that 'technology-enabled relationship marketing will . . . lead to higher level of marketing effectiveness. One dimension of this is the ability not only to respond quickly to customers' needs, but to anticipate those needs'. Anticipating the needs of others is central to the notion of proactivity.

But in what way do CRM systems contribute toward making the FLEs' subjectivity more proactive and toward establishing long-lasting customer relationships? My answer is that they do this by means of the disciplinary power they embody, which has as its main object the FLEs. But before venturing into a disciplinary power analysis of CRM systems and customer databases, let me explain, very generally, just how a modern CRM system appears to the FLEs. When an FLE starts interacting with a customer, the system displays data about the customer as soon as he or she has been identified by it. Exactly what specific data appears on the screen will vary quite a lot because the systems are usually calibrated to suit a specific organization. On a more general level, however, it is possible to say that the systems display information about the customer (Boulding et al. 2005; Greenberg 2001; Jayachandran et al. 2005) pertaining to the services or products he or she has previously bought from the company, the services the customer is currently subscribing to, when the subscription needs to be renewed, what type of add-on service the customer has, and which add-on services the customer is not currently subscribing to. A typical CRM system also includes information about the customer which has been entered by the FLEs when these have been interacting with the customer on previous occasions. Such information might, for example, include: 'The customer is thinking about subscribing to service X but has not decided yet' or 'the customer is dissatisfied with the services provided by company Y (a competitor) and is thinking about switching to us'.

The CRM systems thus provide the FLE with knowledge which he or she can draw on to obtain an image of what business ties the customer has with the organization, as well as what potential business ties the customer lacks (Boulding et al. 2005; Greenberg 2001; Jayachandran et al. 2005). This knowledge provides the FLE with the opportunity to anticipate the needs of the customer (as defined by the organization, that is) and act proactively. More particularly, it provides the FLE with the opportunity to act proactively in relation to, as well as care for, existing business ties: Is the customer subscribing to a service that needs to be renewed in the near future? Is it time for the customer to buy new products? Does the customer have the latest versions of the add-on services that he or she is subscribing to? In addition, the system presents the FLE with the opportunity to act proactively in relation to potential business ties, strengthening the relationship by establishing more ties with the customer: Is it possible to sell the customer more of the core services or products? What add-on services does the customer lack? Based on the information about the customer; what add-on services will be easiest to sell to him or her? The information stored by the system invites the FLE to ask him- or herself questions concerning existing and potential business ties with the customer. The answer to these questions, which the FLEs give themselves, are intended to fuel customer interactions in a way that fosters proactivity, strengthens relationships by establishing more ties between organization and customer, and contributes to the overall profitability goals of the firm.

Perceived in this way, CRM systems can be treated as a form of disciplinary power that targets the FLEs—because it is important to keep in mind the self-evident aspect that it is the FLEs, and not the customers, who primarily interact with the system. As we have seen, the CRM systems thus direct, or at least aim to direct, the actions and thoughts of the FLEs toward caring for the firm's key business ties (Boulding et al. 2005; Jayachandran et al. 2005; Vavra 1994). CRM systems do that, not by taking their point of departure in who the individual FLE is, as is the case with pastoral power, but by means of a general understanding that FLEs are supposed to be, act, and think proactively. The FLEs are thus regulated by placing a general 'proactivity framework' upon them, which they need to adapt to. In this way, CRM systems seek to frame how the FLEs present themselves to the customers when interacting with them. It can thus be argued that CRM systems seek to turn the FLEs into proactive subjects by objectifying them. More to the point, CRM systems subjectify the FLEs by objectifying them in the light of relationship marketing discourse and how this discourse has been adapted to the individual organization—a mode of government that resonates well with the notion of disciplinary power.

Most CRM systems provide managers with the possibility of entering work orders into them. A work order is a task that the system will ask a particular FLE, or group of FLEs, to carry out, e.g. approaching a listed number of customers and offering them a discount on a particular add-on service in order to increase the number of ties that the organization has with these customers. The type of work order to be entered into the CRM systems is normally detected by the marketing department using the customer information that has been stored in the customer database associated with the system. Drawing on that data, the marketing department can detect an interesting customer segment, e.g. a group of customers lacking a particular add-on service. The CRM systems also present managers with the opportunity to monitor how effective each individual employee was when executing the work order, e.g. selling the add-on service (cf. Greenberg 2001; Jayachandran et al. 2005). Managers will be able to relate the performance of each individual employee to the mean for the group, picturing the aggregated result as a steep or a flat normal distribution curve. The statistical data provides knowledge of those who performed above average, on average, and below average, as well as how far from the average they are and how many outliers there are. Accordingly, the system gives the managers the opportunity to detect gaps between the normal and the abnormal, which is a particular feature of disciplinary power

(Foucault 1977). For managers, the most interesting gaps, in most situations, are the ones between the average performers or pre-established goals and the underperformers; these are the gaps they will primarily focus on reducing because they will yield the largest positive effects. Thus, based on the detailed disciplinary feedback that the system is able to generate, managers can target particular FLEs in order to better their performance. And, when managers do this, they can inspire themselves by the above average performers. 'What makes these FLEs so successful?' and 'How do they carry out their work?' are questions that the CRM systems invite managers to ask themselves.

CRM systems thus provide managers with disciplinary opportunities for closing gaps between the outlier and the norm. However, CRM systems should not only be perceived as a form of disciplinary power which fosters a movement toward a proactive subjectivity, but also as a means of generating knowledge of who is deviating from the norm of proactivity and who is not. Exactly how the disciplinary effect of the CRM systems plays out in practice is one of the topics focused on in the next two sections, where we return to the case of the FI and the organizations endeavoring to introduce relationship marketing, in particular.

RELATIONSHIP MARKETING AS
PASTORAL POWER IN PRACTICE

The FI relationship marketing project, which was referred to as Continuously Increasing Customer Value (CICV), is to be perceived as a 'natural continuation', in the words of sales manager David, of the service and market orientation project IWHY, described and analyzed in Chapter 4. As shown in that chapter, IWHY focused on explicating common values or commandments, but not so much on turning them into behaviors, to use the language of the change model presented in the IWHY booklet (see Figure 4:1). The CICV was also influenced by the service quality survey results, or at least management's interpretation of the results: i.e. that the FLEs needed to be more proactive. Because many of the managers argued that relationship marketing 'is known to have proactivity built into it', as one of them put it, they decided to draw on relationship marketing practices when making the subjectivity of the FLEs more proactive.

The interviews with project leader Mary and associate project leader Barbara strongly suggest that relationship marketing is central to the CICV and that relationship marketing fosters proactivity. Mary says:

> Relationship marketing was an important part of [CICV]. Customer orientation and looking after existing customers, creating loyal customers, were prioritized primarily because many existing customers had pointed out the lack of what we perceived to be proactivity, that we

don't suggest improvement measures [in combination with] not priori-
tizing existing customers, that we've had external campaigns focusing
on new customers, where we offered discounts to new customers, but
that this never benefitted the customers who had already chosen us.

(Mary, project leader)

Barbara makes a similar claim:

Relationship marketing was an extremely important parameter, how to
look after existing customers, how to suggest improvement measures,
primarily how to contact the customer during his or her lifespan. We
hadn't focused on that previously. We had shocking examples of a customer who had borrowed from us 14 years ago and we'd never called
him. Looking after customers doesn't mean leaving them in peace.

(Barbara, associate project leader)

The project was, furthermore, directly informed by academic relationship
marketing knowledge. It departed from a collaboration between the FI and
researchers in the field of service and relationship marketing who had conducted, in the role of consultants, according to the FI marketing manager,
'a switching behavior analysis. This was a matter of looking at how many
customers we have who are prone to switching, for instance, in the stock
and how many we have who have no trigger at all. It was all about identifying these triggers then, so to speak'. Switching is a central notion in relationship marketing theory and trigger is the notion used to indicate reasons
or potential reasons for switching (see Roos 1999). One of the researchers
involved in the project specializes in studying switching and the triggers
that provoke switching.

The relationship marketing project, which was initiated during 2004,
was divided up into two phases. As recommended by the literature on relationship marketing (see, for instance, Grönroos 2007b; Gummesson 2008;
Jayachandran et al. 2005; Vavra 1994), the first phase involved the FLEs
developing 'ways of working'—as many referred to it—which aligned with
the managerial rationality of relationship marketing discourse. The second
phase involved the development and introduction of a CRM system. The
first phase will be analyzed first, by drawing on the notion of pastoral
power. After that, the second phase will be addressed, by drawing on the
notion of disciplinary power.

Formal Aim and Fundamental Rationale

Based on the consultancy intervention by the service and relationship marketing scholars, as well as the general understanding that the FLEs needed
to be more proactive, three goals were set up for the project. According to
the marketing manager, these were that:

We'd be working with competitor demortgaging, those demortgaging their loans and moving to competitors. We wanted to do something about them. And we also had to do something about the customers we already had. We wanted additional sales from them. And the customers who come here, they shouldn't be standing in line. And if you have customers standing in line, you have to know which ones to take first. Those three goals are in fact the ones we've been working toward.

(Marketing manager)

Preventing *switching, increasing cross-selling,* and *decreasing waiting times* for new customers were thus the key formal goals, according to the marketing manager, something that Mary and Barbara agreed on.

The FLEs participating in the project had a similar, but less detailed, understanding of the formal goals of the project. When asked about what they believed to be the aim of the project, a typical answer was that the CICV aimed at 'reducing drop-outs and demortgaging'. Minimizing 'demortgaging' means preventing the customer going to a competitor. In the vocabulary of relationship marketing theory, this entails preventing customers from switching. One major way to do this, according to several FLEs, is to sell the customer services over and above the FI's core service, which is home loans. As one of the FLEs put it: 'Additional sales strengthen the relationship with the customer'. Another FLE put it like this: 'The aim of CICV was to achieve additional sales of insurances and savings products, for instance. [In this way] . . . we put ourselves on display to the customer, quite simply. That leads to relationship creation'. Reducing 'drop-outs' means preventing prospective customers from leaving the FI to go to a competitor during the loan application process. Many FLEs felt that this had become more commonplace in recent times because the customer, as one of the FLEs put it, 'shops around these days for home loans the same way that they shop around for cell phones'.

However, the fundamental but more informal rationale of the project, at least from the manager's perspective, was, as project leader Mary said, to turn 'passive order clerks into proactive salesmen and women' or as Barbara put it, 'the FLEs were supposed to be more proactive, the FLEs were supposed to envisage calling the customer, assuming greater responsibility for the entire credit review process, I would say'. Barbara continued like this:

We thought that perhaps a lot of FLEs are order clerks or were order clerks. Yes, kind of when an application came in now, I'll take care of that. And then you did you paperwork and what you were supposed to do and then you sent all that stuff out to the customer beautifully honed now. And then that was that and, wow, now there's a new application so I'll take that and do the very same thing with it.

(Barbara, associate project leader)

The fact that the project was supposed to change the FLEs' ways of perceiving themselves as FLEs was not understood at the outset by the bulk of the FLEs. Or, expressed differently, from the FLEs' position, it was hard to understand, from the outset, the more fundamental effects which organizational change programs informed by relationship marketing discourse aim to accomplish, simply because few of the FLEs had heard about relationship marketing previously, and even fewer had understood the managerial rationality that this regime of government was promoting.

Organizing for Confessions

In order to make the FLEs work more in line with the rationality of proactivity embedded in relationship marketing discourse, project leaders Mary and Barbara, together with one complete work team consisting of 12 FLEs and one team leader, who had been transferred from normal duties for six months, began working on developing relationship marketing informed 'ways of working' (i.e., work practices). These 'ways of working' would ensure, as one of the FLEs put it, 'that existing customers are cared for . . . and that customers stop switching to competitors'. The FLEs were not instructed in detail about how to work but, as Mary points out, and as was pointed out previously, 'they knew that the goal was to reduce drop-outs and demortgaging'. The project leaders were supported by a managerial body of senior managers which consisted, among others, of the marketing and sales managers of the FI. As Mary put it, 'management was involved in framing what was important for the company in order to be able to achieve results and what was important for the customers in order to retain our market position'. These frames were derived from the managers' interpretation of the quality surveys (see Chapter 5) and their understanding of the new and stiffer market situation (see Chapter 3).

Barbara describes the work of the group thus: 'Work was very concrete. We produced call lists. Which questions do you put to the customer and in which way? If you get this answer, how do you continue . . . In the end, it was all about selling more loans, of course. The aim was proactivity.' The role of the project leaders, according to themselves, was to support the FLEs in creating ways of working informed by proactivity. This is corroborated by the FLEs who described the role of the project leaders as 'supporting' and 'facilitating' the work, but not dictating or directing the specific tasks. Of the project leaders, one of the FLEs said: '[The project leaders often said] yes but no, that's not exactly what we meant, what do you say about doing it like this. Maybe you can use a flowchart to describe your interaction with the customer'. Thus, the project leaders tried to get the FLEs to develop ways of working that were informed by the rationality of relationship marketing, but without explicitly ordering them to do so.

The formal organization of the project can be analyzed, by drawing on the notion of pastoral power, in the following way: The project leaders can be perceived as pastors, trying to guide and lead the FLEs toward a proactive way of working. The FLEs can be perceived as the flock of sheep needing to adapt its subjectivity to the ethic of proactivity. Lurking in the background are the high priests, in the managerial body. The high priests seldom enter the story in person, but nevertheless manage the situation by relying on the decrees they send with the pastors and by means of their 'bible', in terms of the IWHY booklet analyzed in Chapter 4. It is the upper management, for instance, that has found out, through its interpretation of the FLEs' 'interaction' with their customers (or God?), an interpretation that has been made by relying on a special medium (in the present case, quality surveys) that proactivity is the ethic that the sheep should strive toward. Pastoral power manages by means of people believing in the ethic governing the social domain it refers to: in this case, the proactive ethic regulating the relationship between the company—especially the FLEs— and the customer. However, in order to realize the rationality it promotes, pastoral power is dependent on the confessions of the sheep revealing information to the pastors, which these can then draw on to manage the sheep. Let us turn to how such avowals were organized within the framework of the relationship marketing project.

Confessing Deviations from Proactivity

Judging from interviews with project management and seven members of the project group, it seems as if the pastoral power advocated to accomplish change has spurred confessions. The FLEs in the group avowed that they had previously interacted with the customer in a way that was not beneficial to the FI and that they needed to change their behavior and ways of thinking about customer relationships. It is possible to interpret these confessions as being colored by the rationality of relationship marketing and, more particularly, by the rationality of proactivity. The general theme in the confessions of the FLEs is that they have behaved reactively and that, in future, they would need to behave more proactively. One of the FLEs said: 'Through our discussions within the group, it became evident that many of us had experienced that customers whom we didn't contact directly after they'd applied for a loan often chose another bank when we eventually contacted them . . . we realized that this wasn't beneficial to us'. Another FLE held a similar position; 'the discussion in the group made me realize that some customers actually change banks . . . help, this won't work, you have to take care of the ones you have. That's the best way to make money'. The project members also shared some experiences. For example: 'They [the customers] call us and say, we've chosen another bank. Then you're just like, no. That's not good for us. Really it isn't. Then we've felt that we have to take care of the existing customers so they don't disappear and maybe get in touch with them a few times and hold on to them . . . That, we discussed in the group' (FLE). A colleague corroborated: 'We realized that we had to take care of it the whole way. We can't just sell stuff and then let things be, because then we won't have any customers left. I mean that we can't just issue loads of loans and leave it at that. I mean, that's not what we make money on. We earn money as long as they're still with us. That's how it is'. Another FLE pointed out that the project made her realize that 'maybe the customers expect slightly better treatment once they've been customers for a while. We've been bad at that but now we're on our way'. One FLE summarizes the experiences of the project members well: 'The customers probably don't stay with us long. They switch'.

Accordingly, the FLEs confessed and avowed that they had lost many customers during the application process. They also agreed that this was bad for business. The FLEs thus realized that they needed to work differently. Implicitly, they acknowledged that the proactive 'way of working', fostering long-lasting relationships with the customer, was something to strive toward. Thus, the managerial rationality of relationship marketing governed their confessions. That this reflects how the FLEs actually worked during the project is corroborated by Mary:

> They got the opportunity to go through their way of working . . . how to make sure of holding onto your customers for longer, how to cut down the time spent on the phone to customers we're interested in, for instance . . . They were given a series of different duties and then they had to sit down and produce ways of working for each respective part—or process you could say, work process. So they went through their ways of working, benchmarked with other companies, and looked at how to make the customer stay put. Who, internally, is best at keeping the customer the longest? Who brings in most customers that lead to loans being issued? And so on. And then they looked at the way of working. How can we make it better and more efficient? How do you talk to the customer on the phone? How can you close the deal? How can you catch the customer who has been a customer for a while and who maybe wants to borrow more or has some other need? How can you be proactive and make suggestions for improvements? And not be passive and wait for the customer to get in touch and so on.
>
> (Mary, project leader)

Barbara follows a similar kind of reasoning: 'The feeling I get now when I think back is . . . that the members of that group became more aware of our ways of working . . . and began to understand why we do certain things and why we really shouldn't do other things from the company's point of view. [They] became more focused on the fact that here it's really sales that count. I can be nice but still sell' (Barbara, associate project leader).

In summary, the FLEs confessed that their current way of working was not optimal. These confessions and the understanding of 'optimal' were framed by the managerial rationality of relationship marketing.

Developing Proactive Subject Positions by Developing New Ways of Working

Informed by these insights, the FLEs developed new ways of working which centered upon their interaction with the customers. Furthermore, these new ways of working focused on the substance of the conversation and what types of phone calls that were supposed to be made. The new ways of working were described by Mary thus: 'In order to hold onto customers, they [the FLEs] realized that they needed to call them up and make them offers . . . [and] that they needed to ask questions in a different way than when the customers called them up'. Thus, the FLEs needed to change what they did—calling up as well as being called up—and how they did it—i.e. approaching the customers differently and asking them different questions when calling them up. The quote from Mary has a pastoral power ring to it. The FLEs 'realized' that their true 'calling' was 'calling' the customers rather than being 'called' by them. No longer were they passively able to sit and wait for the customers to call them, as had previously been the case. Calling up implied a different way of interacting with the customers. Barbara describes the process of realization thus:

> The FLEs themselves thought there were shortcomings in their ways of working and, kind of thing, were able to say; yes, but I don't understand why I don't get as many applications as you get which go all the way to payment. And then they began . . . "ok, is that the way you work". "So you ring the customer at that point". "And I've never done it like that". The ideas were in the minds of the FLEs themselves. They were curious about improving their figures and stuff. So maybe the ideas came from both directions.
>
> (Barbara, associate project leader)

The last sentence is particularly interesting. Arguing that 'the ideas came from both directions', meaning that the ideas about how to develop the organization along the lines of relationship marketing came from both the managers / pastors and the FLEs / sheep. By systematically reviewing their ways of working, the FLEs understood that something was wrong. But they only understood that something was wrong in relation to the norms of relationship marketing, which the managers were responsible for delineating. Thus, the quote nicely summarizes the point that the flock of sheep develops new ways of working governed by the discourse of relationship marketing, as understood by the managers. The quote indicates, furthermore, that the FLEs had understood what the rationality of relationship marketing was all about and that they were able to manage themselves in accordance with this rationality.

This interpretation is corroborated by an inquiry into the new ways of working that the FLEs had developed. Firstly, the substance of the ways of working concerned customer interaction, which is in line with the rationality of relationship marketing as expressed in academic discourse (see preceding). More precisely, the relationship marketing discourse made the FLEs focus on the types of questions that the customers are supposed to be asked and how these questions are to be asked. The new way of asking questions that they had developed was supposed to encourage a proactive attitude during the customer interaction, as exemplified by several FLEs. 'We realized that . . . we needed to ask questions that establish what needs the customers have . . . is this a customer for us? If so . . . how can we help the customer in a beneficial way? . . . We made checklists of how to work this way . . . it then became obvious that we needed to be more active with the customers'. Again, it is interesting to note that the FLEs 'realized' that they were not behaving in the most appropriate way as if they had been struck by an insight from a higher power. Another FLE corroborates the impression that asking questions lay at the center of the new ways of working:

> Part of the work was about coordinating, as a list, what you were able to ask the customer . . . When, for instance, the customer calls, it's a matter of determining his or her needs and checking if he or she is a customer for us and what he or she wants—determining with questions whether it's a rejection or whether it's a customer we can move forward with . . . So that we can make sure that, yes, this is a customer for us.
>
> (FLE)

All the FLEs from the project group I interviewed described the new ways of working by referring to the questions that were asked and how these questions were asked. Hence, the relationship marketing project at the FI led to new and more proactive ways of working being established and proactive subject positions being outlined. 'Via the CICV project, some very proactive things emerged' the team leader associated with the project concluded.

Being a Proactive Subject in the Relationship Marketing Sense

Some of the FLEs adapted themselves to the new ways of working and became more proactive as an effect of the CICV project. Barbara believed that 'they all changed themselves. Not all of them changed themselves extensively, but all of them moved and some of them did so extensively'. The change in subjectivity that Barbara had noted was also referred to by some of the FLEs. 'Now I assume responsibility and call up the customers who have made a loan application and ask if they have any questions . . . previously I never did that' said one FLE, displaying a proactive subjectivity. One of her colleagues makes a similar statement, saying that 'now we call the customer up already when he or she has been granted the possibility to have a loan with us'. Indeed, as an overall effect of the CICV project, most of the FLEs seem to call up the customers more without having been called up by the customer in the first place, or without having been ordered to do so by management. Previously, most of the FLEs called up the customers very seldom, partly because of time constraints and partly because of their reactive "order clerk" mindset. Thus, the CICV project seems to have encouraged the FLEs to take the initiative more often in the customer interface than previously. One of the FLEs summarizes well how he interacts with his customers to create long-lasting relationships with them, as inspired by the CICV project:

> It can start with confirmation being given to the customer: 'Hi, I'm AA and I'm the one who has received your application and I'll be your caseworker from here on. You can expect a decision by tomorrow at the latest.' All the time monitoring the status with the customer; 'your loan has been approved, you'll get the papers tomorrow'. You contact the customer when the papers have been returned and tell them that the postal service has worked ok and that everything has been filled out correctly. 'Payment will be made to your account tomorrow at 11.00'. It can be a matter of monitoring purchase customers maybe within two months of them buying their house. Asking them if the move went ok and asking if they've decorated, asking if they're satisfied with the FI. So it's small, small things that create a good relationship with the customer.
>
> (FLE)

This FLE clearly states that he gives the customer a lot of information and attention, which the customer does not specifically ask for but which the FLE thinks the customer needs, thus displaying a proactive attitude. Several interviews also suggest that the FI, and in particular the FLEs, is more active in the after market as an effect of the CICV project. Several of the FLEs now make what they refer to as post-sales calls, following completion of the CICV project. This entails, a few months after a loan has been issued to a customer, calling that customer up and asking if he or she is satisfied with the service received and if she or he requires any other services from the FI. The previous quote indicates that the FLE sees post-sales calls as a part of normal customer interaction. Another FLE explains: 'Now I make post-sales calls and check how they [the customers] thought it went . . . post-sales calls [entail] calling up a customer one to two months after they've moved into their house. And just by calling and saying; "Hi, have things gone ok, was there anything you thought wasn't so good" you can learn from that and ask if they need anything else'. One of her colleagues explains that a relationship approach to customer interaction implies offering the customer service in addition to just providing them with a mortgage alone: 'We have to, so to speak, catch the customer at an early stage. We have to be able to offer the customer additional services over and above purely a housing loan in that case'. This business of offering customers additional services was alluded to by both managers and FLEs as a means of strengthening the customer relationship because it would be harder for the customers, they believed, to quit a relationship that had many ties. Says one FLE: 'If a customer uses a lot of our services, it'll be difficult for him or her to switch, more awkward kind of thing'. The relationship marketing project and the other service marketing initiatives—e.g. the service and market orientation program, the measurement of service quality and the coaching—seem to have furthered a customer care way of being which is more proactive. One FLE remarks: 'The [CICV] project created a new way of thinking . . . a new mindset'. Some statements by the FLEs indicate that the proactive way of being fosters a virtuous circle. Because proactive FLEs spend more time on the phone with their customers, compared to their reactive counterparts, and because time spent on the phone with the customers, if we are to believe many of the FI's FLEs at least, strengthens the relationship with the customers, proactive behavior cultivates stronger and longer-lasting relationships. One FLE explains: 'It's shown itself to be the case that if you spend a lot of time on the phone, then you'll also be talking a lot to people and with a lot of customers and you'll also be creating a relationship with the customer which makes it difficult for that customer to choose another lender'.

Indeed, it almost seems as though many of the FLEs are relieved that management has finally taken caring for current customers seriously. Some interviews suggest that, for a long time, the FLEs had wanted to do this but that they had previously received no support from management. Even though this has not been explicitly stated, I still get the impression that the FLEs thought that the way the existing customers have been treated in the past has been unnatural (cf. Dibb and Meadows 2001) and that some FLEs have been a bit embarrassed about the low level of customer care on offer to existing customers. One of the FLEs on the relationship marketing project argues: 'The CICV project was all about taking care of existing customers, to make us better at that. We've talked about that previously but it never really came to anything. Now it's finally happened! The relationship marketing project has led to the realization that you always have to take care of what [customers] you have'. Another FLE describes one of the previous organizational structures of the FI where the customers were initially referred to FLEs working on the 'customer front', as it was called, and then, if they really were interested in applying for a home loan—e.g. not just making general inquiries, they would be referred to the caseworkers. The FLE argues that this way of treating customers was bad from a customer relationship point of view. Such a way of working is more aligned with efficient task completion and thus with a bureaucratic way of organizing (cf. Korczynski 2002). In the FLE's own words:

Answer: Customer front it was called. Mostly, we just sat there taking incoming calls, talking about this and that, we never got into details with the customer, instead just passing that on to the caseworkers later. It was rather clumsily thought out, I think, abusing the customer like that: create a relationship first and then start on a new one right after that.

Question: But isn't that function gone now?

Answer: Yes, it is. Now, we work more with getting the customer directly and being able to help him or her from beginning to end.

(FLE)

Resisting the Proactive Subject Position

As Chapters 3 and 4 suggest, it gradually became clear to many of the FLEs, from 2002 onward, that an exclusive focus on efficiency, and the reactive FLE subjectivity that such a focus fostered, was unattainable. Rather, many came to believe that a more customer oriented position, infused with the rationality of proactivity, was needed, even though the FLEs did not always use the word proactivity explicitly. Thus, many FLEs had a positive attitude toward the change initiatives that management had initiated. Most of them had, for instance, learned the hard way that the FI was losing business to its competitors. Many FLEs believed that, if the FI were to continue like that, then they might lose their jobs. Indeed, two smaller customer service centers that had been established during the boom in the housing market, during the first years of the 21st century, had already closed by the time I was conducting my study. The only one remaining was the main customer service office where I carried out my empirical work. Therefore, all of the FLEs taking part in the relationship marketing project approached it with enthusiasm, with many of them also taking part in developing the proactive ways of working.

However, approximately half of the group on the relationship marketing project resisted working in accordance with the new ways of working and quit the project half-way through. Mary explains: ' . . . when some of the group members realized that these [the new ways of working] were being demanded of them, things got very, very tough for some of them'. Barbara argues in a similar manner: 'We [including the FLEs] were also supposed to change ourselves or our ways of working during the project. Not everyone took that into account.' Thus, as the previous analysis has suggested, the FLEs confessed that their current ways of working were reactive, that this way of working was not ideal, and they developed more proactive subject positions or 'ways of working', as they were referred to. However, when they realized that proactivity was being demanded of them, or putting it another way, when they realized what proactive behavior demanded of them—e.g. calling customers up without the customers having made the first move, asking questions differently, taking charge of the phone call, and selling the customers services that they had never explicitly asked for—things became 'tough for them', as Mary put it, or at least for some of them. These FLEs resisted the CICV project and adapted their subjectivity very little to the proactivity prescribed to them by relationship marketing discourse; this was exemplified by one FLE who said, 'I chose to drop out of the project after a while. I couldn't see how it could improve the handling process'. Another of the FLEs who worked with written communication, for instance, said: 'I was working with those templates [for written communication] and felt enough is enough, actually. [I] never really understood how it would contribute toward the real work'.

The resistance relating to the rationality of relationship marketing revolved around the suggested new ways of interacting with the customers. Some of the FLEs, for instance, refused to use the templates that had been developed to guide the customer interaction. One of the FLEs taking part in developing them said: 'Ok. What shall I say about them [the call templates]. Yes, I've looked at them, what they look like of course and stuff, but I don't use them'. Another FLE, in relation to the templates, said: 'You also have to have a bit of a personal touch during it [the customer interaction], I think'. Even Mary admitted 'that one of the risks of implementing call templates is that you lose some of the personal touch'. One FLE not taking part in the project, when talking about the new and more structured way of interacting with the customers emerging from the project, argues. 'We're a bit different. I like to be a bit relaxed. I'm not too [hits table with hand to indicate structured] rigid on the phone. You always have sport to talk about, or some football match. The boss doesn't always like that'. The FLEs are not supposed to talk about sport, but to lead the discussion away from such issues toward home mortgages and the other services offered, in order to behave in a proactive manner. Mary gives her view of the reasons for the resistance:

> Answer: You have to call [the customer]. You can't sit and wait for the customer to call you in 3 years' time, instead you call the customer today—to get the customer to stay with you, you have to start making calls, you have a concrete offer but you have to make calls. When this was realized—together with the fact that you need to ask questions when the customer calls you in a different way than previously—it [the relationship marketing project] became incredibly frightening [to the FLEs]. It was really difficult for them. It was they who defined the new ways of working. But, as the [consequences of the new ways of working] developed, it became extremely difficult for them.
>
> Question: Can you exemplify the questions they were required to ask?
>
> Answer: Yes, it was: "what can we help you with". That simple . . . just that caused half of them to protest. Just a simple thing like asking a question.

According to Foucauldian management scholars, resistance to a particular managerial discourse is mobilized via other available countervailing discourses and it is especially likely to arise when discourses make contesting claims vis-à-vis subjectivity (Covaleski et al. 1998; Quist et al. 2007). It is possible to interpret the resistance of some FLEs toward relationship marketing at the FI on the basis of this reasoning. Relationship marketing offers the FLEs subject positions as proactive FLEs, whereas the institutionalized bureaucratic discourse at the FI fosters reactive subjects. Many FLEs found it possible to balance these claims. But the resisting FLEs were unable to do so. In order to relax what to them appeared as competing and confusing claims, they retreated to their subjectivity colored by the bureaucratic discourse discussed in Chapter 3. They refused to lead themselves reflexively toward the proactive subject position inherent in relationship marketing discourse.

Thus, rather than developing the organization along the lines of the rationality of relationship marketing, Mary found herself comforting angry and disappointed co-workers: 'They sat and cried and were really mad. So most of my energy went into sitting down and talking with them one-to-one to get them to understand why there are reorganizations like these. We more or less had to put the project on ice for a while just to confront this anger which was probably based, I assume, on fear'. This quote illustrates that Mary acted as a pastor and as an agent of pastoral power, because pastors do not force their will on others. Rather, they rely on making their sheep happy, and really try to make them go the right way.

RELATIONSHIP MARKETING AS DISCIPLINARY POWER

According to sales manager David, the common way of introducing relationship marketing is by first acquiring a CRM IT system, implementing it, and then making the employees work in accordance with it. However, FI management was reluctant to start by acquiring a CRM system and associated customer database. Doing that, according to David, would have 'forced' the FLEs to work according to 'the proactivity and customer care built into such systems'. Instead, management thought it would be better to introduce relationship marketing the other way round, i.e. involving the FLEs in developing 'new ways of working' contingent upon relationship marketing rationality and based on that developing the CRM system. As I have suggested in the previous section, this way of introducing relationship marketing can be analyzed and understood by drawing on Foucault's notion of pastoral power. Seen from that perspective, the managers are pastors who invoke confessions from the employees that are framed by the managerial rationality of proactivity embedded in relationship marketing discourse. The confessions make the employees understand that they have not really been working in the best possible way with customer relationships; that is, they have favored reactive approaches over proactive approaches. Guided by this understanding and supported by their pastors, they (as we saw) oriented themselves, or at least some of them did, toward proactive subject positions.

As Covaleski et al. (1998) have pointed out, pastoral power manages from 'the inside out'. It takes into account and departs from the self's image of the self. The individual is treated as a unique subject that needs special attention and treatment in order to change him- or herself in ways that are in line with the rationality governing the situation. For each and every one, the right way is individual but the goal is the same. With disciplinary power, it is different. Here, the subject is treated as an object. The individual's specific characteristics are not formative during the change process. Rather, the distance between the present subjectivity and the ideal subject positions, as given by the discourse governing the situation, is calculated as constituting the distance that needs to be transcended, or the gap that needs to be closed, if disciplinary power is to be realized. What counts is whether or not the subjects close the gap. A type of 'force', as David put it, may thus be involved in processes of disciplinary power. However, this type of force is not the same type of force that is aligned with sovereign power. The person is thus not being forced to do things against his or her will by a power holder, but is forced to act and be otherwise by the power inherent in a truth that has been generated in accordance with a positivistic logic: that is, a truth that corresponds to empirical reality and, as such, has the power to distinguish between actions that are right and wrong.

Acquiring a CRM system before the employees, through the operation of pastoral power, have been persuaded that the rationality of relationship marketing is something to aspire to, or merely introducing such a system without applying pastoral power at all, can, as the conceptual analysis in the first section of the chapter suggests, be analyzed as and understood by relying on the notion of disciplinary power. Indeed, this was the route that the FI embarked on. One effect of the resistance toward the new ways of working, explains Mary, was that 'we had to skip the original plan'. Thus, rather than proceeding in accordance with pastoral power and convincing and allowing all the FLEs of the FI to convince themselves that relationship marketing was the right way for the FI to go, from the point when several members of the project group dropped out of the project and returned to their regular work, the sole focus of the remaining members of the project group, as well as the new members who were added to it, was to develop the CRM system. Mary says: 'When it was finished, we implemented the system throughout the organization. Slowly but surely, they [the FLEs] started to adjust their ways of working to fit in with the system . . . today, everyone works in accordance with it and thinks it's very good'. If we are to believe Mary, the disciplinary power inherent in the FI CRM system—referred to as the Customer Care System (CCS)—influenced the FLEs' ways of working extensively.

Development of the CRM System

The FLEs and managers involved in the relationship marketing project all argued that the CRM system was the major outcome of the project. One of the FLEs put it like this: 'The entire project was about how to keep our customers. There was a lot more than the system; call templates, the web, yes there really was a whole lot, but at the end of the day it was just this system that emerged, it feels like'. Another FLE emphasized the same point: 'The CCS was one of the major things that emerged and it works very smoothly when you contact a customer'. The managers emphasized that the CCS was based on ways of working that had been developed during the first 'pastoral' part of the project and that it had proactivity built into it. Project leader Mary, for instance, argues that: 'The foundation was the new ways of working and then we built the system on that. We developed the ways of working first and then the . . . work processes. Then we built the CCS on that . . . Proactivity was built into the system . . . the system suggests measures contributing toward additional sales and customer loyalty'.

None of the FLEs involved in developing the CCS mentions the notion of proactivity. Accordingly, they do not say that the goal of the project was to make them more proactive. However, proactivity at the FI, as has been noted previously, is a notion primarily used by managers. Many of the FLEs say that the system was supposed to foster additional sales, and most of the FLEs associated proactivity with additional sales, but did not give a formal definition of proactivity. Several of the FLEs argued that the CCS aimed to facilitate additional sales, indirectly suggesting, hence, that the system was designed to foster proactivity. One of the FLEs, for example, argued: 'It was important to build additional sales into the CCS'. Consistent with the conceptual analysis in the first section of this chapter, additional sales, according to the FLEs, were encouraged by the CRM system creating a summarizing image of the customer they were interacting with: 'We created a new system that links up several systems so that we can see everything about a customer in one place, the CCS we call it'. Another FLE asserted: 'We can see everything about the customer in one place as opposed to before when we had to jump into several different systems to look for various things. It was a matter of having everything gathered together in one place in order to simplify additional sales'. The team leader who took part in the development of the new system also emphasized this summarizing picture:

> We've produced an entirely new CCS, which is linked up to all the other systems and exactly all the groups have obtained this now. And it's really good. You can be in one system and if you want to move to the credit system, you just click on a button and it takes you there. Everything goes via one system. The customer enters his or her civil registration number when calling and then his or her entire business relationship with us appears on our screens. We didn't have that before.
>
> (Team leader)

The CRM system at the FI thus seems to be designed to provide the FLEs with the information they need to focus on the important existing and potential ties which the FI has with its customers. As the preceding conceptual disciplinary power analysis of a typical CRM system suggests, it seems to be designed with the intention of directing the FLEs' attention toward acting proactively by creating more ties with the customer, in this way strengthening customer relationships.

That the system creates a shared picture of the customer was also pointed out by Mary who drew attention to the fact that the CCS automatically logs all incoming calls (the latter also was alluded to by some FLEs). Mary says, 'the CCS kind of links up these systems so that you get a more coordinated picture of the customer in one and the same system. You can get to the systems via the CCS and you get an entirely different logging of the customer too. All phone calls are logged automatically'. The latter facilitated the FLEs' interaction with their customers, as one FLE said: 'Something that we also emphasized a lot [when the system was being developed] was that a lot of people call and say that they talked to someone. Who was that someone? They could never tell us. Now all calls are logged so you can see who they've been talking to'. This is also alluded to by another FLE who also argues that the system makes it easier for one FLE to pick up a conversation with a customer at the point where another FLE has left off, increasing the level of customer service.

> An experience we used as a departure point was that return calling customers can never remember who they've talked to. But now when customers call us, the call is logged. It's X who's talked to the customer so then I can make a note there about what I talked to the customer about, a notification for example. So that you can see, yes it was X you talked to last time, as well as what they talked about.
>
> (FLE)

The Disciplinary Power of CRM Systems in Practice

One FLE whom I asked whether or not the CCS was used by the FLEs said: 'Everybody uses it'. Another FLE put it like this: 'We do everything relevant to customer communication in the CCS as soon as we've finished with the credit review in the CRS'. Several FLEs argued that 'you should conduct all contact with the customer via the CCS. You can email or send a SMS to the customer. Then, other administrators [FLEs] will have access to this communication. It's open'. Another FLE, when asked if he had started working with the system yet or if it was too early, said: 'Oh yes, I do work with it. Absolutely . . . I worked with an Excel layout and a loose sheet system for my customers previously. But now there are systems where we do the work'. Team leader John, however, argued that not all the FLEs had started to use the system, during my interview with him (2006–04–03) when the system was still quite new. It was still possible to take and make calls outside of the system, even though the FLEs were supposed to do all that within the system so that the traffic would be logged. John said: 'You make calls via the system because then it'll be logged adequately . . . a few of the customer representatives [FLEs] still neglect to do this'. The interviews with the FLEs were conducted up to one and a half years later, which indicates that the CCS was in more widespread use at the end of the data collection period.

The major benefit of the system for them, most of the FLEs argued, was that they got an overview of the customers calling in. They also argue that it is this overview that contributes toward strengthening the customer relationship. The system contributes toward making the work easier, strengthening the customer relationship at the same time. One FLE argued thus: 'I really think that it [the CSS] strengthens the customer relationship. They [the customers] are impressed that you already have an entire picture on the screen of the objects that are mortgaged . . . yes, that's really provide the basis for good customer support'. Another FLE made a similar point:

> Question: Someone has said that this is to be used to strengthen the relationship with the customer. Is that something you've heard too?
>
> Answer: Of course it does.
>
> Question: How does that work?
>
> Answer: Exactly that you see everything at once. The customers get really impressed when they call and all of their commitments pop up and they say it's me, my name's this and that and my loan number is this, my civil registration number is that. Yes, but listen, I say, I've got you up on the screen here. Wow. They get really impressed.
>
> (FLE)

This suggests that when the FLEs work in the system on a daily basis, which most of them seem to do, their interaction with the customers is structured by the proactive managerial rationality built into it. This is because, based on the information that the CCS provides, the FLEs anticipate what the customers need, without the customers mentioning it. The disciplinary power of the system thus orders the actions and behaviors of the FLEs, at the customer interface, in ways suggested by the preceding conceptual analysis. More particularly, many of the FLEs emphasize that they use the system to plan their interaction with their customers. They also argue that the system gives them the complete history of interaction with the customer, which they draw on during their current interaction. In addition, they also believe that it helps them to carry out their administrative work. One FLE says, thus: 'Yes, the new CCS is really good. People call in and you can make notes to help you remember what you talked about and what the customer's wishes were, what type of customer it was.' Another FLE corroborates this:

If a customer calls us, I can see in the system who it is that's calling. Also, there are links to other systems which I can easily look in. I have templates for letters which I use. I can also register when he calls and then I can write up what we talked about, a notification for instance, then that information will be there next time. And that's really clever because a lot of customers forget about what and to whom they talked. In the system, I can see that you talked with such and such a person and this was what you talked about. So it's actually really very good. And I can see there, kind of thing, if there's a customer I have to call up, who isn't using our services. So it's really clever.

(FLE)

The CRM system thus seems to frame the interaction of the FLEs with their customers. As such, the system orders, at least partly, the actions and thoughts of the FLEs at the customer interface and thus their ways of being FLEs. As do all forms of disciplinary power, this seems to subjectify the FLEs by objectifying them. The FLEs also talk about additional features of the system which they use a lot in order to organize their day-to-day work and which strengthen the disciplinary power interpretation. Several FLEs emphasize the possibility of adding alerts to the system, in this way allowing themselves to be supervised by the system.

Question: What is an alert?

Answer: It could be that you have to call a customer in a week or so or that a customer is taking possession. Taking possession occurs on a rolling basis each month. Via the system, we can keep a check so that we don't miss anybody. Previously, these events were sorted in order just lying in a pile, but now the system reminds me when the time is approaching, so that I don't forget.

(FLE)

It would thus seem as if the CRM system has affected the FLEs in ways that were intended, i.e. that is has made the FLEs focus more on relationship building and maintenance. The CCS has contributed, together with the coaching and the relationship marketing project, toward creating a more equal balance between the reactive subject and the proactive subject positions identified by the disciplinary power of service quality measurement. This is an interpretation that managers definitely agree on. One manager says: 'We've implemented the CCS for all the FLEs. There, we've definitely changed our way of working for the better then, or so that it'll be simpler and easier for everybody really'.

But the CRM system is not just something that the FLEs can use voluntarily. Work orders can be fed into the system, which the FLEs then become responsible for carrying out. The marketing manager put it like this.

Customer data is linked together using the CCS which means that you see customers with certain needs in the system. For example, the marketing department sees that 300 customers have to be called up because they sent in a coupon. Then, we enter those 300 customers into the CCS so that everybody can see them. Here you have 300 customers to call. The customer center divides them up and how they do that is not down to us. But we do make sure that they get the supportive data at the right time and for the right customer etc. Then, it's up to them to implement and respond and then it's up to us to check that things went ok. How many services did we sell to these 300 customers?

(Marketing manager)

One FLE reflects on the practice of putting work orders into the system thus: 'when an attractive customer segment has been detected, the marketing department might put work orders into the system saying: "these customers need to be offered a particular service. Call them about home insurance, for instance, because they don't seem to have any"'. The work orders might be fed into the system for anyone to act upon, as indicated by the marketing manager, but they might also be given to a particular person. Managers found this new possibility interesting. One manager notes: 'When you log on to the CCS in the morning, you get a what-to-do list. This might entail offering customers payment protection insurances or sending loan documents, or anything at all. This offers us new follow-up possibilities'. The last sentence is interesting. The performance of the individual FLEs is benchmarked against the performance of other FLEs, creating pressure and competitiveness—and fostering disciplinary power. The marketing manager again:

Answer: Yes. The system serves very many different purposes really; in part, measuring what people manage to sell. Because, if the marketing department has noticed a customer several times and this customer still doesn't have home insurance, loan protection etc, etc, then you can ask yourself how do you [meaning the individual FLEs] work, kind of thing. Here we have several customers who you've been tasked with selling to but who don't yet have any of our products. Why?

Question: Where another FLE has succeeded in that case.

Answer: Yes, when another FLE has succeeded and here you are not selling anything. Then you can take a look at . . . , is this product being sold the right way. We've been given completely different possibilities of following things up which we've started using in earnest.

(Marketing manager)

Analyzed from the perspective of disciplinary power, the CCS turns the FLE into an object and, more particularly, an object that is supposed to sell home loans and other services. Based on data about the results of sales retrieved from the CCS, the marketing department, as the marketing manager suggests, relates the performance of each individual employee to the mean of all FLEs, picturing the aggregated result as a steep or flat normal distribution curve. This exercise will reveal which of the FLEs have been performing above average, on average, and below average, as well as how far from the average the outliers are. Detecting such gaps between the normal and the abnormal is a key feature of disciplinary power. Accordingly, the marketing department, in ways discussed in the preceding conceptual analysis, uses the system to generate the norm that the disciplinary power promised by the system governs in relation to. Based on this knowledge, managerial initiatives are taken. The weak performers need to be corrected and this is done, for example, via the coaching activities described in the previous chapter. The strong performers can be treated as role models. Several team leaders, for instance, say that they draw inspiration from the strong performers when trying to correct the weak performers. The manager of the customer care center alludes to how the CCI is used to foster these disciplinary means:

> We've developed a customer support system, which is really good . . . It's been outlined, designed, and created by my co-workers here, so it's user-friendly. We're currently expanding it now to make it even better and even more personal toward the customers when they call. We handle the supportive data and facts that the system gives us about the employees in order to work with them in another way than previously.
>
> (Customer care center manager)

In conclusion, the disciplinary power of the CCS and, more particularly, the proactive rationality built into it, order the actions and thoughts of the FLEs at the customer interface and thus their subjectivities as FLEs. The CCS does so by making the FLEs focus on the important customer ties and by means of the possibility of entering work orders into the system. But the CCS should not just be perceived as a form of disciplinary power that fosters a movement toward a proactive subjectivity, it should also be perceived as a means of checking who deviates from the norm of proactivity and who does not, via the feedback it provides the marketing department with.

THE PROACTIVE SUBJECT REVISITED

In this chapter, I have analyzed, conceptually and empirically, relationship marketing discourse and practices by drawing on the notions of disciplinary and pastoral power. The conceptual analysis of academic relationship marketing discourse has positioned relationship marketing as a form of power/knowledge that promotes the managerial rationality of proactivity.

The conceptual analysis has also suggested that the strategic management approaches put forward in the relationship marketing literature can be perceived as practices of pastoral power, whereas the conceptual analysis of the texts on CRM systems perceived these systems to be promoting disciplinary power. The empirical analysis of the relationship marketing project at the FI was well in line with the conceptual analysis. More specifically, it suggested that the project management, during the first phase of the project, which involved a group of FLEs in coming up with ways of working contingent on the rationality of relationship marketing, was acting like pastors. Managers were also guiding and leading the FLEs toward the proactivity embedded in the relationship marketing discourse, based on the confessions the FLEs had made. The latter can thus be positioned as sheep that also guided themselves, to some extent, toward the ethic of proactivity. But the analysis also indicated that some FLEs resisted the new and proactive ways of working. Therefore, managers changed their tactics and implemented the CRM system that had been developed—the CCS—without first having introduced the rationality of relationship marketing, in a pastoral fashion, to the rest of the employees. In the analytical language applied here, they changed their tactics from pastoral to disciplinary. The analysis of the disciplinary effect of the CCS indicates that the FLEs were framed by the proactive rationality built into it. In addition, it also suggested that the marketing department use the data to generate the norms that disciplinary power is dependent on in order to operate and to detect deviations from that norm by individual FLEs. Indeed, it seems hard for the FLEs to avoid the disciplinary power of the CCS. In addition, the chapter also indicates that the power/knowledge of the relationship marketing discourse produced the kind of customerism that the managers had hoped for: i.e. making the FLEs more proactive.

However, the chapter also indicates more ambiguous effects. Many of the FLEs and managers not only argue that the relationship marketing project and the CCS strengthened their relationship with the customers, customer oriented the firm, and made the FLEs more proactive, but also that it made their work easier, provided the customers with better services, and gave the FLEs an overview that contributed toward increasing the efficiency of the handling process. It thus seems as if the relationship marketing initiatives produced and reproduced not only the customer oriented side of the organization, but also the bureaucratic side of it. This is consistent with Korczynski's (2002) reinterpretation of the SMM literature, which argues that SMM practices not only foster customerism, but also efficiency. This theme is something we need to return to in the next and concluding chapter, which seeks to tease out the more general contribution to marketing made by the present study.

7   From Prescribing Marketing Practices to Studying Marketing as Practice

This book makes two important assumptions. The first is that the problematization of marketing management, originating from SMM quarters, has spurred the production of marketing knowledge and practices which facilitate the customer orientation of employee subjectivity rather than the production of knowledge and practices facilitating the customer orientation of products. The second assumption maintains that this problematization reproduces marketing as a managerial, positivistic, and customeristic discipline: a discipline that deflects attention from critically studying the role of marketing and SMM practices in organizations. As an effect of the problem inherent in the second assumption, this book aims to contribute toward marketing in three ways. Firstly, it aims to contribute toward an understanding of how SMM practices facilitate the customer orientation of employees—particularly FLEs—and their customer interaction. Secondly, it aims to contribute toward generating knowledge of the role of marketing in organizations more broadly. Thirdly, the book aims to contribute toward developing an alternative identity for academic marketing research.

I open this chapter by discussing the narrower implications for SMM research, and I focus, more particularly, on the role of disciplinary and pastoral power in the management of the interactive marketing function and the ordering of FLE subjectivity. I then turn to the wider implications for the marketing discipline. Departing from the fact that the marketing concept and the managerial rationality of customerism have played a key role in marketing, I relate the conceptual and empirical analysis of the SMM practices in the preceding chapters to how the marketing concept has been dealt with in previous research. This allows me to critically discuss, on the one hand, the role of marketing in organizations and, on the other, the fundamental nature of academic marketing research. It also allows me to suggest an alternative orientation for the discipline.

INTERACTIVE MARKETING IN PRACTICE

SMM has problematized and redirected marketing research. As argued in the introductory chapter, the pioneers of SMM (see, for instance,

Grönroos 1978; 1982; 1984; Shostack 1977) claimed that the practices of marketing management are insufficient for managing marketing in service firms because they foster the customer orientation of products. In service firms, it was claimed, the customer interaction of the employees constitutes an important, if not the most important, form of marketing. Therefore, marketing was in need of marketing practices that addressed what was referred to as the interactive marketing function. Or expressed differently, marketing needed to advance practices that foster the customer orientation of employee subjectivity, in addition to customer orienting products. This call for research was heard throughout the marketing community. Practices aimed at fostering the customer orientation of organizational members and their customer interaction became a major focus of SMM research, but also in other fields of marketing (Vargo and Lusch 2004). The SMM practices studied in this book—marketing and service orientation initiatives, service quality measurement technologies, coaching, and relationship marketing initiatives—constitute important examples of this orientation.

However, the specific body of knowledge—SMM—that the problematization of marketing management gave rise to does not address what I perceive to be the major problem in marketing research. Indeed, it has instead contributed toward reproducing and concealing this problem. Whereas SMM was breaking away from marketing management, when it came to realizing the customeristic managerial rationality of the marketing concept, SMM in line with marketing management departed from customerism. As argued in the opening chapter, marketing is a largely positivistic and managerially prescriptive academic discipline. Mainstream marketing research has focused on prescribing marketing practices to organizations, but not on studying marketing as a practice. Whereas this one-sided orientation, as suggested in later sections, is unproductive for the marketing discipline as a whole, it has also hampered theory development within the boundaries of SMM. Indeed, whereas the research into SMM has been very successful in generating practices for managing the interactive marketing function, not much is known about *how* the management of interactive marketing is accomplished. Therefore, I decided to study the role of SMM practices within an organization without framing my analysis using the managerial rationality of customerism.

I chose to study the FI because it has a history of drawing on SMM practices. Furthermore, I chose to illuminate the case of the FI from a Foucauldian perspective. The general reason for the latter is that a Foucauldian framework provides the opportunity to problematize SMM discourse. Indeed, Foucault's understanding of discourse, as regimes of power/knowledge, resonates with important points of departure in the SMM discourse, e.g. that the object of management is humans and their subjectivity and that the forms of knowledge produced elicit and promote subject positions. A more specific reason for the choice of analytical framework was the notion that SMM practices can be conceived of as forms of disciplinary and pastoral power. The chapters (4, 5, and 6) devoted to analyzing the SMM practices drawn on by the FI illustrate that this was a feasible idea. The conceptual and empirical analysis of service and market orientation, coaching, and relationship marketing suggest that SMM practices promote pastoral power. In particular, the analysis suggests that these practices are confessional ones that foster a certain subjectivity by positioning managers as pastors who hear confessions and the staff as a flock of sheep who confess how they work and who they are as workers. Furthermore, the analysis suggests that the pastoral care delivered by managers and the confessions of the employees are regulated by the ethic of customerism and that the knowledge of the employees generated by the confessions contributes toward making the subjectivity of the employees more customeristic by means of the managers guiding and supporting the FLEs and by means of the employees managing themselves in the direction of customerism. In addition, the conceptual and empirical analysis of customer-perceived service quality measurement technologies and relationship marketing databases suggests that SMM practices are a form of, and facilitate the operation of, disciplinary power. In particular, the analysis suggests that these practices work as examinations which generate norms of customerism and position the employees in relation to these norms; examinations which make explicit the gap between the ideal customeristic subjectivity and the present subjectivity—revealing the 'subjectivity gap' that the employee needs to transcend; and examinations which focus attention on initiatives for closing the gap between customerism and the customersitic subjectivity and the present 'abnormal' subjectivity.

Thus, the present study argues that the customer orientation and management of employees, as well as the interactive marketing function imposed by SMM practices, can be understood against the backdrop of the notions of disciplinary and pastoral power. This book has shown that the SMM practices are disciplinary and pastoral and, accordingly, that they realize customer orientation in a disciplinary and pastoral way. This knowledge provides a point of departure for studying interactive marketing in future research, for facilitating and managing interactive marketing practice, and for combating the potential, perverse power effects of interactive marketing practices. Hence, whereas the present study is able to illuminate how interactive marketing management is accomplished, it is unable to say anything about what discursive expressions interactive marketing takes. What interactive marketing is, in practice, needs to be studied in future research. In order to generate such knowledge, the actual customer interaction talk of the FLEs of interactive service firms needs to be studied via participant observation. Companies such as the FI, which offers most of their services over the phone, are excellent sites for such studies because the FLEs' customer interaction can be recorded, thus generating 'naturally occurring data' (Silverman 2006).

THE MARKETING CONCEPT AND OTHER 'MANAGEMENT CONCEPTS'

In addition to the managerial and positivistic orientation of marketing delimiting theory development within the boundaries of SMM, it also restricts marketing research as a whole. In order to shed light on this assertion, I take my point of departure in the marketing concept that was articulated in contrast to other 'management concepts', most notably the 'production' and 'selling' concepts. Many marketing scholars associate this distinction with Robert J. Keith's brief and somewhat anecdotal, but influential, article 'The Marketing Revolution' (1960). However, the distinction is also implicitly or explicitly present in other early works on the marketing concept (see, for instance, Aldersson 1957; Borsch 1957; Keith 1960; Levitt 1960; McKitterick 1957) and has been drawn on by marketing management textbook authors for a long time (Brassington and Pettitt 2000; Jobber 2004; Kotler 1967; Kotler and Keller 2006; McCarthy 1964). Phillip Kotler, for instance, has used it to explain what marketing is and to argue for the superiority of marketing over other approaches to management in the opening chapter of all 13 editions of his influential marketing textbook—*Marketing Management*—the first of which was published in 1967.

With a few notable exceptions (e.g. Aldersson 1957), the scholars and practitioners who originally articulated the marketing concept perceived it as incommensurable with, but inferior to, other 'management concepts' (see, for instance, Borsch 1957; Keith 1960; Levitt 1960; McKitterick 1957). This was also the position taken by the authors of early marketing management textbooks (see, for instance, Kotler 1967; McCarthy 1964). In this research, marketing is promoted as the universalistic solution to managerial problems of all kinds. The marketing discipline thus set out along a very uncompromising path at the beginning of the 1960s—a path that the mainstream of the discipline has been following ever since. SMM scholars have, for instance, argued that 'marketing should be positioned at the core of the firm's strategic planning' (Vargo and Lusch 2004: 14; see Grönroos 1997; Gummesson 1987; 2008 for similar positions). The practical implication of this is that the customeristic managerial rationality of marketing and the marketing concept need to dominate the management of organizations at the expense of other 'management concepts' (cf. Morgan and Sturdy 2000).

Accordingly, the marketing concept should not be perceived as a neutral 'concept' but as a regime of power/knowledge competing with other regimes of power/knowledge for hegemony in general management discourse. Whereas the marketing concept prescribes customerism to organizations and customeristic subject positions to organizational members, the production concept is aligned with the ideal type of bureaucracy prescribing high production efficiency, low costs, and mass production to organizations, and bureaucratic subject positions to employees. The selling concept holds that customers will only buy the products of a company following massive commercial campaigns which stimulate interest in that company's products, thus encouraging organizations to develop an effective sales force (see Skålén et al. 2008).

As has been argued previously in this book, the dominant position among marketing researchers is that marketing has lost this battle (Anderson 1982; Hayes and Abernathy 1980; Webster 1981; 2002). In line with Harris and Ogbonna (2003), who showed that the rationality of marketing dominated some parts of the organization they were studying, this position will be questioned in the present chapter. However, in contrast to the study of Harris and Ogbonna (2003), the present study suggests, firstly, that marketing is unlikely to dominate organizational practice and, secondly, that marketing orders organizations in ways other than those predicted by marketing research. In addition, it will be argued that the customeristic power/knowledge of the marketing concept, as well as the uncompromising relationship with the other managerial regimes it has been given, have ordered both marketing research and how marketing researchers have perceived themselves and their cause. The blinders that the marketing concept has provided marketing scholars with continue to haunt the discipline today.

THE ROLE OF MARKETING IN ORGANIZATIONS

It is against the backdrop of the alleged incommensurability between the marketing concept and other 'management concepts' that the applicability of the work of Korczynski (2002) on the customer oriented bureaucracy, introduced at the end of Chapter 3, needs to be perceived. As we remember, in a customer oriented bureaucracy the bureaucratic logic is combined with the customer orientation logic in a number of areas such as HRM. Whereas Korczynski maintains a critical distance to the managerialism of marketing, he nevertheless draws on marketing research, particularly SMM research, in order to articulate the ideal type of the customer oriented bureaucracy. The basic project of Korczynski is to combine the 'organization theory' implicit in marketing research with one of the major organization theories that has contributed toward forming organization studies, i.e. the theory of the bureaucracy. In the vocabulary of marketing, the latter can be referred to as being aligned with the 'production concept'. Translated into the language of marketing, what Korczynski argues, somewhat simplified, with his notion of the customer oriented bureaucracy, is that service firms combine the marketing and production concepts.

Combining the Marketing and Production Concepts

This book questions the argument of the alleged incommensurability between the marketing and production concepts set up in academic marketing discourse, not implicitly or by means of a conceptual discussion, as Korczynski does, but explicitly and by means of conceptual and empirical analysis. The introduction of the SMM practices at the FI, and the customerism they embed, did not replace the institutionalized bureaucratic structures of the organization, which the marketing literature would suggest. Rather, the customerism inherent in the SMM practices supplements the bureaucratic structures. Indeed, the empirical data does not indicate that there is any fundamental incommensurability between the customerism inherent in the SMM practices and the efficiency orientation of the bureaucratic practices. When I asked the FLEs questions that were colored by such an opposition existing at the FI, many of them queried the basic premise of my question. For example, when I asked the FLEs if the FI was an organization that gave priority to customer orientation or efficiency, a typical answer would be as follows:

> It's probably mixed actually. We're trying to become customer oriented and more efficient at the same time . . . If I take an example. Before, we had a customer front: a department which only met the customers and a back office function which took care of the actual credit checks and processing and all that. We changed that in 2002, I think, so that now everybody meets the customers. The customers had to have a point of contact who they could get in touch with about everything. This was a change made on the basis of the customer's needs, to make it easier for him or her. But at the same time, it was also a change that would make things more efficient as everybody would be able to do everything. They took away the time wasted when you receive the customer in order to pass it on to someone else who then calls up the customer. So this made matters easier both for ourselves and for the customer.
>
> (FLE)

This quote reminds me about Korczynski's (2002) discussion concerning the basis of the division of labor in a customer oriented bureaucracy, which combines both efficient task completion and caring for customer relationships. In a customer oriented bureaucracy, customers cannot be sent around to different employees, which the form of minute division of labor associated with bureaucracy would imply, but need to be handled with friendly efficiency by the same employee. As Korczynski points out, this requires systems support such as the credit review and CRM systems used at the FI. Two other FLEs answered the question asking whether they gave priority to customer orientation or efficiency in the following way, also indicating a combination of the rationality of customerism with that of bureaucracy. The first of them said: 'Naturally [we're focused] on doing it as well as possible for the customer . . . But when they come in with applications . . . if they exceed . . . the requirements we have, then we're a bit square'. The second FLE said: 'We adapt to the customers within certain limits, if I put it like that. But we have our basic requirements and these have to be met'. These quotes indicate that the FLEs at the FI customer orient the offering within the boundaries outlined by the bureaucratic rules. Or expressed differently, the bureaucratic rules have evolved to allow for certain forms of customerism. As the financial crisis of 2008, especially the so-called subprime market for home loans in the U.S., has taught us, it is not always customeristic to grant home loans to everyone.

In addition, the empirical material indicates that the FLEs carried out actions associated with customerism and bureaucracy simultaneously. One FLE, for instance, said: 'I always try to wrap everything up on the phone, during the conversation. You do the [loan] application by phone and print out all the documents and make everything ready on the spot. Then it just lies there waiting for the customer to find a property'. Another FLE asserted: 'I talk to the customer about this and that while feeding a few details into the credit review system [the CRS] and when I tell the customer I have a loan guarantee, they are often very surprised. Happily surprised'. These two quotes illustrate that actions associated with customerism and bureaucracy seem to be intertwined with each other. This is not to argue, however, that this combination of work rationalities is unproblematic. The empirical data suggests that the pressure could sometimes be a bit too much for the FLEs, leading to their needing to separate customer focused and bureaucratic tasks. One FLE argues: 'Sometimes, it gets too stressful. That's how it is. Then you have to turn off your phone for a while and just sit and complete one thing at a time, otherwise you'd go crazy'. Another FLE made a similar statement: 'We have the customer loop which we have to be on at certain times, there's a schedule for that. I try to be on that over and above my scheduled time as well, but sometimes I just feel that I have to turn off as I have to sort something out for a customer'. As Korczynski (2002) argues, it is a key role for the management of customer oriented bureaucracies to fashion a fragile order. But it also seems to be important for the FLEs to be able to fashion that order themselves. More importantly, because the present study suggests that customerism supplements rather than replaces the bureaucratic focus on efficiency, marketing scholars need to take the pressure this puts on employees into account when developing theory. Living in the one-dimensional world constructed by marketing scholars and dominated by one managerial rationality is far easier than living in the real world where two or several rationalities intersect.

Furthermore, the SMM practices studied seem to have both customerism and efficiency built into them. You may recall the project leader of the relationship marketing project, Mary, arguing, for instance, that the goal of the CICV project was to 'introduce a CRM system as . . . we haven't kept tabs on our customers. We haven't known whether it was an existing customer sending in an application or a new one until we've entered data into the system and then the entire process is finished. So, for existing customers, you have to do just as much work as for new ones'. From the perspective of customerism, relationship marketing is a good thing because it makes it possible to keep a check on the customers and, in doing so, they can be offered better services. But, according to Mary, relationship marketing is also good for intra-organizational efficiency. The new system saves time when handling existing customers. The conceptual analysis in the previous chapters suggests a similar interpretation, which is in line with Korczynski's (2002) assertion that both customeristic and bureaucratic criteria are embedded in SMM practices such as the gap model. Whereas the fifth and heuristic gap in the gap model, the gap between customer expectations and perceptions, addresses customerism, at least two of the four 'intra-organizational' gaps address bureaucratic issues. Gaps two and three both refer to 'service quality specifications', indicating that it is a management task to develop bureaucratic rules delineating the actions of the FLEs at the customer interface (see Chapter 5). This reminds us that the FLEs' customer interactions are bounded by formal rules and that these rules are informed by previous customer interaction experiences.

The Reactive–Proactive Subject

The preceding discussion also connects with the theme of the relationship between marketing discourse and the subjectivity of employees, which has been the central analytical focus of the present book. Whereas the empirical analysis has claimed that the bureaucratic practices foster reactive subjects, and that the SMM practices foster proactive subjects, it does not suggest that one dominates the other. Rather, the individuals draw on different subject positions—or 'plug-ins' to use the terminology of Latour (2005)—when carrying out different activities. On the one hand, when the employees carry out administrative tasks, their subjectivity is colored by the 'efficiency plug-ins' built into bureaucratic discourse and practices, and on the other, when the employees involve themselves in customer interaction tasks informed by customeristic discourse, their subjectivity is colored accordingly. You may recall that Foucault (1977; 1981a; 1985a) treats subjectivity as subject positions embedded in discourse, not as values and beliefs internalized in individuals, implying that individuals' subjectivity is colored by the discourses that their actions and thoughts are contingent on and aligned with at a particular moment. As the quotes from the FLEs in the previous section illustrate, the subjectivity of the FLEs at the FI is often nested simultaneously in bureaucratic and marketing discourse. For example, the previous quote from the FLE, describing that she often does credit checks while chatting with the customer, indicates that this is indeed the case. Thus, in conflict with some previous research (see Peccei and Rosenthal 2000; 2001), there seems to be no fundamental contradiction between proactive and reactive subjectivities. Other previously cited quotes indicate that, in situations characterized by time constraints, it can be problematic to balance proactivity and reactivity. But the latter should not be taken as an argument against subjects logically being unable to align themselves with both bureaucratic and customeristic discourse, and thus that their subjectivity cannot be simultaneously reactive and proactive, but that it can be practically difficult to balance these claims. It is when opposing managerial rationalities during stressful times intersect that life becomes hard for service workers.

THE ROLE OF ACADEMIC MARKETING RESEARCH: BEYOND INCOMMENSURABILITY

The argument that there is no fundamental opposition between the marketing and production concepts, and the bureaucratic and customeristic—or between the reactive and proactive—subjectivities associated with these concepts, is a potentially liberating one for academic marketing research. It indicates that the uncompromising position given to the marketing concept vis-à-vis other 'management concepts', that has been so central to the formation of the discipline, can finally be dismantled. This implies that the fundamental role of marketing research and its relation to practice need to be rethought, from prescribing marketing to organizations to . . . what? This section attempts to answer this question, based on the previous discussion and analysis.

Translation of Marketing Practices

Marketing has a lengthy tradition of prescribing managerial practices to organizations, but has largely neglected to study the role of the prescribed practices in organizations (Harris and Ogbonna 2003; Svensson 2007; Webster 2002). By empirically studying the marketing practices associated with academic research in an organization, the present study addresses this gap in previous research. Even though more studies of the role of marketing in organizations are needed, the present study suggests that academic marketing practices order and govern organization. This should come as a pleasant surprise to marketing academia where the main position previously held was that managerial marketing has affected practice very little (Anderson 1982; Hayes and Abernathy 1980; Webster 1981; 2002). One reason for the differing results might be that the present study has focused on concrete marketing practices, whereas previous research has focused on the general implementation of the marketing concept. Another reason for the differing results might be that the present study has employed a qualitative methodology, whereas the bulk of the previous research has utilized a quantitative methodology which are not very suitable for studying the micro processes of marketing organization (Svensson 2007; Webster 2002). A third reason might be the approach adopted in the present study. Whereas the bulk of academic marketing research has been guided by managerial aims, the present study has been informed by a reflexive critical sociological approach that perceives academic marketing as a regime of power/knowledge.

The implication of the shift in perspective might be illustrated by referring to service quality discourse as well as the measurement technologies connected with it, studied conceptually and empirically in Chapter 5 (see also Skålén and Fougère 2007). These technologies were perceived as forms of disciplinary power designed to detect and close gaps between the norm and the present state. It was argued that the service quality measurement surveys utilized at the FI had much in common with the most influential service quality technologies developed by SMM researchers—the gap model. The results of the measurement, in combination with the disciplinary power of the measurement technologies, convinced FI managers that their FLEs needed to be more proactive. However, proactivity is not a rationality or notion explicitly associated with the gap model. Despite the fact that it can be related to 'responsiveness', one of the so-called 'quality determinants' composing the gap model, the gap model *per se* is insufficient to draw on in order to explain why managers became convinced that their FLEs needed to be more proactive. The emergence of proactivity, as both a managerial rationality and an ideal subject position, also needs to be related to managers' perceptions of their FLEs as reactive subjects. The managers interpreted the measurement results in the light of that knowledge and that experience. It was, thus, in the unique dynamic that was created between the results of the service quality measurement and the organizational practice of the FI that this norm or ideal surfaced, and it was also in relation to this dynamic that the gap which managers argued had to be transcended was generated. As Foucault (1970; 1972 see also Townley 1994) pointed out, regimes of power/knowledge and their associated practices and technologies not only prescribe ideals, they also generate context-contingent ideals and norms. Thus, it is not possible for scholars to govern organizations via the development of managerial discourse and then expect organizations and their members to act accordingly because the knowledge prescribed will be reinterpreted in accordance with, and adapted, to local needs. The knowledge that flows from managerial practices and technologies is always adapted and contextualized by the specific organization that it enters (see Skålén et al. 2005).

Thus, if the results of the present study are analyzed a bit more deeply, they may not come as such a pleasant surprise to marketing academia after all. Despite the fact that the present study suggests that academic marketing practices order organizations, they do not order them in the way prescribed by marketing. More exactly, the present study suggests that something which can be described as a reinterpretation or 'translation' process (Latour 1987) takes place when marketing practices encounter organizational practice (Czarniawska and Joerges 1996; Skålén et al. 2005). This can, in accordance with a Catch 22 type of logic, explain why quantitative deductive research methods are so poor at explaining the relationship between academic marketing discourse and marketing practice. Whereas deductive research formulates hypotheses based on existing knowledge about marketing, the translation argument tells us that the knowledge which these predictions are based on will be reinterpreted, indicating that the effects of marketing on organizations can never be measured, or indeed seen from the standpoint of previous marketing theory.

Marketing as Practice

Translation processes are always implicit in the operation of pastoral power. The pastor is set to interpret the general ethic governing the situation in relation to the specific situation of his or her flock of sheep. The translation process, which takes place when marketing practices meet organizational practice, remains a black box today which future research needs to open. However, even without opening this black box, the present study suggests that marketing academics need to step down from the conductor's podium they have positioned themselves on and stop trying to direct marketing practice. This advice has serious implications for the marketing discipline because it suggests that the marketing discipline needs to distance itself from the positivism it is founded on today because it is this positivism, and more particularly the truth effect it generates, that grants the marketing discipline the power/knowledge to direct practice and grants marketing scholars the opportunity to adopt the subjectivity of the conductor. It follows, logically, from this that the marketing scholars who have positioned themselves as conductors cannot grasp the marketing practice that results from the translation that takes place at the interface between academic practices and organizational practice. Marketing scholars need to understand and study this at the level of practice and, when doing so, they also need to inform themselves using reflexive analytical concepts. It would have been close to impossible to send out a survey and obtain the longitudinal understanding of the coaching and relationship marketing practices, as well as their role in the organizational change process, that I obtained here. Furthermore, if managerial prerogatives had informed my study, it would have been hard to see, for example, how fundamental pastoral power was for the service and market orientation program in Chapter 4. Thus, managerialism and quantification, together with positivism, need to be counterbalanced by qualitative descriptive/critical research. In this way, marketing would be a less governmental discipline. Indeed, using such an approach, it would be possible to know something about *marketing as practice.*

The analysis in the present book and the discussion in this chapter thus point to the fundamental role of academic marketing research and its relation to practice needing to be rethought, *from prescribing marketing practices to studying marketing as practice.* The role assigned to academic marketing research by Vargo and Lusch (2004: 14), which suggests that 'marketing educators and scholars should be proactive in leading industry toward a service-centred exchange model', is not, on the basis of the present discussion, the most productive one. The problems of marketing, e.g. the lack of 'implementation' of the marketing concept, should not be localized to the level of practice. It needs to be localized to the level of research and to the subjectivity of the researchers. It is academia that is the heart of the problem, not practice. Marketing researchers need to put less emphasis on contributing toward managing organizations and more emphasis on studying marketing, including the role played by the marketing discipline itself. Rather than 'breaking free from product marketing' (cf. Shostack 1977), marketing needs to break free from the customeristic rationality it has produced and to reinvent itself as an analytical social science discipline. In the same way that organization studies and critical management studies 'keep a check' on management theory (see Chapter 1), marketing studies and critical marketing studies need to keep a check on managerial marketing theory.

Appendix
Methodology and Methods

This book studies how SMM discourse facilitates the customer orientation of organizations and their members from a Foucauldian perspective. It does so by studying, empirically, the practices—service and market orientation, service quality, coaching, and relationship marketing—that the FI has been drawing on and, conceptually, the representation of these practices in academic texts. The appendix describes the discourse analytical methodology, as well as the data collection and data analysis method used in the book.

DISCOURSE ANALYSIS

Archaeology and Genealogy

Foucault is considered the founder of discourse analysis (Phillips and Jørgensen 2002; Potter and Wheterhell 1987). In his work, it is possible to distinguish between two overarching discourse analytical approaches, 'archaeology' and 'genealogy', with the methodology of this book drawing inspiration from both. Archaeology focuses on illuminating the rules of formation regulating the emergence of a particular discourse, as well as what can be said and what is valued by a particular discourse (Foucault 1967; 1970; 1973). As shown in this book, marketing, including SMM, emerged into a discourse where research contributing toward making organizations and their members more customeristic is more highly valued than other types of research (see Chapter 2 and Hollander 1986; Skålén et al. 2008). Orthodox archaeological analyses are mostly neutral and do not consider power. The object of analysis is constitutive texts that inform domains of knowledge, e.g. academic or other forms of expert texts: not firsthand empirical data from persons drawing on the truth produced. The analysis in this book, concerning the managerial rationality of customerism embedded in marketing discourse in Chapter 2 as well as the conceptual analysis of the SMM practices drawn on by the FI in Chapters 4, 5, and 6, is informed by archaeology.

Genealogy (Foucault 1977; 1981a) paves the way for political analysis and was developed by Foucualt in tandem with the notion of power/

knowledge. Genealogical analysis can include studies of academic texts, but it can also include studies of other types of texts, e.g. diaries, interviews, or documents produced by organizations—an example of the latter being the IWHY booklet referred to extensively in Chapter 4. Genealogy not only aims to study the formation of academic disciplines, but also regimes of power/knowledge more loosely linked to academia and/or how the truths produced by academia order practice, e.g. how marketing orders organizations and the subjectivity of FLEs. The empirical analysis of the case of the FI is clearly informed by genealogy. So, too, is the power/knowledge aspect of the conceptual analysis.

Discourse Theory

Based on Foucault's original work, several discourse analytical approaches have been developed (see Fairclough 1992; 2001; Laclau and Mouffe 1985; Phillips and Jørgensen 2002; Potter and Whetherhell 1987). Even though it is possible to discern differences between them, they all share the idea that language and discourse not only represent the world, they also produce it. Discourse analysts thus have a performative view of language and discourse. The very basic design of this book has truly been influenced by this supposition because it starts out from the idea that marketing theory not only describes marketing practice, but also prescribes marketing practice, an issue discussed at length in Chapter 7. Discourse analysis is not devoted to producing truth but to studying truth, and its effects on reality. This implies that I do not, in this book, focus on whether SMM theory corresponds with reality or not, but on what SMM theory does to reality. Furthermore, discourse analysis was not designed to develop new managerial rationalities but to draw on, study, and evaluate the effects of managerial rationalities. This implies that I do not elaborate on the customerism inherent in SMM discourse, instead studying how customerism contributes toward the social construction of reality, including the shaping of academic marketing discourse. In discourse analysis, discourse, e.g. SMM discourse, is the object of analysis. Discourse analysis takes as its object that which is believed to be the truth: in the present case, what is legitimated as the truth by academic marketing, what kinds of rationalities such truths stand for, and how they are drawn on in order to socially construct reality.

Of the discourse analytical perspectives that have been developed on the basis of Foucault's work, I most explicitly draw on the 'discourse theory' of Laclau and Mouffe (1985, see Skålén forthcoming 2010; Skålén et al. 2008). Discourse theory is based on the premise that the world is only conceivable through discourse and that discourse is totally constitutive of reality. In contradiction to the critical discourse analysis of Fairclough (1992; 2001), for instance, Laclau and Mouffe break with the Marxist tradition of postulating a dialectic between the discursive and the material. This does not imply that only text and language exist but that it is meaningless to conceive of the material outside of text and language; the material is, so to speak, a part of discourse.

Discourse theory has been drawn on in order to grasp the managerial rationality of SMM, how it orders SMM research and marketing research, more generally, and in order to analyze how SMM practices materialize in organizations and how they customer orient employee subjectivity. This is an ambitious project. It cannot be expected that every aspect of the managerial rationality of a discourse such as SMM can be covered in one book. Delimitation is needed. In the present case, the practices drawn on by the FI provided some limitations. But the case of the FI was also chosen because it utilized practices of key importance to SMM research; my research interest framed the selection of the case and vice versa. Other ways of delimiting the empirical study were provided by the discourse theoretical framework. When the conceptual analysis of the SMM practices that were drawn on at the FI, as represented in the academic literature, was conducted, not every piece of research was reviewed. Rather, the most pivotal contributions or *turning points* were focused upon. The turning point is a notion used by Foucault and historians to refer to significant changes in the object of study, e.g. significant changes in an academic field like the establishment of a new body of knowledge or new directions in an existing body of knowledge like the introduction of SMM into marketing research. Turning points are associated with *problematizations*, the notion Foucault used for lines of argument questioning the existing discursive order and paving the way for a turning point (Dean 1999). The idea in early SMM research, reviewed in Chapter 1 (see also Grönroos 1982; Shostack 1977), that the employees form an integrated part of the service and need, in addition to the products, to be customeristic is one example of a problematization in marketing discourse which brought impetus to a turning point. If problematizations are occurrences that question the existing order, *articulations,* according to Laclau and Mouffe (1985), produce new meaning or redirect existing meaning which eventually might lead to the construction of new discourse or an alternative articulation of an existing discourse. One example is service quality theory (see Chapter 5), which is an example of the articulation of a new (sub-) discourse in general marketing discourse. Another example is the literature on service and market orientation (see Chapter 4) rearticulating the marketing concept. *Nodal points* are the privileged signs of discourse which give discourse a coherent meaning, or in a more technical language, which turn *elements* into *moments*—the latter being the signs that have an exact meaning and compose discourse (Laclau and Mouffe 1985). An obvious example of a nodal point in marketing discourse is the marketing concept, which regulates the meaning of moments such as service quality. However, the closure of discourse is always contingent. Discourse can always be opened up by problematizations and articulations turning moments back into elements, which are signs that lack a clear meaning. The formulation of service quality theory (see Chapter 5), for instance, shows several instances where the quality concept was opened up and given new meaning.

However, the study also has, in line with discourse theory (and Foucauldianism, see Chapter 1), a critical intention. The *hegemony*—the worldview inherent in an articulation that dominates marketing discourse—is also questioned or *deconstructed*—deconstruction being the activity of displaying that the hegemony of marketing discourse is contingent and that it can be articulated differently (Laclau 1993). In the present study, this entails the very basic principles of marketing research being questioned in Chapter 7 by arguing that marketing research needs to distance itself from positivism, managerialism, and quantitative methods. More to the point, it argues that the marketing discipline needs to reorient itself from prescribing marketing practices to organizations to studying marketing as a practice in organizations.

METHODS

Because whether or not, and how, SMM practices order organizations and their members has not previously been subject to any systematic empirical analysis, I adopted an exploratory single case study design (Eisenhardt 1989; Yin 1984). I actively searched for organizations that had been using SMM practices to manage their organization. I visited three of them: a bank, a hotel chain, and the FI. The reason for choosing to study the FI was that it had a clean track record of drawing on SMM practices, something that the other organizations lacked. The FI has, for instance, collaborated with researchers and consultants specializing in the field of service and relationship marketing in order to develop its organization along these lines. An additional reason for choosing the FI was that my contact person, the sales manager of the FI—referred to as David in the empirical chapters—also gave me very good access. I obtained permission to interview whomever I wanted (as long as the interviewee gave me his or her consent) and to contact the respondents myself. David also opened a lot of doors for me by contacting a few interviewees during the early phases of the empirical work and by making my research project known throughout the organization, which made it a whole lot easier to conduct the empirical study. The team leaders were also very helpful in recruiting FLEs for the interviews. All in all, the data collection process went very smoothly.

Data Collection

My main data collection technique was the interview, but documents were also collected. In total, I conducted 41 interviews between March 2006 and December 2007. In order to make the interviewees as comfortable as possible, I used the 'language' of the respondents as much as possible when conducting the interviews (cf. Spradley 1979). Researcher jargon was avoided. In addition, a contract of anonymity was set up with each intervie-wee which stated that I would only be able to reveal the gender and position of the respondents. It was also agreed that the name of the company would remain anonymous.

Each interview lasted between 45 and 90 minutes. In total, I conducted 13 interviews with managers, 6 with back office staff, and 22 with FLEs. The reason for interviewing that many FLEs was that the SMM practices drawn on by the FI were primarily aimed at managing them. An additional reason was that it took a while before theoretical saturation (Glaser and Strauss 1967) was reached in the categories addressing the FLEs. Some of the categories, such as that of reactivity and being an administrator as dis-cussed in Chapter 3, concerned issues that were highly institutionalized at the FI. These can be hard to talk about because of their taken-for-granted nature. Thus, I needed to approach such issues from a few different angles before finding useful ways of asking the FLEs about them. Seven of the respondents—3 managers, 2 back office staff, and 2 FLEs—were inter-viewed twice. These are my main informants and some of them are referred to using fictitious names in the case description. In total, 34 respondents were interviewed, of whom 24 were women and 10 were men.

Following Lincoln and Guba's (1985) guidelines for "purposeful sam-pling" when choosing informants, my main goal was to meet the people who could inform me the most about the role of the SMM practices. The interviewees were thus not randomly selected. Rather, a convenient sam-ple was used. Sometimes, the snowball technique was used, meaning that interviewees were asked about whom to interview on a specific topic and, on some occasions, it seemed like the right time to interview a particular group of employees. As with most case study research, the aim was not to statistically generalize but to make an analytical generalization. When the latter form of generalization is utilized, ' . . . a previously developed theory is used as a template with which to compare the empirical results of the case study' (Yin 1984:. 31), thus supporting, developing, and questioning its claims. In this case, previous Foucauldian analysis of academic marketing discourse (see Skålén et al. 2006; 2008) is elaborated on whereas the posi-tivistic and managerial foundation of the marketing discipline is questioned by drawing on the case study.

An initial round of interviews took place between March and June 2006. After having transcribed all the interviews verbatim, and doing a thorough categorization, I returned to the organization in August and December 2007 for a second and third round of interviews devoted to probing the themes that had emerged (Glaser and Strauss 1967; Spradley 1979). In order to generate knowledge of the role of SMM practices in organizations, as well as how they customer orient employee subjectivity, theoretical sampling (Glaser and Strauss 1967) was used. The process of data collection was thus controlled by the emerging themes. Thus, once a few of the interviews had been conducted, they were transcribed verbatim, and then coded and categorized. As soon as themes started to emerge, these were probed during subsequent interviews. At the same time, openness to the emergence of new themes was retained. This cycle was repeated several times. In order to probe themes, interview questions were used which had emerged from the data analysis. Some of these questions were specific. When interviewing a team leader for the second time, for example, he was asked the following questions about coaching, which had emerged as an important category (see Chapter 5). 'You have been taking a course in coaching: How was it? What is the aim of coaching? In which ways does coaching differ from other management approaches?' However, open questions were included until the interviews had been concluded. In the last five interviews, conducted with FLEs in December 2007, these were asked: 'What is the best thing about working at the FI?' and 'How does a normal workday look for you?'. In addition to the interviews, documents, official public materials (e.g. advertisements, annual reports, etc.), and internal materials (project plans and reports, quality measurement forms, etc.) were also collected and categorized.

Data Analysis

I transcribed and coded the interviews as soon as possible after conducting them—Nvivo 7 was used as the data analysis and organizing software. For the core of the study, I did not start the data analysis on the level of first order coding, as suggested by grounded theory (Glaser and Strauss 1967; Strauss and Corbin 1998) and anthropological approaches to data analysis (Spradley 1979; Van Maanen 1979). Rather, because the aim was to study how SMM practices order organizations and their members, I searched for practices associated with SMM in the data. The result of this was that I found out that the FI was drawing on practices associated with service and market orientation, service quality, coaching, and relationship marketing. These practices can be referred to as the second-order categories or themes of the study. Once identified, I focused on finding out more about these themes and coded the data in relation to them. When empirical saturation was achieved—e.g. when no new themes emerged and when no new types of data associated with existing themes were generated—I terminated data collection.

However, part of the book, especially Chapter 3, does not focus on the SMM practices directly, but on practices associated with the bureaucratic side of the organization. For this part, the data analysis followed a more traditional grounded theory approach, starting out from coding and working toward categories. Once established, the categories were related to the literature and particularly to the notion of the customer oriented bureaucracy (Korczynski 2002) which I found, by iterating between the empirical and theoretical levels, matched very well with the empirical material and was thus used to illuminate the empirical material.

Notes

NOTES TO CHAPTER 1

1. A minority of researchers take the reverse position, believing that critical marketing is already an existing research field with its own empirical agenda. This is the position taken by Schroeder (2007: 26) who argues that: 'It is not enough to bemoan a lack of scholarship, one must critically engage in the critical marketing literature itself, before blithely criticizing'.

2. The term marketing is therefore used to refer to research or practice associated with strategic marketing.

3. There is ambiguity of terminology in naming the school of thought discussed here: should it be service *marketing* or service *management*? In fact, this ambiguity of labeling is inherited from the 'marketing management' school of thought, a label indicating that this school is not only devoted to 'pure' marketing but also to management. Is marketing management a management discipline, or is it a marketing discipline, or is it a combination of the two? Marketing management clearly prescribes a distinct type of marketing where market research has a key role but also a form of customer orientated management. However, the 'management' in marketing management does not signify a management/organization studies kind of approach to marketing because it does not turn marketing into the object of study (see following). Rather, the 'management' in marketing management has more in common with leadership research and management theory, which focuses on prescribing management and not, at least not primarily, on studying management. Perhaps 'marketing leadership' would have been a more correct, but doubtless less catchy, label. In the same way as leadership research, marketing has also had a relationship with management, and it has had this ever since the birth of the discipline in the early 20th century (Skålén et al. 2008). When the label marketing management started to be used to denote mainstream marketing research in the 1960s, it was impossible to distinguish marketing from management and management from marketing.

   This intimacy between marketing and management is further emphasized in service marketing/management (SMM). It is a pity for SMM scholars that the marketing management label was already taken. While the SMM discipline was being born in the 1970s, the term 'service' was used to differentiate SMM from marketing management. As described in what follows, marketing by service firms was perceived to be different and needed a special kind of theory. Today however, when, as Levitt (1972) wrote long ago, 'everyone is in services', and when SMM is emerging, at least according to some marketing scholars, as a dominant logic for management, not only for service organizations but for all kinds of organizations (Vargo and Lusch 2004), the 'service' in SMM is hampering the discipline rather then helping it. Calling a management regime which prescribes management to organizations of all kinds a service-dominant logic is really an oxymoron if common usages of language are to be respected. On the other hand, referring to SMM as marketing management truly makes sense because it prescribes marketing oriented management to all types of organizations. By this, I do not mean that SMM has not contributed significantly to managerial marketing research. As pointed out in what follows, it has shown us that employees not only need to perform marketing now, they also need to embody it because they are an important part of the market offering. At the heart of both SMM and marketing management lies the task of ensuring that the firm is customer and marketing oriented. The main difference between them is the depth and breadth of the prescription of customer orientation. In SMM, both products and people need to be customer and marketing oriented.

Even though, in my view, it would make sense to get rid of the qualifier service and treat SMM as the most advanced form of managerial marketing hitherto developed, I will still adhere to common usage of the terms here. However, I will use the term service marketing and management, or the abbreviation SMM, and not service marketing or service management to clearly indicate that SMM is never just about marketing or management. In SMM, a particular form of marketing is always intimately intertwined with a particular form of management.

4. Several signs point in this direction: SMM articles have been published regularly in leading marketing journals, e.g. *The Journal of Marketing*, since the middle of the 1980s; one of the shared interest groups (SIGs) of the American Marketing Association (AMA)—SERVSIG—is devoted to SMM; several conferences on SMM, e.g. the SERVSIG conference, Frontiers in Services, and QUIS are organized annually or biannually, and several academic SMM journals, including the *Journal of Service Research*, the *Journal of Service Management* (previously the *International Journal of Service Industry Management*), and the *Service Industries Journal* have been established.

5. How the qualitative empirical case study was carried out is described in detail in the methods appendix.

6. Or, to be completely correct: Clegg et al. (2006) place power and efficiency / effectiveness at the center of management / organization theory. Hinings and Greenwood (2002) suggest a slightly different solution in postulating a distinction between management theory focusing on efficiency / effectiveness and organization studies (or the sociology of organization in their terminology) of which power, according to them, is the central concept. Organization studies, then, would have management theory, or its products, as one of the objects of study and would act as some kind of 'discursive police' keeping track of management theory.

NOTES TO CHAPTER 2

1. Thus, the chapter does not review any aspect of Foucault's work or the rich 'post-Foucauldian' work. The intention is, rather, to introduce the notions drawn on in this book.

2. See more about the ontological and epistemological implications of a Foucauldian position in the methods appendix.

3. Because this book is a study of strategic marketing, I focus on management implications when reviewing marketing management discourse. But

let me be clear that the consumers, in addition to the organizations and their products, are the object of the marketing management practices. The practices of marketing management not only aim to make the products of organizations more customeristic but also to influence and manipulate the consumers' buying behaviors and intentions so that they buy existing products from the focal organization involved in the marketing efforts. Marketing management not only aims to create customeristic products but also markets for products (whether customeristic or not) (see Skålen et al. 2008, Chap. 5).

NOTES TO CHAPTER 3

1. This begs the question of whether or not the FI is a call center. Neither the managers nor the FLEs refer to the FI as a call center, which they associate with factory-like service work and a single focus on efficiency and effectiveness. According to FI staff, call centers and their staff are not usually able to handle more complicated services, e.g. issuing home loans. If we turn to the literature, which distinguishes call centers on the basis of the general nature of work and not how complicated it is, parts of the consumer division of the FI would probably be regarded as a call center. Call centers, according to the literature, can give priority to quantity and/or quality (see Callaghan and Thompson 2001; Taylor and Bain 1999; 2001).
2. My main informants—team leaders 'John' and 'Alice', sales manager 'David', project leader 'Mary', associate project leader 'Barbara', and FLE 'Ann'—are referred to using fictitious names.
3. I am aware of the tensions between a Foucauldian and a Labor Process Theory framework when it comes to understanding power, for instance. Whereas Labor Process Theory is based on a classical sovereign understanding of power, Foucault put forward the notion of power/knowledge. But the perspectives also share a general critical orientation making it possible to draw on them in the same study.
4. Edwards distinguished these two types of control from 'simple control', referring to the giving of direct orders by the capitalist or supervisor to the worker. In this system of control, 'power was unmistakably vested in the person of the supervisor' (Edwards 1979: 33). Simple control is not salient in service firms and is omitted from the analysis in this book.
5. It needs to be noted that this section analyzes the social constructions composing the orientation of challenging the ordinary banks, from the perspective of the FI employees. Whether the basis that they draw on in order to construct this image is true or not is not in focus. In line with a Foucauldian standpoint, the focus, in this case, is on what effect truth has on the subjectivity of the FLEs, not on whether or not the truths that build up the FLEs are true.
6. The remaining five percent, the buyer will need to take from his or her own pocket.
7. During periods of data collection, however, the FLEs were granted the possibility of giving customers switching to the FI from other banks up to a 0.3 percent discount on official interest rates.
8. It needs be acknowledged that Korczynski's work on the customer oriented bureaucracy is not an isolated discourse. It should instead be seen as a part of the rich 'post-bureaucratic' stream of literature (see, for instance, Adler and Heckscher 2006; Heckscher and Donnellon 1994; Powell 1990).

NOTES TO CHAPTER 4

1. These early studies have been criticized for resting on a weak empirical basis. Despite this, they have been formative as regards views concerning the effects of the marketing concept on practice within the marketing discipline. This view is critically discussed in Chapter 7.
2. Today, Rick Johnson is the owner of the consultancy firm *CEO strategist*, specializing in leadership training, sales management, and strategy development in the service industry sector. He is a former principal of Disney University, holding other positions at Disney before switching to consultancy. Rick Johnson has done several speaking tours in Scandinavia, and it was probably during such a tour that David met him (see http://sipsi.se/rickjohnson.html; http://www.ceostrategist.com/; both retrieved on 2008–09–18).

NOTES TO CHAPTER 5

1. As research into service quality has pointed out, there is also empirical evidence to support the fact that, when customers are asked about their perceptions of service quality, they compare these against what they have been expecting (Zeithaml et al. 1985; see also Schneider and White 2004). When customers, for example, are asked about their perceptions of the service at a fast food restaurant, they will compare these perceptions with their expectations vis-à-vis fast food dining, which differ radically in most cases from the expectations they will draw on when asked about the service quality of fine dining. According to this reasoning, every single service quality statement checks the gap between perceptions and expectations.

NOTES TO CHAPTER 6

1. Some scholars (e.g. Grönroos 1997; Gummesson 1997; Parvatiyar and Sheth 2000) have put forward the reverse argument: i.e. that today the rationality of relationship marketing orders SMM.
2. The terms relationship marketing and CRM are often used interchangeably. However, CRM is more often used in the context of IT solutions.

Bibliography

Adler, P.S. and Heckscher C.C. (2006) 'Towards Collaborative Community', in C.C. Heckscher and P.S. Adler (eds.) *The Firm as a Collaborative Community: Reconstructing Trust in the Knowledge Economy*, Oxford: Oxford University Press, pp. 11–105.

Alderson, W. (1957) *Marketing Behavior and Executive Action: A Functionalist Approach to Marketing Theory*, Homewood, IL: Irwin.

Alvesson, M. (2002) *Understanding Organizational Culture*, London: Sage

Alvesson, A. and Willmott, H. (1992) 'On the Idea of Emancipation in Management and Organization Studies', *Academy of Management Review*, 17 (3): 432–64.

Alvesson, M. and Willmott, H. (1996) *Making Sense of Management: A Critical Introduction*, London: Sage.

Alvesson, M. and Willmott, H. (2003) 'Introduction', in M. Alvesson and H. Willmott (eds.), *Studying Management Critically*, London: Sage.

Anderson, P.F. (1982) 'Marketing, Strategic Planning and the Theory of the Firm', *Journal of Marketing*, 46 (1): 7–23.

Ansoff, I. (1965) *Corporate Strategy: An Analytical Approach to Business Policy for Growth and Expansion*, New York: McGraw-Hill.

Arndt, J. (1985) 'On Making Marketing Science More Scientific: The Role of Orientation, Paradigms, Metaphors and Puzzle Solving', *Journal of Marketing*, 49 (Summer): 11–23.

Arnould, E.J. and Thompson C.J. (2005) 'Consumer Culture Theory (CCT): Twenty Years of Research', *Journal of Consumer Research*, 31 (4): 868–82.

Bartels, R. (1988) *The History of Marketing Thought*, 3rd edn, Columbus, OH: Publishing Horizons.

Bateman, S. and Crant, J.M. (1993) 'The Proactive Component of Organizational Behaviour: a Measure and Correlates', *Journal of Organizational Behavior*, 14 (2): 103–18

Batt, R. (2000) 'Strategic Segmentation in Front-Line Services: Matching Customers, Employees and Human Resource Systems', *International Journal of Human Resource Management*, 11 (3): 540–61.

Bauman, Z. (1998) *Work, Consumerism and the New Poor*, Philadelphia: Open University Press.

Bergström, O. and Knights, D. (2006) 'Organizational Discourse and Subjectivity, Subjectification during processes of recruitment', *Human Relations*, 59 (3): 351–77.

Berry, L.L. (1983) *Relationship Marketing*, in L.L. Berry, G.L. Shostack, and G. Upah (eds.) *Emerging Perspectives on Services Marketing*, Chicago, IL: American Marketing Association, pp. 25–28.

Berry, L.L. (1999) *Discovering the Soul of Service: The Nine Drivers of Sustainable Business Success*, New York: The Free Press.

Berry, L.L. and Parasuraman, A. (1993) 'Building a New Academic Field: The Case of Services Marketing', *Journal of Retailing*, 69 (1): 13–61.

Bonso, S.K. and Darmody, A. (2008) 'Co-creating Second Life: Market—Consumer Cooperation in Contemporary Economy', *Journal of Macromarketing*, 28 (4): 355–68.

Borden, N.H. (1964) 'The Concept of the Marketing Mix', *Journal of Advertising Research*, 4 (2): 2–7.

Borsch, F.J. (1957) 'The Marketing Philosophy as a Way of Business Life', in *The Marketing Concept: Its Meaning to Management*, Marketing Series No 99, New York: American Management Association.

Boulding, W., Staelin, R., Ehret, M., and Johnston, W.J. (2005) 'A Customer Relationship Management Roadmap: What is Known, Potential Pittfalls and Where to Go', *Journal of Marketing*, 69 (4): 155–66.

Bourdieu, P. (1984) *Distinction: A Social Critique of the Judgment of Taste*, London: Routledge.

Brady, M.K. and Cronin, J.J. Jr. (2001) 'Some New Thoughts on Conceptualizing Perceived Service Quality: A Hierarchical Approach', *Journal of Marketing*, 65 (3): 34–49.

Brassington, F. and Pettitt, S. (2000) *Principles of Marketing*, Harlow: Financial Times Management.

Braverman, H. (1974) *Labor and Monopoly Capital: The Degradation of Work in the Twentieth Century*, New York: Monthly Review Press.

Brown, S.W. and Swartz, T.A. (1989) 'A Gap Analysis of Professional Service Quality', *Journal of Marketing*, 53 (2): 92–98.

Brown, S.W., Fisk, R.P., and Bitner, M.J. (1994) 'The Development and Emergence of Services Marketing Thought', *International Journal of Service Industry Management*, 5 (1): 21–48.

Brownlie D. and Hewer, P. (2007) 'Concerning Marketing Critterati: Beyond Nuance, Estrangement and Elitism', in M. Saren, P. Maclaran, C. Goulding, R. Elliott, A. Shankar and M. Caterall (eds.) *Critical Marketing: Defining the Field*, Burlington, MA: Butterworth-Heinemann, pp. 44–68.

Brownlie D. and Saren, M. (1997) 'Beyond the One-dimensional Marketing Manager: The Discourse of Theory, Practice and Relevance', *International Journal of Research in Marketing*, 14: 147–61.

Brownlie, D., Saren, M., Wensley, R., and Whittington, R. (eds.) (1999) *Rethinking Marketing: Towards Critical Marketing Accountings*, London: Sage.

Burrawoy, M. (1979) *Manufacturing Consent*, Chicago: University of Chicago Press.

Burton, D. (2001) 'Critical Marketing Theory: The Blueprint?', *European Journal of Marketing*, 35 (5/6): 722–43.

Callaghan, G. and Thompson, P. (2001) 'Edwards Revisited: Technical Control and Call Centres', *Economic and Industrial Democracy*, 22 (1): 13–37.

Clegg, S.R. (1989) *Frameworks of Power*, London: Sage.

Clegg, S.R., Courpasson, D., and Phillips, N. (2006) *Power and Organizations*, London: Sage.

Clegg, S.R., Pitsis, T.S., Rura-Polley, T., and Marosszeky, M. (2002) 'Governmentality Matters: Designing an Alliance of Inter-organizational Collaboration for Managing Projects', *Organization Studies*, 23 (3): 317–37.

Cole, R.E. (1999) *Managing Quality Fads*, Oxford: Oxford University Press.

Covaleski, M.A., Dirsmith, M.W., Heian, B.H., and Samuel, S. (1998) 'The Calculated and the Avowed: Techniques of Discipline and Struggles over Identity in Big Six Public Accounting Firms', *Administrative Science Quarterly*, 43 (4): 293–327.

Crant, J.M. (2000) 'Proactive Behavior in Organizations', *Journal of Management*, 26 (3): 435–62.

Cronin, J.J. and Taylor, S.A. (1992) 'Measuring Service Quality: A Reexamination and Extension', *Journal of Marketing*, 56 (3): 56–68

Cronin, J.J. and Taylor, S.A. (1994) 'SERVPERF Versus SERVQUAL: Reconciling Performance-Based and Perceptions-Minus-Expectations Measurement of Service Quality', *Journal of Marketing*, 58 (1): 125–31.

Cruikshank, B. (1994) 'The Will to Empower: Technologies of Citizenship and the War on Poverty', *Socialist Review*, 23 (4): 29–55.

Czarniawska, B. and Joerges, B. (1996) 'Travels of Ideas', in B. Czarniawska and G. Sévon, (eds.) *Translating Organizational Change*, Berlin: de Gruyter, pp. 13–48.

Dabholkar, P.C., Thorpe, D.I., and Rentz, J.O. (1996) 'A Measure of Service Quality for Retail Stores', *Journal of the Academy of Marketing Science*, 25 (1): 3–16.

Day, G.S. (2003) 'Creating a Superior Customer-Relating Capability', *Sloan Management Review*, 44 (3): 77–83.

Deal, T.E. and Kennedy, A.A. (1982) *Corporate Culture: The Rites and Rituals of Corporate Life*, Reading, Mass: Addison-Wesley.

Dean, M. (1995) 'Governing the Unemployed Self in an Active Society', *Economy and Society*, 24 (4): 559–83.

Dean, M. (1999) *Governmentality: Power and Rule in Modern Society*, London: Sage.

Deshpandé, R. and Webster, F.E. Jr. (1989) 'Organizational Culture and Marketing: Defining the Research Agenda', *Journal of Marketing*, 53 (1): 3–15.

Dibb, S. and Meadows, M. (2001) 'The Application of a Relationship Marketing Perspective in Retail Banking', *The Services Industries Journal*, 21 (1): 169–94.

DiMaggio, P.J., och Powell, W.W. (1983) 'The Iron Cage Revisted: Institutional Isomorphism and Collective Rationality in Organizational Fields', *American Sociological Review*, 48 (2): 147–68.

Downey, M. (1999) *Effective Coaching*, London: Orion Business.

Drucker, P.F. (1954) *The Practice of Management*, New York: Harper and Row.

Du Gay, P. (1996) *Consumption and Identity at Work*, London: Sage.

Du Gay, P. and Salaman, G. (1992). 'The Cult[ure] of the Customer', *Journal of Management Studies*, 29 (5): 615–33.

Edvardsson, B. and Enquist, B. (2002) 'Service Culture and Service Strategy: The IKEA Saga', *The Service Industries Journal*, 22 (4): 153–86.

Edvardsson, B., Gustafsson, A., and Roos, I. (2005) 'Service Portraits in Service Research—A Critical Review', *International Journal of Service Industry Management*, 16 (1): 107–21.

Edwards, R. (1979) *Contested Terrain: The Transformation of the Workplace in the Twentieth Century*, London: Heinemann.

Eisenhardt, K.M. (1989) 'Building Theory from Case Study Research', *Academy of Management Review*, 14 (4): 532–50.

Fairclough, N. (1992) *Discourse and Social Change*, Cambridge, UK: Polity Press.

Fairclough, N. (2001) *Language and Power*, 2nd edn, London: Pearson Education.

Featherstone, M., (1991) *Consumer Culture and Postmodernism*, London: Sage.

Fishbein, M. and Ajzen, I. (1975) *Belief, Attitude, Intention and Behavior: An Introduction to Theory and Research*, Reading, Mass: Addison-Wesley.

Fitchett, J. and McDonugh, P. (2001) 'Relationship Marketing, E-commerce and the Emancipation of the Consumer', in A. Sturdy, I. Grugulis, and H. Willmott (eds.) *Customer Service—Empowerment and Entrapment*, Basingstoke: Palgrave, pp. 191–99.

Foucault, M. (1967) *Madness and Civilization: A History of Insanity in the Age of Reason*, London: Routledge.

Foucault, M. (1970) *The Order of Things: An Archaeology of the Human Sciences*, London: Routledge.

Foucault, M. (1972) *The Archaeology of Knowledge*, London: Routledge.

Foucault, M. (1973) *The Birth of the Clinic: An Archaeology of Medical Perception*, London: Routledge.

Foucault, M. (1977) *Discipline and Punish: The Birth of the Prison*, London: Penguin.

Foucault, M. (1981a) *The Will to Knowledge: The History of Sexuality*, Vol. 1, London: Penguin.

Foucault, M. (1981b) 'The Order of Discourse', in R. Young (ed.) *Untying the Text: A Post-Structuralist Reader*, London: Routledge.

Foucault, M. (1985a) *The Use of Pleasure: The History of Sexuality*, Vol. 2, New York: Vintage Books.

Foucault, M. (1985b) *The Care of the Self: The History of Sexuality*, Vol. 3, London: Penguin.

Foucault, M. (1997) *The Politics of Truth*, New York: Semiotext(e).

Foucault, M. (2000a) 'The Subject and Power', in J.D. Faubion (ed.) *Power: The Essential Works of Foucault*, Vol. 3, New York: The Free Press.

Foucault, M. (2000b) '"Omnes et Singulatim": Toward a Critique of Political Reason', in J.D. Faubion (ed.) *Power: The Essential Works of Foucault*, Vol. 3, New York: The Free Press.

Foucault, M. (2006) *Psychiatric Power: Lectures at Collège de France 1973–74*, Basingstoke: Palgrave.

Foucault, M. (2007) *Security, Territory, Population: Lectures at Collège de France 1977–1978*, Basingstoke: Palgrave.

Friedman, W.A. (2005) *Birth of a Salesman: The Transformation of Selling in America*, Cambridge, MA: Harvard University Press.

Fuat Firat, A., Dholakia, N., and Bagozzi, R.P. (eds.) (1987) *Philosophical and Radical Thought in Marketing*, Lanham, MD: Lexington Books.

Gebhart G.F., Carpenter, G.S., and Sherry Jr., J.F. (2006) 'Creating a Market Orientation: A Longitudinal, Multifirm, Grounded Analysis of Cultural Transformations', *Journal of Marketing*, 70 (4): 37–55.

Geertz, C. (1973) *The Interpretations of Cultures*, London: Fontana Press.

Glaser, B.G. and Strauss, A.L. (1967) *The Discovery of Grounded Theory: Strategies for Qualitative Research*, New York: Aldine De Gruyter.

Gouldner A.W. (1954) *Patterns of Industrial Bureaucracy*, Glencoe, IL: Free Press.

Greenberg, P (2001) *CRM at the Speed of Light*, Berkeley, CA: Osborne / McGraw-Hill.

Grönroos, C. (1978) 'A Service Orientated Approach to Marketing of Services', *European Journal of Marketing*, 12 (8): 588–601

Grönroos, C. (1982) 'An Applied Service Marketing Theory', *European Journal of Marketing*, 16 (7): 30–41.

Grönroos, C. (1984) 'A Service Quality Model and its Marketing Implications', *European Journal of Marketing*, 18 (4): 36–44.

Grönroos, C. (1990) *Service Management and Marketing: Managing the Moments of Truth in Service Competition*, Lexington, MA: Free Press / Lexington Books.

Grönroos, C. (1997) 'Value-Driven Relational Marketing: From Products to Resources and Competencies', *Journal of Marketing Management*, 23 (1): 52–60.

Grönroos, C. (2007a) *In Search of a New Logic for Marketing: Foundations of Contemporary Theory*, Chichester, UK: Wiley.

Grönroos, C. (2007b) *Service Management and Marketing: A Customer Relationship Management Approach*, Chichester, UK: Wiley.

Gummesson, E. (1977) *The Marketing and Purchase of Consultancy Services: A Study of Conditions and Behaviour in Swedish Producer Services Markets*, Doctoral Dissertation, Stockholm: Stockholm University, (in Swedish [*Marknadsföring och inköp av konsulttjänster. En studie av egenskaper och beteenden i producenttjänstemarknader*]).

Gummesson, E. (1987) 'The New Marketing: Developing Long-term Interactive Relationships', *Long Range Planning*, 5 (5): 5–20.

Gummesson, E. (1991) 'Marketing Revisited: The Crucial Role of the Part-Time Marketer', *European Journal of Marketing*, 25 (2): 60–75.

Gummesson (1997) 'In Search of Market Equilibrium: Relationship Marketing Versus Hypercompetition, *Journal or Marketing Management*, 13 (5): 421–30.

Gummesson, E. (2008) *Total Relationship Marketing*, London: Butterworth-Heinemann.

Hackley, C. (2003) '"We are All Customers Now . . ." Rhetorical Strategy and Ideological Control in Marketing Management Texts', *Journal Management Studies*, 40 (5): 1326–52.

Hackley, C. (2009) *Marketing: A Critical Introduction*, London: Sage.

Hargrove, R., (2000) *Masterful Coaching Fieldbook*, San Francisco: Jossey-Bass/Pfeiffer.

Harris, L.C. and Ogbonna, E. (1999) 'Developing a Market Oriented Culture: A Critical Evaluation', *Journal of Management Studies*, 36 (2): 177–96.

Harris, L.C. and Ogbonna, E. (2000) 'The Response of Front-Line Employees to Market Oriented Culture Change', *European Journal of Marketing*, 34 (3/4): 318–40.

Harris, L.C. and Ogbonna, E. (2003) 'The Organization of Marketing: A Study of Decentralized, Developed and Dispersed Marketing Activity', *Journal of Management Studies*, 40 (2): 483–512.

Hasselbladh, H. and Kallinikos, J. (2000) 'The Project of Rationalization: A Critique and Reappraisal of Neo-Institutionalism in Organization Studies', *Organization Studies*, 21 (4): 697–720.

Hayes, R.H. and Abernathy, W.J. (1980) 'Managing Our Way to Economic Decline', *Harvard Business Review*, 58 (July–August): 67–77.

Heckscher C. and Donnellon A. (1994) *The Post-bureaucratic Organization: New Perspectives on Organizational Change*, Thousand Oaks, CA: Sage.

Heskett, J.L., Sasser, W.E. and Schlesinger, L.A. (1997) *The Service Profit Chain: How Leading Companies Link Profit and Growth To Loyalty, Satisfaction, and Value*, New York: The Free Press.

Hinings, C.R. and Greenwood, R. (2002) 'Disconnects and Consequences in Organization Theory?', *Administrative Science Quarterly*, 47 (3): 411–21.

Hochschild, A.R. (1983) *The Managed Heart: Commercialization of Human Feeling*, Berkeley, CA: University of California Press.

Hodgson, D.E. (2000) *Discourse, Discipline and the Subject: A Foucauldian Analysis of the UK Financial Services Industry*, London: Ashgate.

Hodgson, D. (2002) '"Know Your Customer": Marketing, Governmentality and the "New Consumer" of Financial Services', *Management Decision*, 40 (4): 318–28.

Hollander, S.C. (1986) 'The Marketing Concept: A Déjà Vu', in G. Fisk (ed.) *Marketing Management Technology as a Social Process*, New York: Praeger.

Homburg, C. and Pflesser, C. (2000) 'A Multiple Layer Model of Market-Oriented Organizational Culture: Measurement Issues and Performance Outcomes', *Journal of Marketing Research*, 37 (November): 449–62.

http://sipsi.se/rickjohnson.html; retrieved on 2008–09–18

http://www.ceostrategist.com/; retrieved on 2008–09–18

http://www.questback.se; retrieved on 2008–03–24

http://www.webserviceaward.com; retrieved on 2008–03–24

Hunt, S.D. (1976) 'The Nature and Scope of Marketing', *Journal of Marketing*, 40 (3): 17–28.

Jaworski B.J. and Kohli, A.K. (1993) 'Market Orientation: Antecedents and Consequences', *Journal of Marketing*, 57 (3): 53–70.

Jayachandran, S., Sharma, S., Kaufman, P. and Pushkala, R. (2005) 'The Role of Relational Information Processes and Technology Use in Customer Relationship Management', *Journal of Marketing*, 69 (4): 177–92.

Jobber, D. (2004) *Principles and Practise of Marketing*, Maidenhead, UK: McGraw-Hill.

Journal of the Academy of Marketing Science (2008) 'Special Issue on the Service-Dominant Logic', 36 (1).

Keith R.J. (1960) 'The Marketing Revolution', *Journal of Marketing*, 24 (3): 35–38.

Kholi, A.K. and Jaworski B.J. (1990) 'Market Orientation: The Construct, Research Propositions and Managerial Implications', *Journal of Marketing*, 54 (2): 1–18.

Knights, D. and McCabe, D. (1999) 'Are There No Limits to Authority?: TQM and Organizational Power', *Organization Studies*, 20 (2): 197–224.

Korczynski, M. (2002) *Human Resource Management in Service Work*, Basingstoke: Palgrave.

Kotler, P. (1967) *Marketing Management: Analysis, Planning and Control*, London: Prentice-Hall.

Kotler, P. (1972) 'A Generic Concept of Marketing', *Journal of Marketing*, 36 (2): 46–54.

Kotler, P. (1992) 'Marketing's New Paradigm: What's Really Happening Out There', *Planning Review*, (September / October): 50–52.

Kotler, P. and Keller, K.L. (2006) *Marketing Management*, 12th edn, Upper Saddle River, NJ: Pearson Prentice Hall.

Kotler, P. and Levy, S.L. (1969) 'Broadening the Concept of Marketing', *Journal of Marketing*, 33 (1): 10–15.

Kotler, P. and Zaltman, G. (1971) 'Social Marketing: An Approach to Planned Social Change', *Journal of Marketing*, 35 (3): 3–12.

Lachman, R. (2000) 'Stepping into the Kitchen: Lay Clients as Co-Producers of a Professional Service', *International Journal of Human Resource Management*, 11 (3): 617–34.

Laclau, E. (1993) 'Power and Representation', in M. Poster (ed.) *Politics, Theory and Contemporary Culture*, New York: Columbia University Press.

Laclau, E. and Mouffe, C. (1985) *Hegemony and Socialist Strategy: Towards a Radical Democratic Politics*, 2nd edn, New York: Verso.

Latour, B. (1987) *Science in Action: How to Follow Scientists and Engineers Through Society*, Cambridge, MA: Harvard University Press.

Latour, B. (2005) *Reassembling the Social: An Introduction to Actor-Network-Theory*, Oxford: Oxford University Press.

Leidner, R. (1993) *Fast Food, Fast Talk: Service Work and the Routinization of Everyday Life*, Berkeley: University of California Press.

Levitt, T. (1960) 'Marketing Myopia', *Harvard Business Review*, 38 (4): 45–56.

Levitt, T. (1972) 'Production-Line Approach to Service', *Harvard Business Review*, 50 (5): 20–31.

Lincoln, Y.S. and Guba, E.G. (1985) *Naturalistic Inquiry*, Beverly Hills, CA: Sage.

Lovelock, C. and Gummesson, E. (2004) 'Whither Services Marketing?: In Search of a New Paradigm and Fresh Perspectives', *Journal of Service Research*, 7 (1): 20–41.

Lukes, S. (1974) *Power: A Radical View*, London: Macmillan.

Lusch, R.F. and Vargo, S.L. (2006) 'Service-Dominant Logic as a Foundation for Building a General Theory', in R.F. Lusch and S.L. Vargo (eds.) *The Service-Dominant Logic of Marketing: Dialog, Debate and Directions*, Armonk, NY: M.E. Sharpe, pp. 406–20.

Lusch, R.F., Vargo, S.L., and O'Brien, M. (2007) 'Competing Through Services: Insights from Service-Dominant Logic', *Journal of Retailing*, 83 (1): 5–18.

Lytle, R.S., Hom, P.W., and Mokwa, M.P. (1998) 'SERV*OR: A Managerial Measure of Organizational Service-Orientation', *Journal of Retailing*, 74 (4): 455–89.

Manley, J.E. (2001) 'The Customer is Always Right? Customer Satisfaction Surveys as Employee Control Mechanisms in Professional Service Work', in A Sturdy, I. Grugulis, and H. Willmott (eds.) *Customer Service—Empowerment and Entrapment*, Basingstoke, UK: Palgrave, pp. 157–69.

Marion, G. (2006) 'Marketing Ideology and Criticism: Legitimacy and Legitimization', *Marketing Theory*, 6 (2): 245–62.

Marketing Theory (2006) 'Special Issue on the Service-Dominant Logic of Marketing', 6 (3).

Martin, J. (2002) *Organizational Culture*, London: Sage.

McCabe, D. (2007) 'Individualization at Work?: Subjectivity, Teamworking and Anti-Unionism', *Organization*, 14 (2): 243–66.

McCarthy, E.J. (1964) *Basic Marketing: A Managerial Approach*, 2nd edn, Homewood, IL: Richard D. Irwin.

McKitterick, J.B. (1957) 'What is the Marketing Management Concept?', in F.M. Bass (ed.) *The Frontiers in Marketing Thought*, Chicago: American Marketing Association.

Mead, C.W. (1934) *Mind, Self & Society: From the Standpoint of a Social Behaviorist*, Chicago: The University of Chicago Press.

Merlo, O., Whitwell, G.J., and Lukas, B.A (2004) 'Power and Marketing', *Journal of Strategic Marketing*, 12 (4): 207–18

Meyer, J.W. and Rowan, B. (1977) 'Institutionalized Organizations: Formal Structure as Myth and Ceremony', *American Journal of Sociology*, 83 (2): 340–63.

Mick, D.G., Broniarczyk, S.M., and Haidt, J. (2004) 'Choose, Choose, Choose, Choose, Choose, Choose, Choose: Emerging and Prospective Research on the Deleterious Effects of Living in Consumer Hyperchoice', *Journal of Business Ethics*, 52 (2), 207–11.

Mills, C.W. (1951) *White Collar: The American Middle Class*, New York: Oxford University Press.

Moorman, C. (1995) 'Organizational Market Information Processes: Cultural Antecedents and New Product Outcomes', *Journal of Marketing Research*, 32 (August): 318–36.

Morgan, G. (1986) *Images of Organization*, London: Sage.

Morgan, G. (2003) 'Marketing and Critique: Prospects and Problems', in M. Alvesson and H. Willmott (eds.) *Studying Management Critically* 2nd edn, London: Sage, pp. 111–31.

Morgan, G. and Sturdy, A. (2000) *Beyond Organizational Change: Structure, Discourse and Power in UK Financial Services*, London: Macmillan.

Morgan, R.M. and Hunt S.D. (1994) 'The Commitment-trust Theory of Relationship Marketing', *Journal of Marketing*, 58 (3): 20–38.

Murray, J.B. and Ozanne, J.L. (1991) 'The Critical Imagination: Emancipatory Interests in Consumer Research', *Journal of Consumer Research*, 18 (2), 129–44.

Narver, J.C. and Slater, S.F. (1990) 'The Effects of a Market Orientation on Business Profitability', *Journal of Marketing*, 54 (4): 20–36.

Narver, J.C., Slater, S.F., and Tietje, B. (1998) 'Creating a Market Orientation', *Journal of Market Focused Management*, 2 (3): 241–55.

O'Malley, P. (1992) 'Risk, Power and Crime Prevention', *Economy & Society*, 21 (3): 252–75.

Oliver, R.L. (1977) 'Effect of Expectation and Disconfirmation on Post-exposure Product Evaluations: An Alternative Interpretation', *Journal of Applied Psychology*, 62 (4): 480–86.

Oliver, R.L. (1996) *Satisfaction: A Behavioral Perspective on the Consumer*, Boston: McGraw Hill.

Parasuraman, A., Zeithaml, V.A., and Berry, L.L. (1985) 'A Conceptual Model of Service Quality and its Implications for Future Research', *Journal of Marketing*, 49 (4): 253–68.

Parasuraman, A., Zeithaml, V.A., and Berry, L.L. (1988) 'SERVQUAL: A Multiple-Item Scale for Measuring Consumer Perceptions of Service Quality', *Journal of Retailing*, 64 (1): 12–37.

Parasuraman, A., Zeithaml, V.A., and Berry, L.L. (1994) 'Reassessment of Expectations as a Comparison Standard in Measuring Service Quality: Implications for Further Research', *Journal of Marketing*, 58 (1): 111–24.

Parvatiyar A. and Sheth, J.N. (2000) 'The Domain and Conceptual Foundations of Relationship Marketing', in J.N. Sheth and A. Parvatiyar (eds.) *Handbook of Relationship Marketing*, London: Sage, pp. 3–38.

Payne, A. and Frow, P. (2005) 'A Strategic Framework for Customer Relationship Management', *Journal of Marketing*, 69 (4): 167–76.

Peccei, R. and Rosenthal, P. (2000) 'Front-line Responses to Customer Orientation Programs: A Theoretical and Empirical Analysis', *International Journal of Human Resource Management*, 11 (3): 562–90.

Peccei, R. and Rosenthal, P. (2001) 'Delivering Customer-Oriented Behaviour Through Empowerment: An Empirical Test of HRM Assumptions', *Journal of Management Studies*, 38 (6): 831–57.

Peters, T.J. and Waterman, R.H. (1982) *In Search of Excellence: Lessons from America's Best-Run Companies*, New York: Harper and Row.

Phillips, L. and Jørgensen, M.W. (2002) *Discourse Analysis as Theory and Method*, London: Sage.

Porter, M.E. (1980) *Competitive Strategy*, New York: The Free Press.

Potter, J. and Wheterhell, M. (1987) *Discourse and Social Psychology*, Sage: London.

Powell, W.W. (1990) 'Neither Market nor Hierarchy: Network Forms of Organization', *Research in Organizational Behavior*, 12: 295–336.

Quist, J., Skålén, P., and Clegg, S.R. (2007) 'The Power of Quality Models: The Example of the SIQ Model for Performance Excellence', *Scandinavian Journal of Management*, 23 (4): 445–62.

Rathmell, J.M. (1974) *Marketing in the Service Sector*, Cambridge, Mass: Winthorp Publishers.

Ritzer, G. (2004) *The McDonaldization of Society*, London, Sage.

Roos, I. (1999) 'Switching Processes in Customer Relationships', *Journal of Services Research*, 2 (1): 376–93.

Rose, N. (1996) *Inventing Our Selves: Psychology, Power and Personhood*, Cambridge, MA: Cambridge University Press.

Rose, N. (1999) *Powers of Freedom: Reframing Political Thought*, Cambridge, MA: Cambridge University Press.

Rosenthal, P., Hill, S., and Peccei, R. (1997) 'Checking Out Service: Evaluating Excellence, HRM and TQM in Retailing', *Work. Employment and Society*, 11 (3): 481–503.

Rust, R.T. and Oliver, R.L. (1994) 'Service Quality: Insights and Managerial Implications From the Frontier', in R.T. Rust and R.L. Oliver (eds.) *Service Quality: New Directions in Theory and Practice*, Thousand Oaks, CA: Sage, pp. 1–19.

Saren, M., Maclaran, P., Goulding, C., Elliott, R., Shankar, A., and Caterall, M. (eds.) (2007a) *Critical Marketing: Defining the Field*, Burlington, MA: Butterworth-Heinemann.

Saren, M., Maclaran, P., Goulding, C., Elliott, R., Shankar, A., and Caterall, M. (2007b), 'Introduction: Defining the Field of Critical Marketing', in M. Saren, P. Maclaran, C. Goulding, R. Elliott, A. Shankar, and M. Caterall, (eds.) *Critical Marketing: Defining the Field*, Burlington, MA: Butterworth-Heinemann.

Schein E.H. (1985) *Organizational Culture and Leadership*, San Francisco: Jossey-Bass.

Schendel, D. and Hofer, C.W. (1979) *Strategic Management: A New View of Business Policy and Planning*, Boston, MA: Little, Brown and Co.

Schneider, B. and Bowen, D.E. (1995) *Winning the Service Game*, Boston: Harvard Business School Press.

Schneider, B. and White, S. (2004) *Service Quality: Research Perspectives*, Thousand Oaks, CA: Sage.

Schroeder J.E. (2007) 'Critical Marketing: Insights for Informed Research and Teaching', in M. Saren, P. Maclaran, C. Goulding, R. Elliott, A. Shankar, and M. Caterall, (eds.) *Critical Marketing: Defining the Field*, Burlington, MA: Butterworth-Heinemann, pp. 18–29.

Scott, W.R. (2003) *Organizations: Rational, Natural and Open Systems*, Upper Saddle River, NJ: Pearson Education.

Shankar, A., Cherrier, H., and Canniford, R. (2006) 'Consumer Empowerment: A Foucauldian Interpretation', *European Journal of Marketing*, 40 (9/10): 1013–30

Sharma, A., Tzokas, N., Saren, M., and Kyziridis, P. (1999) 'Antecedents and Consequences of Relationship Marketing: Insights from Business Service Salespeople', *Industrial Marketing Management*, 28 (6): 601–12.

Sheth, J.N., Gardner, D.M., and Garrett, D.E. (1988) *Marketing Theory: Evolution and Evaluation*, New York: John Wiley and Sons.

Shostack, G.L. (1977) 'Breaking Free from Product Marketing', *Journal of Marketing*, 41 (2): 73–80.

Silverman, D. (2006) *Interpreting Qualitative Data: Methods for Analysing Talk, Text and Interaction*, London: Sage.

Sisodia, R.S. and Wolfe, D.B. (2000) 'Information Technology: Its Role in Building, Maintaining, and Enhancing Relationships', in J.N. Sheth and A. Parvatiyar (eds.) *Handbook of Relationship Marketing*, London: Sage, pp. 525–63.

Skålén, P. (2010) 'A Discourse Analytical Approach to Qualitative Marketing Research', *Qualitative Market Research: An International Journal*, 13(1 or 2): XXX.

Skålén, P. (2009) 'Service Marketing and Subjectivity: The Shaping of Customer-Oriented Employees', *Journal of Marketing Management*, 25 (7–8): 795–809.

Skålén, P., Fellesson, M., and Fougère, M. (2006) 'The Governmentality of Marketing Discourse', *Scandinavian Journal of Management*, 22 (4): 275–91.

Skålén, P. and Fougère, M. (2007) 'Be(com)ing Normal—Not Excellent: Service Management, the Gap-model and Disciplinary Power', *Journal of Organizational Change Management*, 20 (1): 109–25.

Skålén, P., Fougère, M., and Fellesson, M. (2008) *Marketing Discourse: A Critical Perspective*, London: Routledge.

Skålén, P., Quist, J., Edvardsson, B., and Enquist, B. (2005) 'The Contextualization of Human Resource Management and Quality Management—A Sensemaking

Perspective on Everybody's Involvement', *International Journal of Human Resource Management*, 16 (5): 736–51.

Smircich, L. (1983) 'Concepts of Culture and Organizational Analysis', *Administrative Science Quarterly*, 28 (3): 339–58.

Speier, C. and Venkatesh, V. (2002) 'The Hidden Minefields in Adoption of Sales Force Automation Technologies', *Journal of Marketing*, 66 (3): 98–111.

Spradley, J.P. (1979) *The Ethnographic Interview*, Belmont, CA: Wadsworth.

Strauss, A.L. and Corbin, J. (1998) *Basics of Qualitative Research: Techniques and Procedures for Developing Grounded Theory*, 2nd edn, London: Sage.

Sturdy, A. (1998) 'Customer Care in a Consumer Society: Smiling and Sometimes Meaning It?', *Organization*, 5 (1): 27–53.

Svensson, P. (2007) 'Producing Marketing: Towards a Social-Phenomenology of Marketing Work', *Marketing Theory*, 7 (3): 271–90.

Tadajewski, M. (2006) 'The Ordering of Marketing Theory: The Influence of McCarthyism and the Cold War', *Marketing Theory*, 6 (2): 163–99.

Tadajewski, M. and Brownlie, D. (eds.) (2008) *Critical Marketing: Issues in Contemporary Marketing*, Chichester, UK: Wiley.

Taylor, P. and Bain, P. (1999) 'An Assembly Line in the Head', *Work, Employment and Society*, 30 (2): 101–17.

Taylor, P. and Bain, P. (2001) 'Trade Unions, Workers' Rights and the Frontier of Control in UK Call Centres', *Economic and Industrial Democracy*, 22 (1): 39–66.

Teas, K.R. (1993) 'Expectations, Performance, Evaluation, and Consumers' Perceptions of Quality', *Journal of Marketing*, 57 (4): 18–34.

Teas, K.R. (1994) 'Expectations as a Comparison Standard in Measuring Service Quality: An Assessment of a Reassessment', *Journal of Marketing*, 58 (1): 132–39.

Thompson, P. and Ackroyd, S. (1995) 'All Quiet on the Workplace Front? A Critique of Recent Trends in British Industrial Sociology', *Sociology*, 29 (4): 615–33.

Townley, B. (1993) 'Foucault, Power/Knowledge and its Relevance for Human Resource Management', *Academy of Management Review*, 18 (3): 518–45.

Townley, B. (1994) *Reframing Human Resource Management: Power, Ethics and the Subject at Work*, Sage: London.

Townley, B. (1998) 'Beyond Good and Evil: Depth and Division in the Management of Human Resources', in A. McKinlay and K. Starkey (eds.) *Foucault, Management and Organization Theory: From Panopticon to Technologies of Self*, London: Sage.

Van Maanen, J. (1975) 'Police Socialization', *Administrative Science Quarterly*, 20 (3): 207–28.

Van Maanen, J. (1979) 'The Fact of Fiction in Organizational Ethnography', *Administrative Science Quarterly*, 24 (4): 539–50.

Vargo, S.L. and Lusch, R.F. (2004) 'Evolving to a New Dominant Logic for Marketing', *Journal of Marketing*, 68 (1): 1–17.

Vargo, S.L. and Lusch, R.F. (2008a) 'Service-dominant logic: Continuing the Evolution', *Journal of the Academy of Marketing Science*, 36 (1): 1–10.

Vargo, S.L. and Lusch, R.F. (2008b) 'Why Service', *Journal of the Academy of Marketing Science*, 36 (1), 25–38.

Vargo, S.L. and Lusch, R.F. (2008c) 'From Products to Service: Divergences and Convergences of Logics', *Industrial Marketing Management*, 37 (May) 254–59.

Vargo, S.L. and Morgan, F.W. (2005) 'Services in Society and Academic Thought: An Historical Analysis', *Journal of Macromarketing*, 25 (1): 42–53.

Vavra, T.G. (1994) 'The Database Marketing Imperative', *Marketing Management*, 2 (1): 47–57.

Warhurst, C., Thompson, P., and Nickson, D. (2009) 'Labor Process Theory: Putting the Materialism Back into the Meaning of Service Work', in M. Korczynski and C. Lynne Macdonald (eds.) *Service Work: A Critical Perspective*, London: Routledge, pp. 91–112.

Webster, F.E. Jr. (1981) 'Top Management Concerns About the Marketing Function: Issues for the 1980s', *Journal of Marketing*, 31 (Summer): 9–16.

Webster, F.E. Jr. (2002), 'The Role of Marketing and the Firm', in B. Weitz and R. Wensley (eds.) *Handbook of Marketing*, London: Sage, pp. 66–83.

Weick, K.E. (1979) *The Social Psychology of Organizing*, NewYork: MacGraw-Hill.

Weick, K.E. (1995) *Sensemaking in Organizations*, London: Sage.

Willmott, H. (1993) 'Strength is Ignorance; Slavery is Freedom: Managing Culture in Modern Organizations', *Journal of Management Studies*, 30 (4): 515–52

Yin, R.K. (1984) *Case Study Research: Design and Methods*, 2nd edn, London: Sage.

Zbaracki, M.J. (1998) 'The Rhetoric and Reality of Total Quality Management', *Administrative Science Quarterly*, 43 (3): 602–36.

Zeithaml, V., Parasuraman, A., and Berry, L.L. (1985) 'Problem and Strategies in Services Marketing', *Journal of Marketing*, 49 (1): 33–46.

Zeithaml, V.A., Berry, L.L., and Parasuraman, A. (1990) *Delivering Quality Service: Balancing Customer Perceptions and Expectations*, New York: The Free Press.

Zwick, D., Bonsu, S.K., and Darmody, A. (2008) 'Putting Consumers to Work: Co-creation and New Marketing Govern-mentality', *Journal of Consumer Culture*, 8 (2): 163–96.

Index

Note: Page references to tables are in *italics* and those to figures in **bold**.

Printed in the United States
by Baker & Taylor Publisher Services